THE MAKING OF MEDIEVAL HISTORY

YORK MEDIEVAL PRESS

THE MAKING OF
MEDIEVAL HISTORY

Edited by
Graham A. Loud and Martial Staub

THE UNIVERSITY *of York*

YORK MEDIEVAL PRESS

First published 2017

A York Medieval Press publication
in association with The Boydell Press
an imprint of Boydell & Brewer Ltd
PO Box 9, Woodbridge, Suffolk IP12 3DF, UK
and of Boydell & Brewer Inc.
668 Mt Hope Avenue, Rochester, NY 14620–2731, USA
website: www.boydellandbrewer.com
and with the
Centre for Medieval Studies, University of York

ISBN 978 1 903153 70 3

A CIP catalogue record for this book is available
from the British Library

The publisher has no responsibility for the continued existence or accuracy of URLs for
external or third-party internet websites referred to in this book, and does not guarantee
that any content on such websites is, or will remain, accurate or appropriate

This publication is printed on acid-free paper

Printed and bound in Great Britain by TJ International Ltd, Padstow, Cornwall

MIX
Paper from
responsible sources
FSC
www.fsc.org   FSC® C013056

CONTENTS

ILLUSTRATIONS

The editors, contributors and publishers are grateful to all the institutions and persons listed for permission to reproduce the materials in which they hold copyright. Every effort has been made to trace the copyright holders; apologies are offered for any omission, and the publishers will be pleased to add any necessary acknowledgement in subsequent editions.

Otto Gerhard Oexle
(1939–2016)
In memoriam

ACKNOWLEDGMENTS

All but one of these essays are based upon lectures given in 2011–12 at the Universities of Leeds, Sheffield and York, and that by Joep Leerssen at the International Medieval Congress at Leeds in July 2012, as a series sponsored by the White Rose University Consortium, which provided very generous financial assistance to make the lectures and their associated seminars possible. The consortium also provided a subvention towards the costs of producing this book, and reproducing the illustrations therein. We are most grateful for this aid. That it took so long to turn the lecture series into a book – which was always the plan – was largely due to the administrative burdens subsequently laid upon the editors by their respective institutions. Our contributors, several of whom produced finished texts of their contributions not long after they had spoken, have displayed commendable patience. In the meanwhile, Bernhard Jussen kindly offered us an English version of an essay already published in German which expanded our range, addressing the important issues of how medieval history has been presented to a wider public, as well as how 'politicised' the Middle Ages can be in the modern era – a recurring preoccupation of these essays. We thank too our publishers, York Medieval Press and Boydell & Brewer, and especially our commissioning editor Caroline Palmer, for having faith in this project, and also Dr Diane Milburn for offering us her photographs of the Kyffhäuser monument.

The intention behind the project was to examine, and initiate further discussion about, how the writing and study of medieval history over the last two centuries has developed and been conditioned by its environment. Far from being a neutral, or bloodless, activity, the history written about this distant period has always reflected the pre-occupations of the societies in which it was engendered. In addition, we sought to make our range as international as possible, to bring some of the preoccupations of Continental (and in two essays North American) medievalists to the attention of an Anglophone audience which would not necessarily be familiar with them. As historians we need to reflect, perhaps rather more than we normally do, about how and why we study history, as well as to show that the history of the Middle Ages still has a real contemporary relevance.

Finally, to end on a note of commemoration, as we made the last minor corrections before sending this collection to press, the death was announced of the distinguished German medievalist Otto Gerhard Oexle, much of whose work was concerned with the context within which the history of the Middle Ages was written. (In particular, he published extensively about the writing of history during the Nazi era.) Not only was Oexle well known to several contributors to this project, but when it was first mooted, we had asked him if he wished to take part. Sadly, his health was already delicate and he was forced, with regret, to decline. The least that we can do, therefore, is to dedicate this book to his memory.

GAL, MS
June 2016

CONTRIBUTORS

Christine Caldwell Ames is Associate Professor of History at the University of South Carolina, where she has taught since 2005. Her special interests are the history of Christianity, heresy and the inquisition, interreligious relations, and the taxonomy of religion. She is the author of *Righteous Persecution: Inquisition, Dominicans and Christianity in the Middle Ages* (2008) and *Medieval Heresies: Christianity, Judaism, and Islam* (2015).

Peter Biller is Professor of Medieval History at the University of York, where he has taught since 1970, and is a Fellow of the British Academy. He works partly on medieval thought, especially in academic texts, and also on heresy and persecution. He is the author of *The Measure of Multitude: Population in Medieval Thought* (2000) and *The Waldensians, 1170–1530* (2001), and has edited a number of books, including *Inquisitors and Heretics in Languedoc: Edition and Translation of Toulouse Inquisition Depositions, 1273–1282* (2011), and, with John Arnold, *Heresy and Inquisition in France, 1200–1300* (2016).

Michael Borgolte has since 1991 been Professor of Medieval History at Humboldt University in Berlin, where he founded the Institute for the Comparative History of Europe in the Middle Ages in 1998. His interests include both European and Global history during the Middle Ages, as well as the history and theory of Historiography. His books include *Europa entdeckt seine Vielfalt 1050–1250* (2002) [Europe. The Discovery of Diversity, 1050–1250]; and *Christen, Juden, Muselmanen. Die Erben der Antike und der Aufstieg des Abendlandes 300–1400 n. Chr.* (2006) [Christians, Jews and Muslims. The Heirs of Antiquity and the Ascent of Western Europe, 300–1400].

Patrick Geary is the Andrew W. Mellon Professor at the Institute for Advanced Study in Princeton. He has previously taught at several US universities, including the University of California at Los Angeles from 1993 until 2011. He was President of the Medieval Academy of America in 2008–9 and is a Corresponding Fellow of the British Academy. His principal field of research is Continental Europe in the early Middle Ages, with a particular interest in social history, the history of memory, and conflict resolution. Among his books are *Furta Sacra: Thefts of Relics in the Central Middle Ages* (1991); *Phantoms of Remembrance: Memory and Oblivion at the end of the first Millennium* (1996); *The Myth of Nations: The Medieval Origins of Europe* (2002); *Women at the Beginning: Origin Myths from the Amazons to the Virgin Mary* (2006), and *Languages of Power in the Early Middle Ages* (2013).

Richard Hitchcock taught at the University of Exeter from 1966 until his retirement as Professor of Hispano-Arabic Studies in 2003. He has written extensively on Arabic Spain, as well as about Spanish literature, both medieval and of the 'Golden Age', including Cervantes and Lope de Vega; and also on the origins of Hispanic studies in the Anglophone world, and about British travellers in Spain during the eighteenth and nineteenth centuries. Among his more recent publications are *Mozarabs in Early Medieval Spain* (2008) and *Muslim Spain Reconsidered, from 711 to 1502* (2014).

Bernhard Jussen has been Professor of Medieval History at the Johann Wolfgang Goethe-Universität at Frankfurt am Main since 2008. He was before that a professor at the University of Bielefeld. He was a visiting professor at the École Normale Supérieure in Paris in 2008, and a visiting scholar at Harvard in 2008–9. He is the author of *Spiritual Kinship as Social Practice. Godparenthood and Adoption in the Early Middle Ages* (2000), first published in German in 1991, and of *Die Franken* (2013), which has also recently appeared in Italian translation.

Joep Leerssen has been Professor of Modern European Literature at the University of Amsterdam since 1991, and from 1996 until 2006 was Director of the Huizinga Institute (the Dutch National Research Institute and graduate school of Cultural History). He was a visiting professor at Harvard in 2003. His interests include Irish history and literature, and the role of literature in cultural nationalism, especially that of medieval literature in nationalism and nation-building in the nineteenth century. His books include *Remembrance and Imagination* (1996) and *National Thought in Europe: a Cultural History* (2006). He was awarded the Spinoza Prize in 2008.

Christian Lübke has been Professor of the History of Eastern Europe and Director of the Centre for the History and Culture of Eastern Europe at the University of Leipzig since 2007. Before that he was a professor at the University of Greifswald 1998–2007. His books include *Novgorod in der russichen Literatur* (1984) and *Fremde im östlichen Europa. Von Gesellschaften ohne Staat zu verstaatlichten Gesellschaften (9.–11. Jahrhundert)* (2001) [Outsiders in Eastern Europe: from Societies without States to the State Societies, during the ninth to the eleventh centuries].

Jinty Nelson [Dame Janet L. Nelson DBE, FBA] is Professor Emeritus of Medieval History at King's College, London. After working briefly for HM Foreign and Commonwealth Office, she was appointed as Lecturer in Medieval History at King's in 1970, where she taught for thirty-eight years, being promoted to be professor in 1992. Her principal area of research has been the Carolingian world and political ideas in the early Middle Ages. Her books include *Politics and Ritual in the Earlier Middle Ages* (1986), *The Annals of St-Bertin* (1991), *Charles the Bald* (1992), *The Frankish World c. 750–900* (1995), and *Courts, Elites and Gendered Power in the Early Middle Ages* (2007). She was President of the Ecclesiastical History Society in 1992–3, elected a Fellow of the British Academy in 1996, was its Vice-President for Humanities 1999–2001, and was President of the Royal Historical Society 2000–4. She was appointed DBE for services to History in 2006.

Bastian Schlüter is Assistant Professor of German Literature Studies at the Freie Universität, Berlin. His principle areas of research are literature and history from the eighteenth century to the present, and medievalism in German art and politics. He is the author of *Explodierende Altertümlichkeit. Imaginationen vom Mittelalter zwischen den Weltkriegen* [Exploding Antiquity. Concepts of the Middles Ages between the Two World Wars] (2011).

Ian Wood is Professor Emeritus of Early Medieval History at the University of Leeds, where he taught from 1976 until 2015. His research has been concentrated upon the political and religious history of the late-Roman and post-Roman west, but he is also in the broad sense a cultural historian of the Early Middle Ages. He is the author of *The Merovingian Kingdoms (450–751)* (1994), *The Missionary Life. Saints and the Evangelisation of Europe 400–1050* (2001), *Fragments of History: Rethinking the Ruthwell and Bewcastle Monuments* (2007, co-written with Fred Orton), and *The Modern Origins of the Early Middle Ages* (2013), as well as almost a hundred scholarly articles and essays. He was the co-ordinator of the European Science Foundation project on 'The Transformation of the Roman World'.

The Editors

Graham A. Loud is Professor of Medieval History at the University of Leeds, where he was (for his sins) Head of the School of History 2012–15. His principal field of study is the social and religious history of southern Italy from the tenth to the thirteenth centuries. His books include *Church and Society in the Norman Principality of Capua, 1058–1197* (1985), *The Age of Robert Guiscard. Southern Italy and the Norman Conquest* (2000), *The Latin Church in Norman Italy* (2007), *The Crusade of Frederick Barbarossa* (2010), and *Roger II and the Creation of the Kingdom of Sicily* (2012).

Martial Staub has been Professor of Medieval History at the University of Sheffield since 2004. Before then he was a research fellow at the Max Planck Institute of History in Göttingen. His interests lie especially in the religious and urban history of the late Middle Ages, in which field his most important publication is *Les Paroisses et la Cité: Nuremberg du XIIIe Siècle à la Réforme* (2003). He was also co-editor, with Gert Melville, of the *Enzyklopädie des Mittelalters* (2008), which has been published in English as *Brill's Encyclopaedia of the Middle Ages*.

INTRODUCTION

SOME THOUGHTS ON THE MAKING OF THE MIDDLE AGES

Graham A. Loud and Martial Staub

A sense of history, of 'how did we get to where we are now', is integral to any society, in almost any age. More than two millennia ago Aristotle claimed that: 'all men by nature desire to know the things that happened before their time';[1] while from the other side of the world, though of more recent vintage, comes the Māori proverb, 'to have hope and faith in the future, you must first stand on the shoulders of the past' – a sentence that ought to be the motto of any self-respecting University department of History. Yet *how* to stand upon the shoulders of the past is neither necessarily obvious nor straightforward. Classical and Renaissance historians saw the study of the past as a practical, but essentially moral, exercise, to learn how to imitate the good and avoid the wicked.

> The study of history is the best medicine for a sick mind, for in history you have a record of the infinite variety of human experience plainly set out for all to see, and in that record you can find for yourself and your country both examples and warning: fine things to take as models, base things, rotten through and through, to avoid. [2]

But if we have subsequently lost faith in learning lessons from the past, certainly in terms of virtue and vice, neither is history a neutral exercise. Few today would follow the great nineteenth-century historian Leopold von Ranke in considering their discipline as revealing 'how it actually was' [*wie es eigentlich gewesen*]. However much this might be an ideal to aim at, we know that it cannot be achieved. Medievalists are probably even more conscious of this than their modernist colleagues, for we are all too aware of the gaps and inconsistencies in our sources, and how much any modern reconstruction owes to interpretation. Even if we were capable of approaching our subject absolutely dispassionately

---

[1] From the *Metaphysics*, but also quoted approvingly by King Alfonso X of Castile in his *General History* in the 1260s.

[2] Livy: *Titi Livi ab Urbe Condita*, i, *libri i-v*, ed. R. M. Ogilvie (Oxford, 1974), praefatio, p. 2.

and without bias, in itself an unlikely supposition, there is much that we shall never know. So why make the effort at all?

First and most obviously, we still need to understand the past if we are to have any awareness of where we are in the present. How can there be any understanding of modern political issues such as nationalism in the Balkans, the tensions that remain within Northern Ireland, devolution for Scotland and Wales, or the Mezzogiorno debate in Italy, to quote but a few European examples, without some concept of how events and conflicts in the past have created these problems? Nor is it enough to say that we can adequately understand such issues by studying relatively recent history, as though there is some valid conceptual difference between studying the history of the nineteenth and twentieth centuries and that of an allegedly more esoteric and less 'relevant' earlier period. Thus the origins of religious and communal dispute in Northern Ireland stretch back to the Scots settlement in Ulster under James I; those of Shī'a / Sunni strife in Iraq at least as far as the pro-Shī'a policies pursued by the Safavid Shahs of Iran who dominated the Gulf region in that same period;[3] while those in Bosnia date back to the Turkish invasion of the Balkans in the fourteenth century, and arguably further back still, to the missionary activities of Byzantine and German clerics in the ninth and tenth centuries. Moreover, some Scottish nationalists still look back to the Declaration of Arbroath of 1318 as the foundation charter of Scottish independence.[4] Secondly, whereas in Britain a majority of us may, even so, see the study of history, and certainly that of more distant history, as a politically 'neutral' activity, that is hardly the case in many other countries and regions. The furore in parts of the Muslim world which greeted President Bush's unfortunate use of the term 'Crusade' in 2001 should make that clear – although this kerfuffle is somewhat ironic in that until the dawn of the twentieth century the Crusades had largely been forgotten in Muslim countries – it was Kaiser Wilhelm II who drew attention to Saladin's neglected tomb in Damascus just over a century ago, and reminded the Muslims of the Middle East of his achievements, as part of his government's policy of finding allies in that region to counteract British and French influence.[5] And distortions and exploitation of the medieval past have all too frequently

---

[3] G. Parker, *Global Crisis. War, Climate Change and Catastrophe in the Seventeenth Century* (New Haven and London, 2013), p. 418.

[4] There is, indeed, another interesting parallel which appears not to have been noticed. The Scots appealed to Boniface VIII c. 1301 in order to secure their kingdom's independence from England, just as the SNP now wants Scottish independence to be validated by membership of the European community. G. Barrow, *Robert Bruce*, 3rd edn (Edinburgh 1988), pp. 116–19.

[5] J. S. Richter, *Die orientreise Kaiser Wilhelms II. 1898. Eine Studie zur deutschen Außenpolitik an der Wende zum 20. Jahrhundert* (Hamburg, 1997), pp. 86–9; H. Möhring, *Saladin. The Sultan and his Times, 1138–1193*, trans. D. S. Bachrach (Baltimore, 2008), p. 102.

been used to justify modern aggression or exploitation. It was no accident that Himmler saw the Teutonic Knights as precursors of the SS, and an influential school of German historians from the 1920s onwards developed studying *Ostforschung*, the eastwards expansion of the medieval Reich, not as an object of purely academic study, but to justify the eastward expansion of the Nazi era and the exploitation of the Poles and other Slavonic and Baltic peoples.[6] More recently, although admittedly less crudely, Israeli historians have viewed the Crusader settlement in Palestine as in some senses a precursor of the Zionist movement.[7] At the introductory meeting of the lecture series on which these essays are based, at the 2011 International Medieval Congress in Leeds, Gabor Klaniczay spoke eloquently about the use and misuse of medieval history in the context of modern East European nationalism. If we do not study the Middle Ages, and try to understand and explain it in as unbiased a way as we can, then we leave the field open to those who abuse and exploit the past to justify modern injustice.[8]

The lesson therefore is that the Middle Ages still matters. One might also suggest, in a more purely 'academic' context, that if the study of history is worth pursuing at all, and as university professors who have spent a lifetime studying and teaching history we would obviously argue that it is, then one ought to study all history, and not just some of it. The ludicrous suggestion (soon withdrawn after a storm of criticism) by Charles Clarke, the former Education Secretary, back in 2003, that medieval historians in universities were in some way purely ornamental and unworthy of support, not only revealed how absolutely unfitted for his post Mr Clarke was, but also that he had a complete lack of understanding of how history is taught and studied within higher education. Few undergraduate students simply study the Middle Ages alone. They rather study medieval history as part of a wider chronological and thematic span, and for a proper understanding of the significance of history it is right that they should. And why not take the 'Clarke argument' to its ultimate *reductio ad absurdum*? Do students, or for that matter ordinary intelligent people, need to know about the Reformation, or the English Civil War, or the French Revolution? Well surely they do! The seventeenth century, for example, arguably laid the groundwork for modern parliamentary democracy, and many of the rights and powers of the modern British parliament date back

---

[6] How politicized an issue this was is made clear, for example, by Michael Burleigh, in 'Albert Brackmann (1871–1952) Ostforscher: the years of retirement', *Journal of Contemporary History* 23 (1988), 573–88, with respect to one of the leading German medievalists of his time, whose seventieth birthday was marked by telegrams from Hitler and other Nazi leaders.

[7] R. Ellenblum, *Crusader Castles and Modern Histories* (Cambridge, 2007), pp. 57–61.

[8] See now, *Manufacturing Middle Ages: Entangled History of Medievalism*, ed. P. J. Geary and G. Klaniczay (Leiden, 2013).

to the Glorious Revolution of 1688. But then how does one understand the debates and conflicts of that century without some knowledge of the historical precedents that were of immense importance to men of that time? The trial of Charles I, for example, was not simply a critique of that monarch's failings as a ruler, but also an historical debate about the precedents, powers and limitations of monarch and parliament, stretching back into the Middle Ages. And at exactly the same time, the Levellers traced contemporary social inequalities back to the impact of the Norman Conquest – 'What are the nobles and knights but William the Conqueror's captains and sergeants?' At the Putney Debates of 1647, General Ireton, the spokesman of the army high command – the new 'establishment' – argued with his Leveller opponents about such issues as to what extent monarchical authority had existed before the Conquest, and what role the Commons had played in such seminal events as the promulgation of Magna Charta and the deposition of Richard II.[9] Furthermore, we might also address this same argument about the importance of the distant past to other subjects. Could one study English literature without Shakespeare, Ben Jonson or Chaucer, or French without Molière and Racine, or for that matter Rabelais or François Villon? But there is a further and different argument as well. Precisely because it deals with a distant, unfamiliar world, with different attitudes and values from that of today, medieval history *is* more difficult and less approachable than the history of the very recent past. Medieval men and women were not the same as those of today. As students often lament, medieval history *is* difficult. If history is to be studied as an intellectual discipline, and as a training-ground in the analysis and making sense of significant amounts of often difficult evidence (a 'transferable skill' as the jargon goes), how much more important is it to make this training as rigorous as possible, and to study the difficult parts, and not just recent periods that may already be familiar to students from what they have done at school or contemporary media coverage?

But the other side of the coin is that history is not a static discipline, but an evolutionary one. What happened in the past, in terms of events, may not have changed, but how we approach it certainly does. One of the most distinguished of contemporary medievalists, Jacques Le Goff, for example, argued that the past 'is constantly being reconstructed and re-interpreted'.[10] Furthermore, as Jinty Nelson writes in her essay: 're-inventing keeps history alive and well'.[11] If scholars of the nineteenth and early twentieth centuries thought of history, medieval *and* modern, primarily in terms of political, constitutional and legal history, and of the development of government and states, our vision now is

---

[9] *Puritanism and Liberty, being the Army Debates (1647–49) from the Clarke Manuscripts*, ed. A. S. P. Woodhouse, preface by I. Roots, 3rd edn (London, 1992), pp. 96, 120–1.

[10] *History and Memory. European Perspectives*, trans. S. Rendall and E. Claman (New York, 1992), p. 108.

[11] Below, p. 17.

much, much broader. Economic and social history has of course long been part of our remit. But the definition, particularly of the latter, has become much wider and richer. Few historians of two or three generations ago would have posed research questions such as 'did the increase in the cultivation of chestnuts in the early medieval Mediterranean lead people to eat less pork?', nor would it have occurred to many of them to do so. (The answer to the question seems to be: yes, it did.)[12] The influence of the *Annales* school pioneered in the inter-war years by Marc Bloch and Lucien Febvre has, however, led us to think in terms of long-term social and economic structures, as well as of 'mentalities' or 'thought-worlds'. [13] The former has increasingly come to include geography, climate and the environment as dominant forces in pre-modern economic history. This interest has been made even more significant by modern concerns with climate change.[14] The investigation of mentalities has laid great stress on memory, as an historical phenomenon to be investigated, and has led to a revival, and to much greater subtlety, in the study of documents and archives. How and why archives were compiled and structured is now viewed as part of the 'construction' of the past, and the workings of historical memory.[15] The significance of cognate disciplines for the historian, and especially the medievalist, has become greater. Early medievalists, in particular, have for fifty years or more drawn upon anthropology for methodological insight, and above all archaeology for new evidence; and as medieval archaeology has developed as a discipline our view of the social and economic history of the late Roman and early medieval world has been transformed. In recent years the sciences too have been co-opted: such as microbiology for the study of epidemics, and palaeo-pathology for that of archaeological sites – for example the work of Piers Mitchell on Crusader sites, which has done much to advance both the study of the Crusades (another area, like the early Middle Ages, where the written sources are finite) and also that of medieval medicine.[16] Medieval historians may lack the technical expertise to conduct such work themselves, but they can still draw upon and interpret such evidence.

---

[12] P. Squatriti, *Landscape and Change in Early Medieval Italy. Chestnuts, Economy and Culture* (Cambridge, 2013), pp. 73–80.

[13] See P. Burke, *The French Historical Revolution: the Annales School, 1929–1989* (Cambridge, 1990), and more recently André Burgière, *The Annales School: an Intellectual History*, trans. J. M. Todd (Ithaca, NY, 2009).

[14] One recent example among many: F. Ludlow and C. Kostick, 'The dating of volcanic events and their impact upon European society 400–800 CE', *European Journal of Post-Classical Archaeology* 5 (2015), 7–30.

[15] Notably by P. Geary, *Phantoms of Remembrance: Memory and Oblivion at the end of the first Millennium* (Princeton, NJ, 1996).

[16] P. Mitchell, *Medicine in the Crusades: Warfare, Wounds and the Medieval Surgeon* (Cambridge, 2004).

New fields of study, which previous generations of medievalists would have ignored, or indeed barely have been able to imagine, now abound: the history of medicine is one, and those of women, marriage and sexuality are other obvious examples. Categories of source material which were once largely shunned, or were the preserve of a few narrow specialists, are now studied as evidence for different types of history: penitential handbooks, saints' lives, sermons and canon law collections are obvious paradigms. These have been used to great effect, for example, for the study of popular religion, medicine, death and commemoration, marriage and contraception in the Middle Ages (this last by, among others, one of this project's organizers, Peter Biller).[17] Modern social concerns, such as with minorities and with cultural differences, have led to an efflorescence in the study of medieval heresy, and of the role and significance of non-Christian minorities within medieval Christendom, notably the Jewish community. Furthermore, we now interpret more 'traditional' fields of study in new ways. The history of religion has developed away from the history of ecclesiastical institutions towards a broader understanding of how religious belief was understood, and a religious life actually lived, once again pointing us towards a history of 'mentalities', but also to what such attitudes might tell us, in the broadest sense, about medieval society, and not just the society of the powerful, but also that of the poor. The pioneer in this field was the German historian Herbert Grundmann (1902–70), whose *Religious Movements in the Middle Ages* was published in 1935. This work received little interest at the time from contemporary German medievalists, and given the political context of that time, its concern with the impact of religious experience would not have been welcomed sympathetically. But in the years since 1945 its sociological approach to religion, and concern with the 'other', religious experience on the margins, have gained increasing currency. If the Anglophone world was relatively slow to adopt such an approach – and Grundmann's masterpiece only appeared in English translation long after his death[18] – an equally pioneering role has been played by the late Roman historian Peter Brown (born in the same year that *Religious Movements* was published, 1935), and especially by his famous essay on the role of the Holy Man in the late Roman world, which showed *inter alia* precisely how the 'outsider' status of eremitic holy men enabled them to mediate in disputes, replace an increasingly urbanized and absentee upper class as 'patrons', and allay anxiety about the natural world and the afterlife in the dynamic, but often contentious, society of fifth- to seventh-century rural

---

[17] P. Biller, 'Birth control in the west in the thirteenth and early fourteenth centuries', *Past and Present* no. 94 (1982), 3–26.

[18] H. Grundmann, *Religious Movements in the Middle Ages*, trans. S. Rowan, introduction by R. E. Lerner (Notre Dame, IN, 1995), translated from the 2nd German edn of 1961.

Syria.[19] But Brown perhaps most succinctly expressed how he differed from more traditional approaches to religious history in a book review, written a year or two earlier.

> To delineate the role of orthodox Christianity the historian must go beneath history. He has to turn ethnographer and social anthropologist. He must collect folk tales and immerse himself in the rhythms of village life.[20]

Brown himself has investigated such concerns at greater length in his various studies of late Antiquity;[21] and similar themes in religious thought and practice have been developed with regard to the central and later Middle Ages, notably by André Vauchez[22] and Caroline Walker Bynum.[23] Two of the essays in our collection, by Peter Biller and Christine Ames, explore the historiography of these issues. Alongside such newer developments, more 'traditional' areas of study have been revived and re-invigorated by new ideas and the use of hitherto-neglected sources. Examination of liturgical commemoration, using especially monastic *libri memoriales*, has provided new insights into both the family structures of the medieval aristocracy and their relationship with the Church. The political history of the Middle Ages has been re-examined in the light of the social rules, often unspoken and only revealed unconsciously or in passing by our written sources, and rituals prevalent, again especially in aristocratic society. And it is notable that both these fruitful and flourishing areas of study have been developed by German historians: the former especially by the late Gerd Tellenbach and Joachim Wollasch,[24] the latter above all by Gerd Althoff.[25] This

---

[19] P. Brown, 'The rise and function of the holy man in Late Antiquity', *Journal of Roman Studies* 61 (1971), 80–101 [reprinted in his *Society and the Holy in Late Antiquity* (London, 1982), pp. 103–52]. Brown himself is generous in acknowledging the influence upon his work of others, notably N. Baynes (1877–1961) and his own contemporary É. Patlagean (1932–2008).

[20] P. Brown, *Religion and Society in the Age of St Augustine* (London, 1972), p. 157: from a review of S. Runciman, *The Great Church in Captivity* (Cambridge, 1968).

[21] Notably, *The Body and Society: Men, Women and Sexual Renunciation in Early Christianity* (New York, 1988).

[22] A. Vauchez, *The Laity in the Middle Ages: Religious Beliefs and Devotional Practices*, trans. M. J. Schneider (Notre Dame, IL, 1993); *Sainthood in the Later Middle Ages*, trans. J. Birrell (Cambridge, 2005).

[23] For example in her *Jesus as Mother: Studies in the Spirituality of the High Middle Ages* (Berkeley, CA, 1982) and *Holy Feast and Holy Fast: the Religious Significance of Food to Medieval Women* (Berkeley, CA, 1987).

[24] E.g. *Studien and Vorarbeiten zur Geschichte des großfränkischen und frühdeutschen Adels*, ed. G. Tellenbach (Freiburg im Breisgau, 1957); J. Wollasch, *Mönchtum des Mittelalters zwischen Kirche und Welt* (Munich, 1973), amid many other studies.

[25] G. Althoff, *Family, Friends and Followers. Political and Social Bonds in Early Medieval Europe*, trans. C. Carroll (Cambridge, 2004) [first published in German 1990]; *Spielregeln*

reminds us that Anglophone historians cannot, and must not, ignore what is going on elsewhere, nor limit themselves to 'English history written by Anglo-Saxons'. One of the principal aims of these essays, and the lecture series that preceded them, is to reveal more of the concerns of medievalists in Continental Europe to an Anglophone audience than has hitherto been easily available.

In addition, not only do modern medievalists examine new types of source, or old sources in new ways, but the work of palaeographers and textual editors brings more source material into public view, at least for the history of the eleventh century onwards. Yet, while it is unlikely that many, or perhaps any, completely new written sources or documentary collections will be revealed – most archives containing medieval documents are known, if not always explored – there is still a great deal to do to make these available in print to facilitate study. Thus more than half the chartularies from pre-1204 Normandy remain unpublished. Similarly, in the largest surviving medieval archive in southern Italy, that of the abbey of Holy Trinity, Cava, there are some 3,000 documents dating from the twelfth century, and 2,500 from the thirteenth, most of them originals, of which only a handful have been published.[26] And for medieval England, some 130 years endeavour by the Pipe Roll Society has completed editions of the accounts of the royal administration and related documents only from the 1150s until the early 1220s: and the pace of publication is likely to slow because these accounts became ever longer and more complex as the thirteenth century progressed. Of course, many fine scholars have laboured, and continue to do so, among these manuscripts – yet the more that is eventually revealed in print (or increasingly on the internet) the greater the possibilities will be – not least for students who may lack the technical skills needed for archival work. Modern technology, notably digital photography and publication on the world wide web, nonetheless offers unparalleled opportunities for the dissemination of both sources and results, and is also making available rare editions hitherto confined to a handful of libraries. Such new technologies have not invalidated the older type of diplomatic edition; but they also allow unpublished sources to be made more widely available and more quickly and cheaply than if we were dependent on diplomatic editions alone. The online *Regesta Imperii* [www.regesta-imperii.de] and *St. Gallen Klosterarchiv* [www.stiftsarchiv.sg.ch] projects are outstanding examples of how new technology can enhance a traditional discipline. Furthermore, translations (into English and other modern languages), while they cannot entirely replace original

---

der Politik im Mittelalter. Kommunikation in Frieden und Fehde (Darmstadt, 1997); Die Macht der Rituale. Symbolik und Herrschaft im Mittelalter (Darmstadt, 2003). Althoff's theories have not, however, been without their critics, notably P. Buc.

26 G. Vitolo, 'L'Archivio della badia della SS. Trinità di Cava', in S. Leone and G. Vitolo, *Minima Cavensia. Studi in margine al IX volume del Codex Diplomaticus Cavensis* (Salerno, 1983), p. 192.

sources in Latin and other medieval languages, allow students to access and study new fields. Thus the translation of Greek and Arabic sources has done much to open up the study of the Crusades and Byzantine history to those of us who do not read oriental languages, as well as to our students.

Alongside all this activity in studying the Middle Ages themselves, we are now far more conscious of, and concerned with, how this distant history has been studied, and sometimes distorted, in previous years. The study of historiography can, if pursued unimaginatively, be a sterile discipline, summarising the outdated views of long-deceased and largely (and sometimes rightly) forgotten historians. But it can also, particularly if conducted as an investigation into the way history has been studied, tell us much about the time of study, establishing a living debate between the past and the present, hugely challenging and invigorating. One of the contributors to this volume, Ian Wood, has recently published such a book, a magisterial study of how the fall of the Roman Empire and the creation of the so-called 'barbarian' successor kingdoms has been viewed and debated by the European intelligentsia from the later seventeenth century until the present day.[27] The audience for this study is, or should be, just as much historians of the Ancien Régime, the Enlightenment, the Risorgimento or indeed of the twentieth century as medievalists. The 'relevance' of medieval history has rarely been more lucidly or learnedly demonstrated. Ian Wood's work was certainly an important spur to the commissioning of these essays, and of the original lectures on which they were based. For just as it is important for society to understand whence it has developed, so too as historians we need to have a clear idea of the tradition to which we belong, and of how our predecessors have enriched and developed our discipline. Furthermore, we need to do this, not just in an appropriately interdisciplinary manner which reflects how medieval history is studied today, but by understanding the *international* tradition which has moulded the modern-day study of the Middle Ages.

Medieval history resonates in a particular way with the present. Indeed, it has been constructed for at least the last two centuries as its opposite – for good or ill – often as a consequence of unreflective assumptions, not just about the Middle Ages but also about the nature of modern society.[28] For any reference to the Middle Ages as a time of religious fanaticism, how many suggestions of this period being a golden age of communitarian ties? True, this once stark opposition has been nuanced as our picture of the Middle Ages has become more diverse and our understanding of the millennium or so between the fifth and the early sixteenth centuries has grown deeper. Historians have eventually contributed to a more complex picture of medieval history, as indeed have non-historians

---

[27] I. N. Wood, *The Modern Origins of the Early Middle Ages* (Oxford, 2013).

[28] O. G. Oexle, 'The Middle Ages through modern eyes. A historical problem: the Prothero Lecture', *Transactions of the Royal Historical Society*, 6th series, 9 (1999), 121–42, especially p. 122.

too, from novelists to creators in the film, advertisement and, more recently, video-game industries, to mention only a few fields. Yet, for all this impressive collective effort, the opposition between the Middle Ages and Modernity keeps structuring our understanding of the past.

The essays collected in the present volume reflect on this opposition and aim to take stock of changes that have affected it. Such an inventory is necessarily incomplete, given the growing number and variety of interventions that have occurred over time. Albeit partial, it seems particularly timely, however.

Many observers have noticed that our time is obsessed by the present. The historian François Hartog has even gone so far as to diagnose a form of 'presentism' at the heart of contemporary perceptions of time.[29] According to his interpretation, the present functions like a vortex into which both the past and the future disappear. The heritage industry, on the one hand, and the precautionary principle imperative of ethics and politics, on the other, are seen as evidence of that phenomenon.

While medieval history is as any other history affected by 'presentism', the unsettled relationship between the Middle Ages and our present may be a particularly interesting vantage point from which to put contemporary approaches to the past at a critical distance. Again, there are limits to what a collection of essays can achieve, however important individual contributions may be. Yet a reflection on the possibility of critical history under the conditions of 'presentism' seems overdue.

What can a volume centred on the writing of medieval history then contribute to understanding history in the making – as opposed to making, that is constructing and representing, the past? It may be advisable to return to some of the aspects of the 'presentism' of our time identified by Hartog. Rather than to the rise of the heritage industry, about which much has been written,[30] the following reflections will pay attention to the precautionary principle that has established itself in the last couple of decades or so as one of the cornerstones of international law and ideas of social responsibility.

Hartog points to the precautionary principle imperative as a consequence of certain contemporary reluctance to engage with the future, which being concomitant of an equally clear tendency to shun true engagement with the past, is evidence of 'presentism'. Yet not so much the diagnostic itself is of interest here as the origin of the precautionary principle or, more precisely, the role played by German philosopher Hans Jonas in the formulation of the related imperative of responsibility. A disciple of Martin Heidegger, Jonas was keen to stress, against the background of both the Cold War and the rise of environmental concerns,

---

[29] François Hartog, *Regimes of Historicity: Presentism and Experience of Time*, trans. S. Brown (New York, 2015).
[30] D. Lowenthal, *The Heritage Crusade and the Spoils of History* (Cambridge, 1998), for example.

that the potential scale of action open to mankind exceeded by far its predictive knowledge. Scientific uncertainty, he added, is best taken into account, when it comes to action, by a principle which is itself uncertain, but turns uncertainty into a fact. The practical rule which can be drawn from it is 'to give in matters of a certain magnitude—those with apocalyptic potential—greater weight to the prognosis of doom than to that of bliss.'[31]

Jonas derived human responsibility towards the world from speculations on the existence of a 'non-omnipotent' God that was deeply rooted in Jewish reflection 'after Auschwitz', on the one hand, and contribution to the post-war debate on the nature of modernity that another of Heidegger's disciples, Karl Löwith, had initiated, on the other.[32] Following in the footsteps of Carl Schmitt's Weimar 'political theology', Löwith ultimately saw modern secularization as a continuation of Christian eschatology, not unlike Ernst Kantorowicz. Yet it was Eric Voegelin who proved the most influential by shifting the terms of the debate about the origins of modernity from Christian eschatology to Gnosticism. Modernity is Gnostic, Voegelin contended, in as far as it is the result of the 'immanentization of the eschaton'.[33]

While Hans Blumenberg suggested that modernity be seen, instead, as a novel answer to the Gnostic challenge of the world as evil which had concerned late medieval thought,[34] Jonas speculated that the lesser God of the created world had become a transcendent power in modern times, albeit one whose nature was very different from that of the omnipotent Creator God of the Jewish-Christian tradition. Two consequences followed from that. For one thing, there is a world of integrity on which the future of mankind depends. For another, mankind has only limited power at its disposition to preserve it. The imperative of responsibility was Jonas' practical response to this situation. Not surprisingly, however, it also recovered a central intuition of the classical Gnosis to which Jonas had devoted his early scholarship.[35] By placing mankind in a situation

---

[31] H. Jonas, *The Imperative of Responsibility: In Search of an Ethics for the Technological Age*, trans. H. Jonas and D. Herr (Chicago, 1984), p. 34.

[32] Y. Hotam, 'Gnosis and modernity – a postwar German intellectual debate on secularisation, religion and "overcoming" the past', *Totalitarian Movements and Political Religions* 8 (2007), 591–608 (pp. 600–1).

[33] This rather obscure phrase may be interpreted as follows: Voegelin was fascinated by the eschatological writings of Joachim of Fiore (d. 1202), whom like Löwith he saw as a precursor of modernity. Both saw Joachim as having given a meaning to the immanent course of history. But in contrast to Löwith, Voegelin saw this as a result of Gnostic thinking through the transformation of the hidden reality into the worldly reality. Modernity can therefore be described as 'immanentization of the eschaton'. See E. Voegelin, *The New Science of Politics: An Introduction* (Chicago, 1952), pp. 29, 120–1.

[34] Hotam, 'Gnosis and modernity', pp. 599–600.

[35] H. Jonas, *Gnosis und spätantiker Geist*, Part I: *Die mythologische Gnosis* (Göttingen, 1934).

in which it is expected to emancipate itself from the world in order to retrieve from it the divine spark, Gnosticism ties the present to eternity, thus effectively promoting 'presentism' over historical temporality.[36]

As Voegelin, Jonas and Blumenberg knew all too well, the pre-requisite to any interpretation of Gnosticism and ultimately modernity lay in the proper understanding of the Middle Ages. At a time at which the diagnostic of the Gnosticism inherent in modernity resurfaces in all but name, a collection of essays devoted to the making of medieval history ought to offer answers, however partial and transitory they may be, to this most intimate and intriguing relationship between modernity and its attributes (such as secularization and 'presentism'), on the one hand, and the Middle Ages, on the other. In this way, this volume is also part of a conversation about 'the legitimacy of the modern age', to quote the title of Blumenberg's seminal contribution to it.[37]

The broad disciplinary scope covered by this book as well as the attention paid to public narratives, be it as texts or images, in the form of official art and events, private advertising technique or individual happenings, remind us, first and foremost, that making medieval history has more often than not been akin to making the Middle Ages present. While some of these attempts amounted to mysticism of some sort (one thinks of *das Geheime Deutschland* of Stefan George and his 'circle' or of Michel Mourre's disruption of the mass at Notre-Dame of Paris in 1950), myth-making for the sake of nation-states and other political organizations and causes, including the European unification process, has been ripe. Not only have historians played a central role in these developments, but they have more often than not shaped their scholarship – in some cases, unashamedly so; in most of them, however, more discreetly or even unwittingly so.

Yet the contributions to this volume suggest that, for most, medievalists have been aware of the remaining distance between the Middle Ages and their present. Another perspective on the essays collected here consists therefore in tracking the ingenuous scholarship that has been born of the necessary confrontation between the Middle Ages as an object or range of objects subjected to historians' skills and the continued relevance of the period or some of the main developments which took place between 400 and 1500 to the present. While expressed in very different ways, from rhetorical invention to language and nomenclature, to mention the first and the last essay, the proposed approaches are all carefully crafted and any one of them is too subtle and nuanced to be pigeonholed according to Schools and even less so to be boiled down to scholars' mere interests. In line with recent and more complex developments, in which

---

[36] D. J. Levy, 'Mythic truth and the art of science', *Eric Voegelin Society Papers* (2002), 17.
[37] H. Blumenberg, *The Legitimacy of the Modern Age*, trans. Robert M. Wallace (Cambridge MA, 1983).

the impact of scholarship and, more particularly, of making history on society at large requires attention in its own right, the contributions gathered in this volume represent an honest attempt to reflect on medieval history in the making – from the eighteenth century to the present.

Medieval history is a thriving and dynamic discipline. If through this book we can reveal something of the richness, diversity and dynamism of how historians have interpreted, and continue to reinterpret, the Middle Ages, and through this enthuse a new generation of medievalists, then we shall have succeeded in what we have envisaged.

PART ONE

IMAGINING / INVENTING
THE MIDDLE AGES

1

WHY REINVENTING MEDIEVAL HISTORY IS A GOOD IDEA

Jinty Nelson

My title takes its cue from Pete Biller in his online thoughts on the lecture series on which these essays are based: 'Examining how medieval history has been and is being "made" is not a luxury activity ... [but] a necessary activity.'[1] The Middle Ages were, and go on being, not born but made: firstly in a particular early modern time, and re-made ever since in successive comings-to-terms with things present through things past.[2] And then, as Thomas Hobbes astutely observed, 'of our conceptions of the past we make a future'.[3] Conceptions of the past are a yeasty mix of understandings and imaginings, anything but inert. Historians doing their professional best to improve understandings, and critically assess imaginings, do not so much control as re-invent. Whether opening out to grand narrative, or focused on smaller themes, re-inventing is, for a historian, less of an option than an inevitable and necessary default mode. Re-inventing keeps history alive and well. In our profession, progress depends, as Biller put it, on being determined to re-examine and (I infer) re-make – or re-invent – medieval history, 'rather than just repeat what we have been doing'. This is work in continual need of being re-done, as new agendas in the present prompt new focuses, new anxieties, new selections, new meanings in the past. There is a delicious Italian word, *aggiornamento*, for which no real synonym exists in other languages: it means bringing into line with the needs of today (perhaps, in current parlance, 'updating') – and in that sense is not so far off

---

[1] P. Biller, 'The Making of Medieval History, some thoughts' (online at: www.makingmedievalhistory.com/discussion.htm).

[2] See J. Arnold, *History. A Very Short Introduction* (Oxford, 2000), pp. 20–33, 98–100, and *What is Medieval History* (Cambridge, 2008), esp. pp. 16–22; cf. for relevant nineteenth-century inventions, see D. Matthews, 'From mediaeval to mediaevalism: a new semantic history', *The Review of English Studies* 62 (2011), 695–715.

[3] T. Hobbes, *Behemoth* (1679), quoted by Christopher Hill, 'The Norman Yoke', in his *Puritanism and Revolution* (London, 1958), pp. 50–122 (at 55).

from a similarly hard-to-translate German adjective, *zeitbedingt*, usually applied to ideas, and meaning 'required by the time(s)'.

Perhaps the Middle Ages lend themselves *particularly* to being re-invented. Here is a case in point: in 1958 the English writer Terence H. White published *The Once and Future King* – a strange fantasy-book about the young Arthur.[4] (J. K. Rowling has admitted to having been strongly influenced by it as a child.)[5] In 1960, Lerner and Loewe's musical *Camelot*, based on White's book, opened on Broadway. Weeks later J. F. Kennedy was elected president of the United States of America. His years in power were chronicled as they happened by a leading contemporary US historian, Theodore H. White, who happened to be an old friend and contemporary at Harvard of Senator Joseph Kennedy, JFK's father. A week after JFK's assassination on 22 November 1963, his widow Jacqueline summoned White to her residence for an interview, to be published in *Life* magazine. In it she developed the theme of King Arthur. She said that JFK often listened to the *Camelot* theme-song last thing before going to bed: 'Don't let it be forgot, that once there was a spot, for one brief shining moment, that was known as Camelot.'[6] In the United Kingdom in 1966 a leading archaeologist, Leslie Alcock, began to excavate the iron-age hill-fort at Cadbury Hill, Somerset, which according to the antiquary John Leland writing in 1542 was believed by locals to be the site of Arthur's citadel. In 1970 Alcock announced to a delighted world that he had discovered Camelot.[7]

Before going further into inventions of the Middle Ages, consider how the words *invent* and *invention* were used *in* the Middle Ages, in Latin. Invention, whether in the context of rhetoric or law or religion, seems to have been considered an entirely positive activity. It was not something done instantly or fortuitously or falsely.[8] Through questioning, discussing, and metaphorically digging away, you invented an effective argument or wise judgement. Matthew Kempshall's book on rhetoric in medieval historiography has a substantial chapter on Invention.[9] Through literally digging, you invented relics, that is, discovered them, prompted by a heavenly sign or message, as the Empress Helena, mother of Constantine, invented the True Cross on 6 March 326. Ordinary finding was something else. You could find (*repperire*) 'in ancient places' (*in antiquis locis*)

[4]   T. H. White, *The Once and Future King* (London, 1958).
[5]   See entry 'T. H. White', on *Wikipedia*.
[6]   *The Wall Street Journal*, 22 November 2013.
[7]   See the annual reports in *The Antiquaries Journal* 47–50 (1967–1970); L. Alcock, *Arthur's Britain* (London, 1971).
[8]   In Classical Latin, the verb *invenire* was normally value-neutral, but could (though seldom) mean 'invent' in the sense of make up falsely, with damaging effects: Tacitus, *Annales*, i.74; for inventing not necessarily in a pejorative sense cf. orators' *inveniendi copia*, Quintilian, *Institutionis oratoriae Libri Duodecim*, X. i. 69.
[9]   M. Kempshall, *Rhetoric and the Writing of History, 400–1500* (Manchester, 2011), 'Invention and Narrative', pp. 265–49.

ancient vessels made (*fabricata*) by pagan art which could be put to re-use after being exorcized.[10] *Repperire* is value-neutral in classical and medieval Latin. *Invenire* is value-loaded, positively.

Punctually with the Renaissance came a negative sense in some vernaculars – inventing as fabricating, making up – which did not oust the positive sense as used by Shakespeare in the prologue to *Henry V* ('O for a Muse of fire that would ascend / the brightest heaven of invention…') but competed with it and in many contexts superseded it. In law and religion, for instance, a judgement or a truth was and is found, not invented, though rather strikingly 'invent' and its derivatives retained and retain a positive sense in the case of 'inventions' and 'inventors' in science and the technical arts; and an inventive person is not one who makes things up.

Inventing the Middle Ages

Inventing the Middle Ages was the title of a book by Norman Cantor published in 1991.[11] It is an often highly critical account of the work of twenty twentieth-century historians. It caused something of a scandal for reasons that will be well-remembered by some, and will shortly become clear to others. A careful re-reading of this book has convinced me that Cantor's view of invention was in fact positive – as is mine. I want, first, to say something about my re-reading of Cantor. I shall then consider some recent forms of invention especially, though not exclusively, of the *earlier* Middle Ages which is my patch, though not, as it happens, either Cantor's, or Pete Biller's or that of any of the medievalists Professor Biller commends in his excellent think-piece. Finally I shall talk about biography, 'the bastard art', as Virginia Woolf called it. On this, I am currently doing some re-inventing of my own.[12]

Norman Cantor argued that medieval history is peculiarly attractive to inventors and susceptible to inventions. His first important point, in a kind of manifesto, was that the invention of the Middle Ages could only happen in modern times, and not before then, because the scholars of the early modern period had, so to speak, pre-invented the Middle Ages as a dark and dismal age of superstition and barbarism, and the Enlightenment only reinforced that view. The Romantics and their nineteenth-century intellectual heirs could do little better, for, despite their achievements in creating scholarly infrastructure – the *Monumenta Germaniae Historica*, the École des Chartes, the Rolls Series – their

---

[10] See C. I. Hammer, 'Recycling Rome and Ravenna', *Saeculum* 56 (2005), 295–325 (at 297–309, 320), for the relevant exorcism-prayers in sacramentaries and pontificals.

[1] *Inventing the Middle Ages. The Lives, Works and Ideas of the Great Medievalists of the Twentieth Century* (New York, 1991, and Cambridge, 1991).

[2] See H. Lee, *Virginia Woolf* (London, 1996), p. 10, quoting Woolf's Notebooks, October 1934.

accounts of the Middle Ages were hammered into 'hastily generalized and over-determined evolutionary schemes' and interpretative models that were 'vulgarly simple'.[13] Only in the late nineteenth and twentieth centuries was their work made obsolete by modernism: Durkheim and Freud above all were responsible for new understandings of human social and institutional functioning, and human psychology. The creation of functioning social structures, on the one hand, ambivalence and ambiguity, complexity and contradiction, on the other hand, once they had been recognized as *characteristics* of the Middle Ages, made that world look 'much closer to our own'. This allowed modern people – not just professional medievalists but students, consumers of medieval stories and iconography via large and small screens, novels and fantasy fiction (and you might add theme-parks cheaply reached by package-holidays) – 'to find in the Middle Ages the mirror image of themselves or parallel manifestations to trends and happenings in the twentieth century', and in our own contemporary world to see that 'medieval civilisation stands towards our postmodernist culture as the conjunctive other, the intriguing shadow, the marginally distinctive double, the secret sharer of our dreams and anxieties'.[14] I find this linking of medievalist work with modernity helpful in locating our field on the intellectual map of Humanities scholarship.[15]

In chapter 2, Cantor's prime example of a new modernist medievalist was F. W. Maitland (1850–1906). Cantor pinned Maitland down as 'cool-eyed social scientist', part of 'an intellectual revolution', because Maitland's view of medieval English law shared the functionalist and structuralist assumptions and insights of Durkheim, that is, English common law performed 'critical functions in the society of that time' and could be dispassionately viewed as having 'rationally served the immediate interests of particular social groups and political forces' within medieval England's 'self-referential operations', its cultural structure and market economy.[16] After Maitland, in short, medieval English law no longer had to be filtered through a Stubbesian 'thick prism of teleology, piety and cant'.[17] 'Had Maitland lived another ten years [...] his name would now figure prominently in biographies of Virginia Woolf

[13] *Inventing*, chapter 1, pp. 28–47, esp. p. 29, and cf. 27.
[14] *Inventing*, chapter 1, p. 47. Cf. my comments on H. Fichtenau, *Das karolingische Imperium*, below, n.19.
[15] See for example *Medievalisms in the Postcolonial World: The Idea of "the Middle Ages" Outside Europe*, ed. K. Davis and N. Altschul (Baltimore, 2009), sympathetically reviewed by S. Yarrow, *Early Medieval Europe* 19/4 (2011), 457–9; *Why the Middle Ages Matter: Medieval Light on Modern Injustice*, ed. C. Chazelle, S. Doubleday, F. Lifshitz and A. G. Remensnyder (London, 2011). Cf. T. Reuter, 'Medieval: another tyrannous construct', first published 1998, reprinted in Reuter, *Medieval Polities and Modern Mentalities*, ed. J. L. Nelson (Cambridge, 2006), ch. 2, pp. 19–37.
[16] *Inventing*, ch. 2, pp. 48–78, citations at pp. 78, 52–3, 57, and 51–2.
[17] *Inventing*, p. 52.

and John Maynard Keynes'.[18] At first it surprised me to find that Cantor's comments seemed to have found no sympathetic resonance whatsoever in recent appreciations of Maitland or indeed other medievalists; but some of Cantor's judgements were ill-tempered and manifestly unjust.[19]

In the rest of Cantor's book, a string of twentieth-century historians are claimed, more or less convincingly, as exemplars of modernist medievalism.[20] Percy Ernst Schramm (1894–1970) and Ernst Hartwig Kantorowicz (1895–1963), each interested in both individual and mass psychology, showed how ritual and iconography and ideas about the body shaped medieval imaginations. Chapter 3 is, however, misleadingly entitled 'The Nazi Twins', a travesty – particularly with regard to Kantorowicz, a Jew who despised the Nazis, from whom he ultimately had to flee.[21] In Chapter 4, 'The French Jews', Cantor situated Louis Halphen (1880–1950) and Marc Bloch (1886–1944) in 'the old humanistic Jewish

---

[18] *Inventing*, p. 57. Both Woolf (née Stephen) and Keynes were related to Maitland by marriage. For comment on British medievalists considered by Cantor (Maitland, Lewis, Tolkien, Powicke, Knowles, Southern, Power and Postan), see Nelson, 'European History', in *A Century of British Medieval Studies*, ed. A. Deyermond (Oxford, 2007), pp. 71–130, esp. 74–5, 83, 106. For Maitland, see *The History of English Law. Centenary Essays on Pollock and Maitland*, ed. J. Hudson (Oxford, 1996), *passim*, and P. Wormald, *The Making of English Law* (Oxford, 1999), esp. pp. 15–20. For materials that make possible a just appraisal of Southern, see *History and Historians. Selected Papers of R.W. Southern*, ed. R. J. Bartlett (Oxford, 2004).

[19] For instance on Heinrich Fichtenau (1912–2000) and John Michael Wallace-Hadrill (1916–85), see *Inventing*, p. 139; for more sympathetic judgments, see J. L. Nelson, 'Why Heinrich Fichenau's "Das karolingische Imperium" still needs to be read', in *Urkunden – Schriften – Lebensordnungen. Neue Beiträge zur Mediävistik*, ed. A. Schwarcz and K. Kaska (Vienna, 2015) [a memorial volume in honour of Fichtenau], pp. 113–22, and I. Wood, 'John Michael Wallace-Hadrill', 1916–1985', *Proceedings of the British Academy* 124 (Oxford, 2004), pp. 333–55. Robert Bartlett's judicious review of *Inventing*, in *The New York Review of Books*, 14 May 1992, gets the measure of the man and the book.

[20] The exceptions are the 'passive retromedievalism' (pp. 203–4) of the 'formalists' discussed in chapter 5, Erwin Panofsky, art historian, and Ernst Robert Curtius, historian of literature and high culture, and the scholars of administrative history dealt with in Chapter 7, 'American Pie', who in any case belong far more firmly in an American cultural context.

[21] *Inventing*, Chapter 3, pp. 79–117. Cf. especially R. E. Lerner, 'Meritorious academic service: Kantorowicz and Frankfurt', in *Ernst Kantorowicz*, ed. R. L. Benson and J. Fried (Stuttgart, 1997), pp. 14–32, and see the essay by Bastian Schlütter in this volume. Schramm's case is more problematic, given his role as the official historian of the OKW during the Second World War. János M. Bak, however, who knew Schramm personally, and wrote a thoughtful memoir of him, 'Percy Ernst Schramm (1894–1970)', in *Medieval Scholarship. Biographical Studies on the Formation of a Discipline, vol. 1: History*, ed. Helen Damico and Joseph Zavadil (New York 1995), pp. 247–62, acquitted him of any real sympathy for the Nazis; and it is unlikely that Kantorowicz, or Walter Ullmann, another notable exile from the Third Reich, would have remained, or, in Walter's case become, his friends had he shown any such sympathy.

culture' of Western Europe. They were interested in different versions of social history, Halphen in Charlemagne's recruitment of 'learned intelligence' to impose 'a kind of order' via 'meritocratic principles', Bloch in how a society's structure, its 'original character', was 'durable over long stretches of time', its social developments related, in a distinctively modernist manner, to 'material and environmental factors'.[22] Cantor, in Chapter 5, 'The Formalists', is less sympathetic to Erwin Panofsky (1892–1968), an art historian, and Ernst Robert Curtius (1886–1956), a specialist in medieval Latin literature: he turns up his nose at their 'passive retromedievalism', yet he celebrates their articulating and preserving of European culture.[23] Notwithstanding the title of Chapter 6, 'The Oxford Fantasists', Cantor is much more sympathetic to C. S. Lewis (1898–1963), J. R. R. Tolkien (1892–1973) and F. M. Powicke (1879–1963), who were so actively committed to recapturing medieval mentalities, and, especially in the case of Lewis and Tolkien, to interesting 'the masses' in a medieval elite culture which Cantor claims, explicitly borrowing the language of Freud and Lacan, was recognisably 'our other'.[24] The continued popularity of Tolkien's *Lord of the Rings* in the twenty-first century might not have surprised Cantor, who would surely not have been at all surprised by such retro-medieval travesties as *Game of Thrones*. In Chapter 7, 'American Pie', Cantor presents Charles Homer Haskins (Harvard) (1870–1937) and Joseph R. Strayer (Princeton) (1904–87) as 'liberals', whose distinctive approach to medieval administrative government, though hardly modernist, linked it with modern analogues in the USA: their intellectual heirs, Thomas N. Bisson (Harvard) and William C. Jordan (Princeton), are 'as American and as durable as Grandma's recipe for apple pie, and as tasty'.[25] The faintly disappointing Chapter 8, 'After the Fall', on the Roman Catholic medievalists David Knowles (1896–1974) and Etienne Gilson (1884–1978), is frank about the constraints imposed by the Church, yet Cantor engagingly notes that 'the Catholic inventing of the Middle Ages carries with it a sharpness, an immediacy, and an emotional evocation' which he evidently admires but finds hard to fathom or consider critically. Gilson had studied with Durkheim but, says Cantor, 'should have listened more closely to [him]'.[26]

János M. Bak, however, who knew Schramm personally, and wrote a thoughtful memoir of him, 'Percy Ernst Schramm (1894–1970)', in *Medieval Scholarship. Biographical Studies on the Formation of a Discipline, vol. 1: History*, ed. Helen Damico and Joseph Zavadil (New York 1995), pp. 247–62, acquitted him of any real sympathy for the Nazis; and it is unlikely that Kantorowicz, or Walter Ullmann, another notable exile from the Third Reich, would have remained, or, in Walter's case become, his friends had he shown any such sympathy.

[22] *Inventing*, ch. 4, pp. 118–60, with citations at 157, 137, 142.
[23] *Inventing*, ch. 5, pp. 161–204, with citation at 203–4, and cf. 193, 196–8.
[24] *Inventing*, ch. 6, pp. 205–44, with citations at 213, 215.
[25] *Inventing*, ch. 7, p. 246.
[26] *Inventing*, ch. 8, citations at pp. 295–6, 335.

The climax of the book is Chapter 9, devoted to R. W. Southern, described as 'The Once and Future King'. The phrase, echoing an epigram on King Arthur recorded by Malory, was borrowed from T. H. White.[27] Cantor, who had been Southern's doctoral student at Oxford, tells a story of betrayal at once personal and institutional. Cantor believed that, like King Arthur, Southern had 'disappointed apocalyptic expectations'. *The Making of the Middle Ages* (1953) and *Western Society and the Church* (1970) were the only books in which Southern offered a big picture. In later works his scope narrowed to that of an intellectual historian focussed on twelfth- and thirteenth-century England.[28] Cantor's charge was far more serious, though: Southern, having 'articulated the intellectual rebellion and imaginative stretching of an emerging generation of medievalists ... and humanists in general', made no attempt to break, or break with, the Oxford establishment, or to found an innovative institute or identifiable school, instead surrounding himself with students who were 'an ordinary, conformist, anal-retentive lot that excelled in reintegrating Southern's ideas where they were most radical and fertile back into the anodyne, established view of the Middle Ages and making sure that horizons would be sparsely adorned but not expanded'.[29] Cantor's own hopes of radical change were cruelly disappointed. It is unclear whether Southern himself ever harboured such hopes (p. 358). There are still Oxford-trained medievalists who have never forgiven Cantor for *his* betrayal.

Cantor's final chapter bundles five 'Outriders': Johan Huizinga (1892–1945), Michael Postan (1899–1986) and Eileen Power (1889–1940), Carl Erdmann (1898–1945) and Theodor Ernst Mommsen (1905–58), bringing out forms of medievalist modernism in some of their work: Huizinga grasped the importance of ritual not only at court but within popular culture;[30] Postan posed 'disturbing questions' that de-sentimentalized and complicated England's medieval economic history in ways that stimulated further research;[31] Power's early writings on women's history inspired later generations (Cantor, who tended to admire feminist scholars, overestimated the quality of *Medieval English Nunneries*, but underrated Power as an economic historian);[32] Carl Erdmann, of the bundled five, produced work that has had perhaps the largest and most enduring posthumous impact, notably in his critical examination of the origins of the

---

[27] See above, n. 4.
[28] See Nelson, 'European History', pp. 83–4.
[29] *Inventing*, p. 349. Cantor grudgingly conceded that Southern had had *some* distinguished students but his failure to create and leave a school meant that there was no legacy, and thus a missed opportunity for radical change at Oxford.
[30] *Inventing*, p. 381.
[31] *Inventing*, pp. 384–7, 391–5 (with citation at 395). See C. Dyer, 'Economic History', in Deyermond ed., *A Century of Medieval Studies*, pp. 159–79 (at 171–2), on Postan's 'conjunctural agenda'.
[32] *Inventing*, p. 387; but compare his prescient recognition of the importance of Caroline Walker Bynum's work, *Inventing*, p. 364.

crusading idea;[33] Ted Mommsen's essays contributed much to the history of Christianity and its profound involvement in political culture.[34] In the end, though, Cantor considered his 'Outriders' united by their 'dissenting, critical ... essentially negative attitude' towards the Middle Ages, and here he parted company with them.[35] Cantor's heart was with the other 'inventors' who basically admired, even adored, the aspects of medieval civilization they wrote about. Cantor rejoiced that it was their Middle Ages that prevailed, and when he epitomized that in the image of 'a cathedral tower shining on the verdant horizon of the placid twelfth-century countryside', he was not being ironic (I don't think Cantor *did* irony), but absolutely serious: 'There is something about the Middle Ages that appears integral to the collective memory of Western civilisation.'[36] Cantor ended by predicting that the core values embodied in the twentieth century's inventions would be carried through into the twenty-first century. For students in US universities, the social sciences would be unable to compete: medieval studies would hold their own, especially because of the appeal of medieval literature, 'the medieval intelligentsia's perception of its own culture and society'.[37] For Cantor, 'prospective retromedievalism [...] comes down to two things: civil society or privatism and enterprise protected by the rule of law [he spells this out as 'turning back the welfare and regulatory state from impinging drastically upon [...] society'], and tough love or sentimental formalism' [meaning, 'institutions and structures that recognize the privilege of private feeling and personal love'].[38] In 1991, it was possible to see – or apparently to foresee – that all the world was – or would be – America: the land of the liberal arts college, the land with its own highly marketable brand of liberalism.

Twenty years on, post-9/11, post-2008, and re-viewed from somewhere else, things look otherwise. Does prospective retro-medievalism begin to capture how medieval studies are now in the UK? And if so, can you or I regard re-inventing the Middle Ages as a Good Idea? Retro-medievalism is big in heritage, in entertainment, in the cultural and creative industries, even in politics – having a referendum on Scottish independence in 2014 means: think Bannockburn! Celebrations of the centenaries of Magna Carta, Agincourt and Waterloo have

[33] *Die Entstehung des Kreuzzugsgedanken* (Stuttgart, 1935), trans. M. W. Baldwin and W. Goffart as *The Origin of the Idea of the Crusade* (Princeton, 1977), see *Inventing*, pp. 402–4. Erdmann's illuminating essays on early medieval political ideas were posthumously edited by F. Baethgen, *Forschungen zur politischen Ideenwelt des Frühmittelalters. Aus dem Nachlass des Verfassers* (Berlin, 1951).

[34] T. E. Mommsen, *Medieval and Renaissance Studies*, ed. E. F. Rice (Ithaca NY, 1959, reprinted London, 1982). Cantor writes particularly movingly about Mommsen's life, *Inventing*, pp. 371–4, 398–402, 404–7.

[35] *Inventing*, p. 407.

[36] *Inventing*, citations from pp. 409 and 410.

[37] *Inventing*, pp. 412–14.

[38] *Inventing*, p. 416.

come wrapped in shiny chauvinism. Sociologists, social psychologists, people in film studies and museum studies are in business here, and the business is global, or as they say these days, trans-national. Of course, some intellectual fodder can be retrieved from all this, but whatever forms that takes, important questions remain. One is: how do medieval studies fit the agendas of the students who are coming *to* the UK? Another is: how can the Middle Ages, however re-invented, be thought useful to medieval scholarship (and medieval history in particular) *in* the UK. Curricula in schools and universities are evolving here. New forms of evidence require new skills to connect with the work of scientists and social scientists, as well as traditional linguistic skills that are frankly becoming increasingly hard to acquire to the requisite level. When, as now in the UK, the Department for Education is 'responsible for issues affecting people in England up to the age of 19' and the Department for Business, Innovation and Skills is responsible for 'economic growth', it is not just the language that sounds ugly.[39] Politicians seem unsure how to offer potential students the choice of intellectually stimulating and life-enhancing objects of study.

It is hard to see Cantor's retro-medievalism as the answer.[40] Though of broadly European sympathies, he wrote primarily for Americans, especially young Americans being educated in liberal arts colleges. He did not often visit Europe, or other continents. He didn't anticipate the trend towards comparative and global history. His Middle Ages were culturally isolated. They began in the eleventh century, and they were not accessed through archaeology or other hard sciences (though they did attract psychological investigation). Cantor himself did little re-inventing: rather, he synthesized, with flair and discrimination, the re-inventions of others, in ways that, I have argued, contribute significantly to the intellectual history of Europe's dark twentieth century. Towards the end of that century, in a time of general European optimism, a huge European Science Foundation-funded project, The Transformation of the Roman World (TRW), signalled multiple, unsynthesized, re-inventions of the early Middle Ages.[41] They came, as it were, too early to fit with Cantor's own post-1000 interests, and certainly too late for him to have considered them in *Inventing*; and they included a great deal of archaeology. Yet I will end this first half of my paper, which has been in effect a review of *Inventing*, with praise for Cantor's fundamental integrity as a historian. He was always willing to engage, if selectively, with new thinking about the discipline of history. He was elected a Fellow of the Royal Historical Society in 1973, and he remained a Fellow until his death. More than one president of the Society received letters from Cantor that contained

---

[39]   The language is quoted from the Departments' websites.
[40]   *Inventing*, pp. 411–17.
[41]   I. Wood, 'Report: the European Science Foundation's Programme on the Transformation of the Roman World and the Emergence of Early Medieval Europe', *Early Medieval Europe* 6 (1997), 217–28.

observations on History as practised in the UK, and expressed his willingness to advise on the Society's direction of travel. He was after all Canadian-born, and had been a Rhodes Scholar at Oxford. Whatever his regrets about aspects of that Oxford experience, he was never the anti-British figure portrayed by the author of his obituary in the *Telegraph*, 1 October 2004.

Twenty-first century inventions and reinventions

In the second half of this paper, I turn to new inventions of medieval history with agendas for applying new methods to make new discoveries. My examples will be early medieval, though some, for instance plague, and migration, have later resonance as well. Some of the 'new' agendas are actually old – but at the same time new, because the means of interpreting data allow new hypotheses, new explanations. There is more need than ever now to co-operate not only with other medieval disciplines, literary and linguistic, and archaeological, but also with colleagues in ancient and modern history; and with non-European, or global, historians; and, last but not least, with other disciplines than just the mainstream Humanities: I have in mind digital humanities, history of medicine and history of science, geography, and non-medieval archaeology, and the thriving fields of the social sciences, including one that Cantor commended, psychology. Interdisciplinary co-operation often tends to mean team-work... But not always, for, as my first examples will show, the lone scholar is alive and well.

Underlying Chris Wickham's *Framing the Early Middle Ages* are comparative as well as interdisciplinary approaches, enriched in the 1990s by the work of the TRW project in which Wickham himself was a leading light.[42] His over-arching argument in *Framing* is that, as the Western Roman Empire fragmented, the demise of the tax-based state left resources in the countryside that actually improved peasants' standards of living. Though mass-produced, good quality pottery dwindled after the sixth century, there were revivals of local production, under the stimulus of aristocratic demand, and of regional markets, controlled by kings. In the East, by contrast, strong states survived in Byzantium and the caliphate, engaged in nurturing multiple local societies, and producing not just one narrative but many. The sweep is exhilarating. Wickham wants readers to get used to diversity. His more recent *The Inheritance of Rome*, partly going over *Framing*'s ground, has extended the time-span to *c*. 1000. This produces, on the one hand, the huge advantage of including a fine account of the reign of Charlemagne and the Carolingian period, with a clearer contrast of western with eastern, Byzantine and Islamic, regimes, and also a fair slice of necessary attention to the Church and Christianization, where *Framing* had largely left the Church

---

[42]   C. Wickham, *Framing the Middle Ages. Europe and the Mediterranean, 400–800* (Oxford, 2005)

pre-800 as, to borrow Ian Wood's phrase, 'the elephant in the sitting room'.[43] On the other hand, making, or retaining, so-called feudal mutation (from the French) *c.* 1000, as the book-end seems something of an unreconstructed choice. The work of Charles West, Sarah Hamilton, and Simon MacLean, amongst others, is reinventing the tenth century as a bridge comfortably spanning the year 1000 and joining up the eleventh-century to the post-Carolingian world, and also rediscovering diversely regional fragments as building-blocs of a cultural edifice large enough to include elephants literal and metaphorical.[44] Coincidentally, Charlemagne's elephant has recently been recognized as a religious symbol recognisable in West and East.[45]

Peter Sarris is another lone scholar with a strong line in reinvention. *Empires of Faith 500–700* covers 500–700, a crucial formative phase in the histories of Latin Christendom, Greek Christendom, and Islam.[46] Sarris sees social and economic changes as fundamental: on a population drastically thinned by plague, and hugely reduced productive capacity, political and military power was constructed anew; and while tax-based states persisted in Byzantium and the Near East, western European kingdoms – states of a new kind – operated through consensus between trans-regional aristocrats and kings. But it was religious beliefs and religious institutions that powered and cemented all three major new formations: hence, empires of faith. Sarris is particularly convincing when he compares the developments of holy war ideologies in Byzantium and early Islam, and identifies 'core instincts and gut reactions' rather than theological complexities as what motivated and rallied believers.

There are obvious differences in the accounts of Wickham and Sarris, for instance in the assessment of the impact of plague, and the use made of archaeological evidence, but I want to highlight similarities symptomatic of early twenty-first century reinventions and likely (I am wielding my crystal ball) to reappear in future. First, scholars who began as Marxist or *marxisant* now accord much more weight to belief as a personal driver and collective force, rather than seeing organized religion as mere mystifier or superstructural adjunct. Is this reinventing the wheel? No indeed, given the critical finesse, and

---

43 I. Wood, 'Landscapes compared' [a review-article of Wickham, *Framing*, and of J. M. H. Smith, *Europe after Rome: a New Cultural History, 500–1000* (Oxford, 2005)], in *Early Medieval Europe* 15 (2007), 223–37, esp. 235–7.

44 C. West, *Reframing the Feudal Revolution: Political and Social Transformation Between Marne and Moselle, c. 800-c.1100* (Cambridge, 2013); S. Hamilton, *Church and People in the Medieval West, 900–1200* (Harlow, 2013); S. MacLean, *Queens, Queenship and the Shaping of Post-Carolingian Europe* (forthcoming 2016).

45 P. Cobb, 'The Gift of the Elephant: on the meaning of Abulabaz', a paper given at the Leeds International Medieval Congress in July 2011, and A. T. Hack, *Abul Abaz. Zur Biographie eines Elephanten* (Badenweiler, 2011).

46 P. Sarris, *Empires of Faith. The Fall of Rome to the Rise of Islam, 500–700* (Oxford, 2011), with citation below at p. 258.

the social and psychological insights, shown in different but connected ways by both Wickham and Sarris. Second, a mental map of Europe has been overlaid by a larger one that includes the Mediterranean world and the Near East. Medieval European history has burst its buttons, and to me this is not cause for alarm, or symptomatic of trendy retro-orientalism, but a sign of healthy conceptual growth. Thirdly, and consequently, there is a determined comparative take; and as anyone who has tried to write comparative history well knows, this is hard to do convincingly without a huge amount of extra homework, which, if it doesn't demand the acquisition of an extra suite of languages, most definitely means seriously collaborating with people who do have those. Fourthly, this kind of history, though it can in principle be done within a national framework, will always tend to look beyond the nation too.

One further and contrasting case of reinvention is Wendy Davies's paper on medieval economic growth. It is about Ireland and discusses chiefly archaeological data.[47] The number of known early medieval sites has rather suddenly hugely increased to over 2,000, many discovered as a consequence of much increased numbers of digs in the contexts of road building and construction projects in the last fifteen years or so, but also thanks to government legislation and co-ordination. Very many of the excavated sites are settlement sites, and 38 early medieval watermills have been dug and recorded just in this small country – more than for anywhere else in the world at that period, apparently. The dates of many of these are pre-Viking, that is pre-ninth century, with numerous others dating from the ninth century. Davies infers economic growth, attributable to (i) the activity of ecclesiastical communities, mostly new monasteries and (ii) Viking activity evidenced by much increased numbers of silver-hoards showing bullion in circulation, but not found in areas of Viking settlement, hence indicating Viking purchases from local producers. Is this an early medieval Celtic Tiger? Or, rather, many small tigers, for these are micro-studies of very local things. The research costs of such digs are not large, given laws that require firms to support excavation and well-established relatively cheap and now widely used tree-ring dating (which can be precise to a year, so, much more useful than C14's plus or minus 70 years date-spans, invaluable though those are when tree-rings aren't available).[48] Davies's is a model study of many small-scale local efforts producing reinventions of the Middle Ages as it were in one country. The comparative and trans-national implications, though, are huge.

At the other end of the scale is a project based at the University of Leicester, directed by Joanna Story, and funded to the tune of just under £1.3m. by the

---

[47] W. Davies, 'Economic change in early medieval Ireland: the case for growth', in *L'Irlanda e gli Irlandesi nell'alto medioevo*, Settimane di studi del centro italiano di studio sull'alto medioevo 57 (Spoleto, 2009), pp. 111–33.

[48] Cf. on dendro-dating, below, n. 68.

Leverhulme Trust which, like the UK research councils, invests only after much careful calculation of the value of outputs and outcomes. The project is entitled, 'The impact of diasporas on the making of Britain: evidence, memories, inventions'.[49] The object was to investigate how far the making of Britain was the product of a series of far-flung and necessarily trans-marine population shifts, and to apply a range of new (or new-ish) research methods for assessing the shifts' effects. The immigrants in question were Anglo-Saxons, and later, Scandinavians. Six scholarly disciplines are involved in the project: history, onomastics (the study of personal names and place-names), linguistics, social psychology, genetics, and archaeology. There is division of labour, and association of labour. Quantifying the volumes and tempos of migrations over time, identifying the densities of settlement, are problems being tackled collaboratively by historians, geneticists and archaeologists. The historians do the texts. The geneticists in this context use molecular biology to study the DNA of modern populations, and the archaeologists, using analysis of ancient DNA (the technology is expensive but getting less so) to study historic populations. Interdisciplinary teamwork is at the heart of this project. Researchers work in the same room, learning the tools and the talk of each others' trades. Onomasticians and linguistic specialists link their studies of modern and pre-modern names of people and places, pooling their results with each other, and then with the geneticists and archaeologists. Linguists and historians of language work applying similar methods to languages used now, and those traceable historically. Social psychologists work with linguists to study how diasporas are recorded in historic texts and memories embedded in those, and in modern memories, through interview techniques and oral history. Finally, each set of findings is mapped on to the rest. So looking at the Anglo-Saxons, between, say, the fourth century and the seventh, it should become possible to pin down more precisely where they settled, and how densely, and to get a clearer impression of what might have been the overall, and over-time, volume of settlers compared with indigenous people. In order to establish how gender affects other pictures, results reached by different methods are compared and matched, to assess convergence and if possible to identify impacts in terms of the presence of Anglo-Saxon women relative to men, or the scale of intermarriage between migrants and locals. The whole series of procedure is replayed (with necessary variations) for Scandinavians at a somewhat later period, from the ninth century to the eleventh. And last but not least, since all these questions have been exercising investigators already for a long time, it becomes possible to

---

[49] See the University of Leicester website for the Leverhulme Trust-funded project directed by Professor Joanna Story, 'The Impact of Diasporas on the Making of Britain: evidence, memories, inventions' [www2.le.ac.uk/projects/impact-of-diasporas]. The appearance of 'inventions' in this context is very welcome.

ask how the project's results alter pre-existing pictures, for instance, in terms of the scale and localized divergences and social impacts of immigration.

A strident answer to that last question can be found on the web if you scroll down a couple of centimetres from the University of Leicester Project site to a site with a banner-headline: 'University of Leicester to play catch-up on "Roots of the British", the BNP's ground-breaking study'. Here online is the British National Party claiming not just a place but first place in the research firmament – they *know* that the ancestors of the bulk of the British population long predated these migrations, and the effects of early medieval immigrants were therefore more or less marginal. As a long-term migrant worker in London with an acquired penchant for Cockney rhyming slang, I can only say: would you Adam and Eve it? A serious response would be: yes, you would, because any scholarly risk-assessment must include the potential misuse of research. The research itself, however superlatively deployed, is of course also risky. Findings in historic DNA studies are constantly and necessarily being critiqued and revised, and sometimes completely superseded. To fail is also to learn. That technologies get cheaper, and faster, makes it increasingly possible, and reasonable, to risk time, and to fail cheaply. But, without prejudging what is still very much work in progress, it may be unrealistic to expect clear or incontrovertible findings across this huge piece. The Leverhulme has put its money on a project with risks attached. That's what so-called 'blue skies' research is about. Some genetic findings may not tally with others; they may or may not show from archaeologically-salvaged ancient DNA the relative roles of maternally-inherited genetic features (inherited by sons and daughters in mitochondrial DNA) and paternally-inherited features (inherited father-to-son via Y-chromosomes) in any consistent patterns. The linguistic, onomastic and textual findings, medieval and modern, less newsworthy, may be more likely to confirm or deny the relative long-term regional stability of immigrant populations; and it will be interesting indeed if migration, exclusion and foreignness can be proved to have persisted as themes in collective memory evidenced in texts, ancient and modern, and in oral traditions, from specific UK regions. Proving negatives has merits of its own. Believe me, I think this project is terrific; but I know that real-life research lacks the thrills of Time Team.

From microbiology, I turn briefly to chemistry – which offers a way of identifying isotopes, variants of chemical elements C12 and C13, which survive naturally and stably in bones and especially tooth enamel. They can be not just dated but located in a specific climatic, animal and vegetal environment. A couple of years ago the British quality press thrilled to the finding of the remains of the Anglo-Saxon princess Eadgyth, or Edith, wife of the German king Otto I. She died in 946, aged 36, and was buried in Magdeburg Cathedral. Her tomb had in fact been reopened in 2008, and contained some very old-looking bones, but careful German osteo-archaeologists, uncertain as to whether these were the real things (Edith's remains had been moved more than once before), with exquisite diplomatic tact sent the bones in January 2010 to England, to the University of Bristol where a team of osteo-archaeologists were ready to investigate. The focus was less the bones than the teeth. It transpired that the woman whose teeth these were had lived as a child in Wessex. Repaying the diplomatic compliment, the British team returned the remains to Magdeburg, where they were reinterred on 22 November 2010. This story is an invention in both senses, and even a third, for Edith has been digitally invented in Pauline Stafford's revised version of the queen's entry in the *Oxford Dictionary of National Biography (ODNB)* online.[50]

Invention through science is a continuing story in the study of medieval plague. Debates that have long surrounded the nature and impact of plague in the Middle Ages are currently live as never before. The evidence of ancient DNA from enough mass-graves should have settled the question of whether or not this plague was bubonic, rat-borne. But DNA is hard stuff to handle, and it is not surprising that the jury is still out on this one. As of now, the bubonic hypothesis seems more likely than not to be confirmed. If so, then it would strengthen the argument for seeing the Justinianic plague of the 540s, which recurred in waves, like the Black Death, but in this case for some 200 years, down to c. 750, as bubonic.[51] In any case, that plague was endemic, and devastating, for two centuries, suggests population did not rise then significantly, with all that that implies for other kinds of history, social, economic, global.

Re-invented too, in more than just European terms, is the history of climate. Writing the history of climate (and hence the consequences for harvests) is not new as a way of reinventing history, of course: it is well over forty years since Emmanuel Le Roy Ladurie invented un *ancien régime biologique*.[52] But the precise co-ordinating of different measures is new. The science of volcanic activity, and ash-clouds blocking out solar heat and hence causing severe winters, has been applied historically in interdisciplinary work published by a Harvard specialist on early medieval historiography, a Canadian connoisseur of Carolingian literature, and an atmospheric physicist at MIT.[53] Evidence for the phenomenon

---

[50] See Wikipedia entry, 'Eadgyth'; also Pauline Stafford's revised entry in the online *ODNB*. See further R. Fleming, 'Bones for Historians: Putting Body back into Biography', in *Writing Medieval Biography, 750–1250. Essays in Honour of Frank Barlow*, ed. D. Bates, J. Crick and S. Hamilton (Woodbridge, 2006), pp. 29–48.

[51] P. Sarris, 'Bubonic Plague in Byzantium: The Evidence of the Non-Literary Sources', in *Plague and the End of Antiquity: The Pandemic of 541–750*, ed. L. K. Little (Cambridge, 2007), pp. 119–32; M. McCormick, 'Molecular Middle Ages: early medieval economic history in the twenty-first century', in *The Long Morning of Medieval Europe. New Directions in Early Medieval Studies*, ed. J.R. Davis and M. McCormick (Aldershot, 2008), pp. 83–97; L. K. Little, 'Plague historians in lab. coats', *Past & Present* 213 (2011), 267–90.

[52] E. Le Roy Ladurie, *Histoire du climat depuis l'an mil* (Paris, 1967), trans. B. Bray, *Times of Feast, Times of Famine. A History of Climate since the year 1000* (Garden City NY, 1971).

[53] M. McCormick, P. E. Dutton and P. A. Mayewski, 'Volcanoes and the Climate Forcing of Carolingian Europe, AD 750–950', *Speculum* 82 (2007), 865–95.

known as climate forcing comes from (i) annual snow deposits on the Greenland Icesheet and the advance or retreat of Swiss glaciers; and (ii) mentions of extreme winters in Frankish annals. The data are presented in tables showing that physical evidence of spikes in severe winters correlate neatly with annalistic mentions of severe winters. The spikes are generally fairly regular, but there is an unusual gap between the extreme winter of 763–4 and that of 821–2 with another in 822–3. The historical climate-evidence for this period from Byzantium and the Near East is, unfortunately, much thinner than that supplied by western sources, but up to a point the ending of two centuries of endemic plague, and the absence of climate forcing, are phenomena visible in Byzantium and the Near East as well.

I am working round to an invention, or re-invention (for McCormick saw this), of my own. What coincided, roughly, with the ending of plague c. 750, and with the absence of climate forcing from c. 764 to 821, was the life of Charlemagne (748–814). And as someone writing a biography of Charlemagne, I am interested in the extent to which times and contingent circumstances condition human agency. Of course, the favourable environmental factors were not the only factors: during the reign there were recurrent annalistically well-documented famines, not all of them merely local or regional, in 778/9; 791/2; 805/6, symptomatic of the biological *ancien régime*. These have rightly been called times of crisis.[54] But Charlemagne surmounted the crises, and part of the explanation for his capacity to do so was that the labour force was gradually growing, and so were harvests, and these conditions, so to speak, at the beginning of a Malthusian cycle, favoured all families and all landlords. Social harmony, political consensus, became relatively easier to achieve. Charlemagne, like any ruler, faced opposition; but opposition could well have become easier to manage and contain.[55] Any performance assessment must take this into account without ever mistaking possibilities for certainties. You could say Charlemagne was lucky, as his contemporaries were. There is a further dimension: these environmental conditions extended across the Mediterranean world, promoting not just more stable and extensive regimes in Byzantium and the Near East as well as in western Europe, but intensified communications and connectivity (to

---

[54] F. L. Ganshof, 'Une crise dans le règne de Charlemagne, les années 778 et 779', in *Mélanges d'histoire et de littérature offerts à Monsieur Charles Gilliard* (Lausanne, 1944), pp. 133–45; A. Verhulst, 'Karolingische Agrarpolitik: Das *Capitulare de Villis* und die Hungersnöte von 792/93 und 805/06', *Zeitschrift für Agrargeschichte und Agrarsoziologie* 13 (1965), 175–89, reprinted Verhulst, *Rural and Urban Aspects of Early Medieval Northwest Europe* (Aldershot, 1992), chapter 6; Verhulst, *The Carolingian Economy* (Cambridge, 2002), pp. 123–4, 133–4; Hubert Mordek, 'Karls des Großen zweites Kapitular von Herstal und die Hungersnot der Jahre 778/779', *Deutsches Archiv für Erforschung des Mittelalters* 61 (2005), 1–51.

[55] Nelson, 'Opposition to Charlemagne', Annual Lecture of The German Historical Institute, London, for 2008.

echo the terms of Mike McCormick, and Peregrine Horden and Nicholas Purcell) between regimes that were also empires of Faith.[56] The elephant famously sent by the caliph to Charlemagne is symptomatic: he belongs in the world of late antique diplomatic gift; he exemplifies a creature celebrated in the Koran; and his name echoes the name given by Islamic scholars to the Koranic elephant. That name, when it resonates in Frankish annals, strongly suggests Frankish recognition – Charlemagne's recognition – of the elephant's religious as well as its diplomatic habitat.[57] McCormick's recent book, *Charlemagne's Survey of the Holy Land*, is packed with information about Charlemagne's information-gathering mission to the Near Eastern holy places: 'the most detailed portrait […] of any major Christian church before Domesday Book'.[58]

A dozen or so scholarly books on Charlemagne have been published, in various languages, in the last fifteen years or so, all of them wholly or partly biographical, in different ways admirable, and therefore necessary for a merely aspiring biographer to read very thoroughly. But I intend my book to interest a reading public whose thirst for historical biography is apparently insatiable, not least where medieval people are the subjects. A few years ago, it was possible to declare that a biography of Charlemagne was 'not really possible to write' because the sources simply did not permit access to this man as a person.[59] Historians are getting more ambitious in this respect, and not just in Charlemagne's case. Obviously, even the most determined early medieval historian cannot write a biography comparable to the much more fully-sourced biographies of, say, the emperors Frederick Barbarossa, or Frederick II, or the massively archive-based biographies of post-Conquest English kings, or of Tudor monarchs or prelates, or of Adolf Hitler. Virginia Woolf, daughter of Leslie Stephen, editor of the original *Dictionary of National Biography*, was a woman closely acquainted with the hazards of the genre: and, remember, she called it a bastard art. Whether or not Cantor would have agreed with that view, his *Inventing* could certainly be considered a series of biographies that were not merely intellectual. His biographical subjects were not medieval people, though, but medieval*ists*. Michael Prestwich wrote in reviewing Cantor's book, '[he] does not stop at an examination of […] the time in which historians write; he is much concerned with their inner condition'.[60] This 'analysis of personality' doesn't just make the book readable, it makes an important methodological point about how seriously the personal and the

---

[56] M. McCormick, *Origins of the European Economy. Communication and Commerce* (Cambridge, 2001); P. Horden and N. Purcell, *The Corrupting Sea. A Study of Mediterranean History* (Oxford, 2000), pp. 123–72; Sarris, *Empires*.

[57] See above, note 45.

[58] McCormick, *Charlemagne's Survey of the Holy Land* (Washington DC, 2011)

[59] R. Collins, *Charlemagne* (Basingstoke, 1998), p. viii.

[60] The extract from Prestwich's very perceptive *TLS* review (31 January 1992) can be accessed online at: Inventing the Middle Ages – Norman Cantor – RootsWeb.

individual must be taken, whatever historical person or group you study. This connects with Cantor's stress on modernity, which for him meant in principle (though this was not his aim in *Inventing*) including psychology among the skills required to study people in the medieval past. It is impossible to psychoanalyse medieval subjects, but it is perfectly possible to search out, and treat as rigorously as possible, the kind of material psychoanalysts work with: childhood memories, relationships with siblings and parents and children, friendships, education, sex, religious belief and practice, sense of humour, dreams, use of language, leisure pursuits, physical condition and health, consciousness of the ageing process, dying. None of those things can be detached from the times in which the subject lived: they are *zeitbedingt*. Their effects, and the accidents of their transmission in texts, vary with circumstances and with chance. Weighing up these elements and accidents is never easy; and it is all *too* easy for the biographer-investigator to construct the subject so as to make him or her 'say' what he or she wants to hear.[61] But there is more to historical biography than illusion, or authorial self-delusion. The bastard art can be a legitimate art, and from the reader's standpoint, a very useful one, provided the canons of disinterested interrogation of textual and material sources are applied. A medieval biography that works, idiosyncratically yet quite brilliantly, by way of dissecting, and treating separately, the various aspects of the subject's personality in three successive phases of his life, is Michael Clanchy's *Abelard*.[62] Even more so than in the case of an intellectual, the life of a ruler really has to be set in times, as if in a sense of real time, for even in the Middle Ages a week could be a long time in politics. The public figure needed to connect constantly with those surrounding and attending them, expectantly. The biographer, keeping public and private somehow in synch, and hypothesizing as plausibly as possible in light of known unknowns, is on the look-out for moments of psychological self-awareness.

Meanwhile, to get at some aspects of my subject's 'inner condition', I have published one or two preliminary sketches of what might be considered easy bits of the story: an episode of Charlemagne's boyhood experience which combined religion and publicity-seeking;[63] devotion to St Peter coexisting with ambivalent feelings towards an actual pope;[64] recurrent intense rivalries with close kin,

[61] P. Bourdieu, 'L'Illusion biographique', *Actes de la recherche en sciences sociales* 62/1 (1986), 69–72, writing as a sociologist about oral testimony. Cf. comparable risks attached to inquisitors' records: J. H. Arnold, *Inquisition and Power. Catharism and the Confessing Subject in Medieval Languedoc* (Philadelphia PA, 2001), esp. pp. 74–110, 113–15.
[62] Clanchy, *Abelard. A Medieval Life* (Oxford, 1997).
[63] Nelson, 'Charlemagne the man', in *Charlemagne. Empire and Society*, ed. J. Storey (Manchester, 2005), pp. 22–37, at 24–8.
[64] Nelson, 'Charlemagne, the man', pp. 28–31; and 'The role of the gift in early medieval diplomatic relations', *Le relazioni internazionali nell'alto medioevo*, Settimane di studi del centro italiano di studio sull'alto medioevo 67 (Spoleto, 2011), 225–48.

especially males;[65] strong affective relationships with successive wives and other female kin;[66] the importance of oaths in sustaining relationships between *fideles*, faithful men, and their lord;[67] concern with the representation, staging and performance of power, including the construction of large public works whose scale can be verified by dendrochronological findings;[68] an insistence on moral correction and self-correction, conveyed in written instructions, especially in the years when Aachen had become a capital and officials waited, booted and spurred, to make Charlemagne's orders and exhortations known in the counties and the villages, driven by their lord's personal conviction of having been called by God to rule – a conviction that grew with age.[69]

One thing I certainly will not complain about is lack of material. It has often been said, for instance, that only a single letter of Charlemagne's survives.[70] But some twenty-three lost letters sent to Pope Hadrian are preserved, in part or in gist, within the papal responses to them.[71] A good number of charters (including judgements) convey something of the force and immediacy of letters patent: that is, they show and help to explain the connexion of personal traits with official roles and relationships, and the ways in which information is contextualized and catalysed in the flow of events.[72] Even so, and even with, by early medieval

---

[65] Nelson, 'Making a difference in eighth-century politics: the daughters of Desiderius', in *After Rome's Fall. Narrators and Sources of Early Medieval History. Essays presented to Walter Goffart*, ed. A. C. Murray (Toronto, 1998), pp. 171–90; and 'Opposition to Charlemagne'.

[66] Nelson, 'The siting of the Council at Frankfort: reflections on family and politics', in *Das Frankfurter Konzil von 794: Kristallisationspunkt theologischen Denkens in der frühen Karolingerzeit*, ed. Rainer Berndt (Mainz, 1997), pp. 149–65; 'La cour impériale de Charlemagne', in *La royauté et les élites dans l'Europe*, ed. R. Le Jan (Lille, 1998), pp. 177–91; and 'Did Charlemagne have a private life?', in *Writing Medieval Biography*, ed. Bates and others, above), pp. 15–28. See further the shrewd insights of S. Hamilton, 'Review article: early medieval rulers and their modern biographers', *Early Medieval Europe* 9 (2000), 247–60.

[67] Nelson, 'How Carolingians created consensus', in *Le monde carolingien*, ed. W. Falkowski and Y. Sassier (Paris, 2010), pp. 69–83.

[68] Nelson, 'Evidence in question: dendrochronology and medieval history', in O. Kano ed., *Mélanges Shoichi Sato* (Paris, 2015), pp. 213–35, and cf. *Großbaustelle 793. Das Kanalprojekt Karls des Großen zwischen Rhein und Donau*, ed. P. Ettel, F. Daim, S. Berg-Hobohm, L. Werther and C. Zielhofer (Mainz, 2014).

[69] Nelson, 'The Voice of Charlemagne', in *Belief and Culture: Studies in the Middle Ages presented to Henry Mayr-Harting*, ed. R. Gameson and H. Leyser (Oxford, 2001), pp. 76–88. See now J. R. Davies, *Charlemagne's Practice of Empire* (Cambridge, 2015).

[70] Epistolae Variorum no. 20, MGH *Epistolae Karolini Aevi* ii, ed. E. Dümmler (Berlin,1895, reprinted Munich, 1994), pp. 528–9.

[71] A. T. Hack, *Codex Carolinus. Päpstliche Epistolographie im 8. Jahrhundert*, 2 vols. (Stuttgart, 2007), II, 966–72.

[72] See for instance MGH *Diplomata Karolinorum* i, ed. E. Mühlbacher (Hannover, 1906, repr. 1991), p. 95 no. 65, p. 112 no. 78, pp. 201–4 no. 148–9, no. 149, pp. 244–5 no. 181, p. 264

standards, much evidence, it is not easy to grasp political interactions between the king and his subordinates, powerful and less powerful, which have almost always to be inferred and reconstructed from evidence of action off-camera, so to speak. It is not easy to understand Charlemagne the man – unless, so I have come to think, by approaching him not only through political relations of fidelity and the work of governing, shared by Charlemagne in his palace and *patresfamiliae*, fathers of families, in their households, but also through a more consistently visible part of the everyday being-in-the-world of the man and his contemporaries, namely, their religion, and, central to that, a shared and social interest in intercessionary prayer for Charlemagne and his family, and for the Franks.[73] This was fundamentally a matter of psychology as well as morality, a disposing of minds to righteous action, an 'inner condition', to recall Prestwich on Cantor – or what Charlemagne himself called *conversatio*, 'right-living', a word with an inbuilt semantic sense of movement, of 'turning-round'. Charlemagne may have had the advantage of generally favourable economic conditions, which he benefited from though hardly controlled, but his continuous and constant task, shared with his people, high and low, was the invention of faithfulness. This paper's end returns to its beginning, and the meaning of timely, time-required, positive, medieval-style invention. In that sense, my own task now is inventing Charlemagne.

---

no. 196.

[73] Nelson, 'Religion in the reign of Charlemagne', in *The Oxford Handbook of Medieval Christianity*, ed. J. Arnold (Oxford, 2014), pp. 490–514.

2

LITERARY COMPOSITION AND THE EARLY MEDIEVAL HISTORIAN IN THE NINETEENTH CENTURY

Ian Wood

Ranke may not seem the obvious way to begin a discussion of the relationship between history and nineteenth-century historical novels which take the early Middle Ages as their subject. After all, in the preface to his *History of the Latin and Teutonic Nations from 1494 to 1514*, first published in German in 1824, he commented that 'A strict representation of facts, be it ever so narrow and unpoetical, is, beyond doubt, the first law.'[1] Moreover, the German scholar had scarcely any impact on the writing of early Medieval History, despite his importance for early modern and modern historians. Although he is frequently described as the mentor of Georg Waitz, a greater influence was the latter's senior at the MGH Georg Heinrich Pertz. On the occasions that Ranke appears in Pertz's autobiography he does not come over as an intellectual influence, despite the fact that they belonged to the same circle, but rather as a committee man, with useful court connections, and as a walker.[2] In any case scholars working on Antiquity and the Middle Ages were already paying attention to source criticism long before Ranke came along.[3]

In addition to his reputation for being a stickler for facts, Ranke was also famously concerned which how things really were: *wie es eigentlich gewesen*. The phrase appears in the preface to the *History of Latin and Teutonic Nations* (without its dates of 1494 to 1514 the title can deceive the early medievalist). One insight into what Ranke meant may perhaps be gleaned from Philip Ashworth, the translator of the *History*, who visited the old German scholar shortly before he died. In the course of the interview Ranke remarked: 'Great as is the respect

---

[1] L. von Ranke, *History of the Latin and Teutonic Nations from 1494 to 1514*, trans. P.A. Ashworth (London, 1887), p. vi.

[2] *Autobiography and Letters of G. H. Pertz, edited by his wife (Leonora Pertz)* (London, 1894), pp. 91, 102, 107, 115, 163, 183, 185, 195.

[3] G. E. Iggers, 'The Professionalisation of Historical Studies', in *A Companion to Western Thought*, ed. L. Kramer and S. Maz (Oxford, 2002), pp. 225–42 (at pp. 229–30).

and veneration in which I hold Sir Walter Scott, I cannot help regretting he was not more available for the purposes of a historian than he is. If fiction must be built upon facts, facts should never be contorted to meet the ends of the novelist. What valuable lessons were not to be drawn from facts to which the great English novelist had the key; yet, by reason of the fault to which I have referred, I have been unable to illustrate many of my assertions by reference to him.'[4]

The historical novel, then, if fully footnoted, so that one could identify what was accurately recorded, could be used by the historian as source material. Manzoni, the Risorgimento novelist, dramatist and cultural theorist, in his treatise *Del romano storico*, made a series of observations about the historical novel, as well as epic and tragedy, which connect at a number of points with Ranke's yearning to use Scott, whom the Italian called 'the Homer of the historic novel'. 'How many times', he asked, 'has it been said, and even written, that the novels of Walter Scott were truer than history!'[5] Surely, *wie es eigentlich gewesen*. The historical novel, as a mixture of history and invention ought, according to Manzoni, to be an impossibility[6] (we are not far here from Virginia's Woolf's description of biography as a bastard art), but could be a success in the hands of a master. More important, from our point of view, he also pointed out that historical novels had become increasingly based on fact,[7] and indeed from the eighteenth century onwards they started to include footnotes.[8] Manzoni made a comparison with drama: 'Shortly after the middle of the last century, a French actor or actress (I do not know which) introduced a general reform in costuming to make it conform to the time in which the dramatic action was set.' In relation to all this he used the concept of the verisimilar (*verosimile*).[9]

In what follows, I shall not be looking for accurate facts in historical novels written in the nineteenth century. Rather, I wish to consider a number of literary works written by men who were also scholars, to see whether there could be a serious interpretative purpose in the historical novel. Essentially I shall look at five novels: Chateaubriand's *Les Martyrs*, Sismondi's *Julia Sévéra, ou l'an quatre cent quatre-vingt-douze*, Collins's *Antonina*, Kingsley's *Hypatia*, and Dahn's *Kampf um Rom*, although I will also look briefly at two dramatic works: Werner's *Attila, König der Hunnen* and Manzoni's *Adelchi*. The shadow of Sir Walter Scott will, of course, be ever present, but as none of his novels deals with the end of Rome or the post-Roman period, he will remain a shadow.

[4]   Ranke, *History of the Latin and Teutonic Nations*, p. vi.
[5]   A. Manzoni, *Del romano storico*, trans. S. Bermann, *On the historical novel by Alessandro Manzoni* (Lincoln NB, 1984), pp. 69, 126.
[6]   Bermann, *On the historical novel by Alessandro Manzoni*, p. 72.
[7]   Bermann, *On the historical novel by Alessandro Manzoni*, pp. 67–9.
[8]   S. Goldhill, *Victorian Culture and Classical Antiquity. Art, Opera, Fiction and the Proclamation of Modernity* (Princeton NJ, 2011), pp. 158, 183.
[9]   Bermann, *On the historical novel by Alessandro Manzoni*, p. 120.

Scott, although the greatest historical novelist of the period was by no means the first. One might categorize some English Gothic novels as being attempts to conjure up the past. More scholarly, and perhaps more important, was Marmontel's *Bélisaire*, published in 1767.[10] This tells the story of Belisarius, the general of Justinian, who fell from grace and was, in some traditions, imprisoned and blinded. The novel recounts the blinded hero's return home. As he begs his way back to his castle he meets a number of his earlier opponents, including the Vandal king Gelimer and also the Bulgars, who are overcome with pity for him, and take vengeance by killing one of the Romans who had betrayed him in Italy. The news of his progress reaches Justinian, who decides to follow him incognito, with the young general Tiberius. When Belisarius himself reaches his castle, his wife dies in a moment of joy and grief, on seeing him blind. One critic unkindly suggested that she was very sensible to die at that moment, because it meant that she did not have to listen to the political discourses between Belisarius and Justinian that take up the rest of the book.[11] Marmontel disarmingly states in the preface that he knows that it was only a popular tradition that Belisarius was blinded (actually although the story is probably fictional, it is a remarkably early tradition, as shown by Lord Mahon in 1829):[12] but he claims that everything else in the novel is derived from historical fact, essentially taken from Procopius and Agathias, though not, he insists, the *Secret History*, which he did not regard as an authentic work of Procopius.[13]

Marmontel's claim to historical accuracy is certainly not justified, although he clearly knew his sources very well, and makes frequent allusion to them. In fact, however, the novel was inspired by a famous image of the blind Belisarius, originally by Van Dyck, but known to Marmontel from an engraving by Abraham Bosse, and the idea of writing the novel came from Diderot.[14] Its purpose was not to say anything about the past, but rather to debate the Bourbon present. Marmontel himself had been imprisoned in the Bastille on the false charge of having slandered the duc d'Aumont.[15] To read Marmontel in the hope of discovering historical verisimilitude, to use the notion stressed by Manzoni, would be a disappointing experience, despite the claims of the preface.

A much more ambitious, and indeed bizarre, attempt to conjure up the past was Chateaubriand's *Les martyrs*, begun in 1802, just as he was completing the

[10] J.-F. Marmontel, *Bélisaire* (Paris, 1767), ed. R. Granderout (Paris, 1994). See I. N. Wood, *The Modern Origins of the Early Middle Ages* (Oxford, 2013), pp. 64–8.
[11] Marmontel, *Bélisaire*, ed. Granderout, p. 52, n. 1.
[12] P. H. Stanhope (Lord Mahon), *The Life of Belisarius* (London, 1829), pp. 441–73.
[13] Marmontel, *Bélisaire*, p. 5.
[14] M. Fried, *Absorption and Theatricality: Painting and Beholder in the Age of Diderot* (Chicago, 1980), pp. 144–60.
[15] Marmontel, *Bélisaire*, ed. Granderout, p. iii.

Génie du Christianisme, and published in 1809.[16] *Les martyrs* is set at the end of the Great Persecution: it tells the story of Eudore, a young Christian, and Cymodocée, daughter of a pagan priest, who, as a descendent of Homer was responsible for the upkeep of the shrine of the great poet. Most of the first half of the novel is taken up with the exploits of Eudore. He had been a soldier, whose postings had taken him through much of the Empire, including a spell in Rome, where he had been educated with Ambrose and Augusine: for a brief period as slave to Clothilde, the wife of the Frankish leader Pharamond, before becoming commander in Armorica, where the druidess Velleda fell for him – the episode would be the ultimate basis for the libretto of Bellini's *Norma*.[17] In the course of his wanderings he ended up excommunicated, and as a result was subject to a long period of penance. It was while he was a penitent that Cymodocée saw him and fell in love with him. She, however, was lusted after by the governor Hiéroclès. Eudore saved her from the governor, and sent her off to Jerusalem, where she entered service with Helena. He himself went to Rome where he represented the Christians before Diocletian, who is presented as wise but weak, and as a result was persuaded by Galerius and Hiéroclès to sign the Edict of Persecution and then to abdicate. Eudore warned Constantine to flee to Britain, before himself being tried, condemned, and imprisoned with just about every other martyr who ever existed. The outbreak of persecution meant that Helena could not protect Cymodocée, who headed into the Judaean desert, and was baptized in the Jordan by Jerome. She then made her way to Rome to join Eudore in the Colosseum, where he managed to place a ring on her finger before they were eaten by wild beasts.

It is difficult to do justice to the narrative of *Les martyrs*, not least because alongside the earthly story there are scenes in Heaven and Hell, and even a brief trip to Purgatory. The scenes on Earth are heavily footnoted: they are underpinned with a barrage of citations of classical and early Christian sources, as well as references to objects and sites that Chateaubriand knew or had read about. In the preface Chateaubriand insists that there is a factual basis for what he has to say. He does, however, admit, disarmingly, that there is a certain amount of apparent anachronism (which is more than a slight understatement, seeing that the material he draws on stretches from the Archaic Age to the fifth century

[16] Rather than the first edition of 1809, I cite the more accessible reprint. F. R. de Chateaubriand, *Les Martyrs* (Paris, 1873), p. 8. Wood, *The Modern Origins of the Early Middle Ages*, pp. 138–9.

[17] Although Felice Romani derived his libretto from Alexandre Soumet's *Norma, ou l'infanticide* of 1831, this in turn was inspired by Chateaubriand's novel. See J.-M. Gautier, 'L'épisode de Velléda dans *Les Martyrs* de Chateaubriand', in *Nos ancêtres les Gaulois, Actes du Colloque International de Clermont-Ferrand*, ed. P. Viallaneix and J. Ehrard (Clermont-Ferrand, 1982), pp. 145–52, and J. Joly, '"Oltre ogni umana idea": le mythe, la tragédie, l'opéra dans la *Norma* de Bellini', ibid., pp. 153–61.

A.D.), but he urges the reader not to be disturbed by any apparent discrepancy, arguing that Augustine and Jerome behave as they would have done had they been there, and that if one thinks that a figure like Pharamond, Clodion or Mérovée, is out of place, one should just imagine that it was another person of the same name as the individual known from Fredegar: there were, after all, lots of Pharamonds, Clodions and Mérovées in history (Chateaubriand's view, not mine!).[18] For the modern reader the historical anachronisms may seem easier to stomach than the scenes in Heaven and Hell, which are unfootnoted, but which are partly dependent on *Paradise Lost*, as Chateaubriand states in the preface. Indeed the whole work is conceived as a confrontation between Homer and Milton.[19] Heaven and Hell are every bit as real as the Roman Empire in the novel: effectively the world conjured up by Chateaubriand is that of religious art, which in precisely the same decade was being revived with, for instance, plans for the decoration of the dome of the Panthéon, which was to have represented Napoleon and Joséphine in heaven with Charlemagne, St Louis and the shrine of Geneviève, Clovis and Clothilde: the scheme, of Antoine Gros, had to be modified to represent the restored Bourbons in place of the emperor and empress.[20] There were those whose religious understanding meant that their reading of history was cosmic. And if *Les martyrs* for us lacks historical truth, Manzoni's verisimilitude, for Chateaubriand it was concerned with eternal truth: the work represented an attempt to put the arguments of the *Génie du Christianisme* into a novel, so as to reach a wider audience. It is a text that lies at the heart of the catholic revival of the nineteenth century, and would inspire a long line of catholic historians, most of whom have been forgotten, but who were of significance for the development of ecclesiastical, and more broadly religious history: Frédéric Ozanam, founder of the Société de Saint Vincent de Paul, and subsequently himself a saint, as well as author of major work on the early medieval Church,[21] Montalembert, author of *Les moines d'Occident*,[22] and the Prince de Broglie, Prime Minister of France, and author of a very creditable account of the fourth-century Church, which, although it was attacked by the abbé Guéranger, founder of Solesmes, was defended by none other than Pius IX.[23]

Yet while Chateaubriand had his devotées (and we shall return to yet another of them shortly), he also had his opponents, of whom the most interesting was perhaps Jean Charles Léonard Simonde, better known by his adopted name of Sismondi. He set about writing his historical novel, *Julia Sévéra, ou l'an quatre*

---

[18] Chateaubriand, *Les Martyrs*, pp. 6–7.
[19] Chateaubriand, *Les Martyrs*, p. 3.
[20] F. Macé de Lépinay, *Peintures et sculptures du Panthéon* (Paris, 1997), pp. 26–8.
[21] Wood, *Modern Origins of the Early Middle Ages*, pp. 140–4.
[22] Wood, *Modern Origins of the Early Middle Ages*, pp. 144–7.
[23] Wood, *Modern Origins of the Early Middle Ages*, pp. 147–9.

cent quatre-vingt-douze in 1819/20, just after he had begun writing his *Histoire des français*, twenty-nine volumes of which would appear between 1821 and 1842. The first volumes of his *Républiques italiennes* had appeared in 1807/8, though the work was not completed until 1817.[24]

Stripped to its bare bones, Sismondi's narrative is not unlike Chateaubriand's. Boy meets girl, they fall for one another, but they are only united after a series of picaresque adventures. In this instance the boy is Félix Florentius and the girl Julia Sévéra: her other suitor is none other than the Frankish king Clovis. She is pushed forward by the catholic clergy in order to ensure his conversion. The objection of the lovers leads them to be kidnapped by the agents of bishop Volusianus of Tours in a wonderful episode set in a ruined castle, which has more than an echo of the English Gothic novel. Félix's objection leads to him to be exposed in church as a demoniac: Volusianus exploits the liturgy to whip up public opinion in a scene which deserves full operatic performance. Félix's subsequent attempts to get justice lead to his falling in with the *Bagaudae* (bands of dispossessed and dissidents), before he and Julia are finally united.

This being Sismondi, rather than Chateaubriand, established religion comes off badly: as a Genevan Calvinist Sismondi had no love for the Catholic episcopate, which he saw as the enemy of all liberty.[25] Yet equally, and more important for us, being Sismondi a very considerable amount of detail is devoted to the socio-economic reality of the period.[26] We are told a good deal about slavery, and the depiction of the *Bagaudae* is as well founded as any scholarly treatment of the subject: essentially we are given a close reading of Salvian by a man for whom the inadequacies of Adam Smith had been exposed by a tour of the industrial cities of the North of England.[27]

In his preface Sismondi is explicit about his aims. He wished to present the conditions of peoples, the relations of inhabitants, dominant opinions and domestic habits.[28] This is not the intention of your average historical novelist. He seems to have intended to write a series of novels setting out such aspects of the past for a whole sequence of periods, but in the event he only produced the one for the late fifth century, where he brought together Romans, Armoricans, *Bagaudae*, Franks and others. He explains that he wished to set out an image

[24] J. C. L. Simonde de Sismondi, *Julia Sévéra, ou quatre cent quatre-vingt-douze* (Paris, 1822); Wood, *Modern Origins of the Early Middle Ages*, p. 87.

[25] A. Lyttelton, 'Sismondi's *Histoire des Républiques italiennes* and the Risorgimento', *Annales Benjamin Constant* 31–2 (2007), 351–66 (at pp. 351–66); S. Patriaca, 'Indolence and regeneration: tropes and tensions of Risorgimento Patriotism', *American Historical Review* 110 (2005), 380–408 (at pp. 397–9).

[26] Sismondi, *Julia Sévéra*, pp. 10–11, 214–32.

[27] J.-R. de Salis, *Sismondi 1773–1842. La vie et l'œuvre d'un cosmopolite philosophe* (Paris, 1932), pp. 21–4, 405.

[28] Sismondi, *Julia Sévéra*, p. 5.

of society as it really was, and not to present a particular religious or political system.[29] Shades of Ranke *avant la lettre*. The comment on a religious system is surely a swipe at Chateaubriand. Not that he really avoided setting out his own anticlerical and libertarian religious and political views. Even so, we can, I think accept that the novel really was an attempt to present his interpretation of late Roman and early Frankish society to a broad audience.

As for that audience, we might guess that it included his mother, but also his wife and her friends. He had married Jessie Allen, sister-in-law of Josiah Wedgwood, and aunt of Charles Darwin, in 1819. It would seem that he also wrote his *History of the Fall of the Roman Empire*, a very smart modification of Gibbon, for Jessie and her friends, for it appeared in English in 1834 months before it appeared in French.[30] That an English audience was envisaged for *Julia Sévéra* might be deduced from the use of epigraphs from contemporary sources, in the manner, as Sismondi put it, of the Scottish novelists (he clearly had Scott in mind).[31] In fact *Julia Sévéra* appeared in both French and English, though the French edition came first. The English text actually appeared at more or less the same time as the publication of the first American review, which announced that this was a book that was so bad that it most certainly did not deserve translation.[32] This is a little unkind: it may lack the verbal glories of Chateaubriand: indeed much of it is in rather plain prose (though the scenes where Sismondi's own feelings about liberty and catholic oppression break out are rhetorical tours de force). But it is a serious attempt to present the early Middle Ages as Sismondi understood them (which was pretty well) to the general public. And as he comments in his preface, most of the characters are attested in the sources: the events are rarely in conflict with what was known of the period in the first half of the nineteenth century, and there is only one unquestionable anachronism (which is admitted by Sismondi): the hermit, Senoch, in whose cell Félix and Julia are united, lived fifty years after the supposed date of the story.[33]

Sismondi's decision to use historical characters was expressly rejected by Wilkie Collins in 1850. In his preface to *Antonina: or the Fall of Rome. A Romance of the Fifth Century*, he explained that '[t]o the fictitious characters alone is committed the task of representing the spirit of the age'. He wanted to ensure that his novel was 'free from the fatal displays of learning which have hopelessly

[29] Sismondi, *Julia Sévéra*, p. 6.
[30] de Salis, *Sismondi*, p. 382; T. Roscoe, 'Life of M. Simonde de Sismondi', in *J. C. L. Simonde de Sismondi, Historical View of the Literature of the South of Europe*, 4th edn (London, 1877), pp. 9–24 (at pp. 22–3).
[31] Sismondi, *Julia Sévéra*, p. 6.
[32] *The North American Review* 15, 36 (1822), pp. 163–77.
[33] Senoch: Gregory of Tours, *Liber Vitae Patrum*, XV, ed. B. Krusch, *Monumenta Germaniae Historica, Scriptores Rerum Merovingicarum* I, 2 (Hanover, 1885), pp. 270–4: trans. E. James, *Gregory of Tours: Life of the Fathers* (Liverpool, 1985), pp. 104–8.

damaged the popularity of the historical romance in these times', but at the same time he claimed that 'exact truth in respect to time, place, and circumstance is observed in every historical event introduced in the plot'.[34] He is at pains to explain that what he presents is an account of the first Gothic siege of Rome, and not the more famous third siege which culminated in the city's sack.[35] He had also visited Rome as a twelve- and thirteen-year-old in 1837 and 1838,[36] and was clearly intent on presenting as accurate a picture of the city as he could manage. Collins thus treads a delicate line between fiction and historical truth. While writing what is presented as a 'romance', he went out of his way to comment on the state of Rome: 'Slaves in their season of servitude, masters in their hours of recreation, they presented as a class, one of the most amazing social anomalies ever existing in any nation; and formed, in their dangerous and artificial position, one of the most important of the internal causes of the downfall of Rome.'[37] So too, he talks of the hatred between Romans and Goths, caused by years of exploitation.[38] His model may have been Bulwer-Lytton's *Last Days of Pompeii*,[39] and his information may have come largely from Gibbon, but while Dorothy Sayers claimed that 'Goths and Romans alike hail from Wardour Street',[40] he actually made a genuine attempt to distinguish between Goths and Romans, Christians and Pagans.

As a good Anglican Collins also has a dig at Catholicism: in describing St Peter's as 'more like a vast Pagan toy-shop than a Christian church,'[41] he was conjuring up not only the post-Constantinian church as he envisaged it, but also the Catholic Church of his day. Three years after the initial publication of *Antonina*, Charles Kingsley also used the format of a historical novel to criticize Catholics and Anglo-Catholics. The Patriarch of Alexandria, in *Hypatia*, was thought to be a portrait of bishop Phillpotts of Exeter, and both cardinals Newman and Wiseman were the butt of his depiction of Cyril's fanatical followers.[42] The obviously polemic elements in the novel, and the fact that Kingsley, despite holding the Regius Chair of History at Cambridge, was regarded as a light-weight,[43] have led to a neglect of the quality of the research underlying the novel. Yet Kingsley

---

[34] Wilkie Collins, *Antonina: or the Fall of Rome. A Romance of the Fifth Century*, rev. ed. (London, 1861), pp. v, vii, citing the prefaces of both the second and the original three-volume edition (London, 1850).

[35] Collins, *Antonina*, p. 414.

[36] A. Lycett, *Wilkie Collins: a Life in Sensation* (London, 2013), p. 36.

[37] Collins, *Antonina*, p. 45.

[38] Collins, *Antonina*, p. 236.

[39] For the importance of Bulwer-Lytton, Goldhill, *Victorian Culture and Classical Antiquity*, p. 194.

[40] Cited by Goldhill, *Victorian Culture and Classical Antiquity*, p. 13.

[41] Collins, *Antonina*, p. 54.

[42] Goldhill, *Victorian Culture and Classical Antiquity*, pp. 157, 174, 223–4.

[43] Goldhill, *Victorian Culture and Classical Antiquity*, pp. 163–4, 256.

had done his homework, as he makes plain in his preface: 'I have, in my sketch of Hypatia and her fate, closely followed authentic history, especially Socrates' account … To Synesius's most charming letters, as well as those of Isidore, the good Abbot of Pelusium, I beg leave to refer those readers who wish for further information about the private life of the fifth century.'[44] Unlike *Antonina*, *Hypatia* is one of those nineteenth-century novels that makes use of the footnote. Moreover, Kingsley's researches into Classical and Late-Antique Egypt also resulted a work of scholarship in the form of his lectures on *Alexandria and her Schools*.[45] The preface to *Hypatia* gives a brief account of the early history of the early Church, which fares rather better than it does at the hands of Collins: 'And thus an age, which to the shallow insight of a sneerer like Gibbon, seems only a rotting and aimless chaos of sensuality and anarchy, fanaticism and hypocrisy, produced a Clement and an Athanase, a Chrysostom and an Augustine.'[46] Admittedly this rather ignores the extent to which Gibbon underpinned Kingsley's own account of the monks following Cyril.[47] Perhaps in order to make plain the historical importance of the early fifth century Kingsley rather incongruously introduces a group of Gothic soldiers stationed in Alexandria. It allowed him to alert the reader to that fact that 'even for the Western Church, the lofty future which was in store for it would have been impossible, without some infusion of new and healthier blood into the veins of a world drained and tainted by the influence of Rome. … And the new blood, at the era of this story, was at hand. The great tide of those Gothic nations … was sweeping onwards.'[48] Here we should remember his own work on *The Roman and the Teuton*.[49] Not that Kingsley's Goths in *Hypatia* come across as particularly impressive examples of new blood. They are rather comic figures who we initially meet trying to sail up the Nile to find Asgard, the home of the gods Odin and Thor. When everything goes pear-shaped in Alexandria they resolve to go '[b]ack to Adolf; back to our own people' – a rather unfortunate spelling of Athaulf, given twentieth-century developments.[50] Despite the buffoonery, Kingsley's Goths, like Collins's, are already a people caught up in their own Northern traditions and myths.[51] At the same time, there is a genuine attempt to understand North Africa in the early fifth century, and

[44] C. Kingsley, *Hypatia or New Foes with an Old Face* (London, 1853: reprinted, Gloucester, 2005), p. 8–9.
[45] C. Kingsley, *Alexandria and her Schools: four lectures delivered at the Philosophical Institution, Edinburgh* (Cambridge, 1854).
[46] Kingsley, *Hypatia*, pp. 4–5
[47] Goldhill, *Victorian Culture and Classical Antiquity*, p. 170.
[48] Kingsley, *Hypatia*, p. 5.
[49] C. Kingsley, *The Roman and the Teuton* (Cambridge, 1864).
[50] Kingsley, *Hypatia*, p. 445.
[51] Goldhill, *Victorian Culture and Classical Antiquity*, p. 205, presents the Goths of Collins and Kingsley entirely in their nineteenth-century context.

for most readers in late nineteenth-century Britain Kingsley would have been the main source of information on late-antique Egypt.[52]

At almost exactly the moment that Sismondi turned to write up the fifth century in novel form Augustin Thierry embarked on a rather more radical combination of history and fiction. As Thierry himself explained, it was reading *Les martyrs* that inspired him to write about the past, and it was *Ivanhoe* that provided him with a model of how to write.[53] The two influences came together most fully in his *Récits mérovingiens*. The first of these appeared as journal articles in 1829, but they were gathered together in 1840.[54] These works of Thierry can perhaps best be described as 'faction'. They are painstakingly accurate reworkings of sections of Gregory of Tours, to which very little has been added except description and direct speech. Essentially Thierry presents his material as if it were a novel, but the accuracy of the reproduction of his source material is exemplary. And, it is underpinned with a vast apparatus criticus, quoting large sections of the source material in Latin, and adding discussion of points of detail – all of which, in the later articles, was done from memory, for Thierry suffered terribly from disease which left him blind and crippled,[55] and able only to dictate to an amanuensis.

But while Thierry cannot be faulted in his presentation of his material, his interpretation essentially lay in his choice of episodes, which consistently brought out the worst in the Franks, and of the Merovingians in particular. Thierry saw himself as both a *Gaulois* and a *roturier*, a Gaul and a worker:[56] in certain crucial respects the two categories overlapped. To be a *Gaulois* in France was not to be a Frank: and for generations, but above all since the publications of Henri de Boulainvilliers in the 1720s, the Franks had been associated with the aristocracy, while the *Gaulois* had been thought of as essentially the peasant class of France.[57] In the eighteenth century aristocratic writers had been keen to present themselves as descendents of the Franks. During the Revolution this association was inevitably rather less popular, and there was a growing desire to be thought of as a descendent of the *Gaulois*.[58] It was this feeling that Thierry encapsulated. Essentially he reversed the old picture of the invading Franks as champions of aristocratic equality, overthrowing the despotism of Rome, and instead stressed the extent that they were oppressors. He could have found the material to effect

52   Goldhill, *Victorian Culture and Classical Antiquity*, p. 32, notes the eleven editions of *Hypatia* in the 1880s alone.
53   A. Thierry, 'Autobiographical Preface' and 'Preface to the Narratives', in his *The Historical Essays* (Philadelphia, 1845), pp. xi, 109, 112.
54   A. Thierry, *Récits mérovingiens* (Paris, 1840); English trans. in Thierry, *The Historical Essays*, pp. 109–204.
55   Thierry, *The Historical Essays*, pp. v-vi, xviii.
56   Thierry, *The Historical Essays*, p. xii.
57   Wood, *Modern Origins of the Early Middle Ages*, chs. 2–3.
58   Wood, *Modern Origins of the Early Middle Ages*, p. 103.

that reversal of ideas in the writings of Boulainvilliers, Montesquieu and Mably, but it was, by his own account, English historiography of the Norman Conquest and Scott's depiction of the oppression of the Anglo-Saxons in *Ivanhoe* that led him to present the Merovingians in unremittingly dark terms.[59]

It was a vision of the Frankish past that had a remarkable impact on the realization and representation of the early Middle Ages. The *Récits merovingiens* would be illustrated above all by Jean-Paul Laurens in 1880,[60] but the notion of the degenerate Merovingians had already become a popular subject for painters from the middle of nineteenth century. Laurens was one of the artists commissioned to decorate the Panthéon, which has a number of medieval cycles: depicting Geneviève, Clovis, Charlemagne and Jeanne d'Arc. The Huns, the Franks, and the Alamans are all presented as out-and-out savages (although among the clergy surrounding Clovis in the depiction of his baptism by Paul-Joseph Blanc one can make out Antonin Proust, Léon Gambetta and Georges Clémenceau!).[61] Not that all the images in the Panthéon present the period as savage. By the 1870s when the designs were being drawn up an alternative reading of the early Middle Ages was becoming established: that of Fustel de Coulanges, with its emphasis on Roman continuity, which found its presentation in the paintings executed by Puvis de Chavannes.[62] Important for all these artists, however, Laurens as much as Puvis, is an attempt at accuracy, even if it is not always achieved, and anachronisms are not avoided. The paintings present the latest in archaeological reconstruction, and they portray fibulae, and other jewelry, as well as weapons, as they had been revealed by excavation.[63] These paintings are in many respects the equivalents of Thierry with his extensive citation of sources.

Thierry's writings were enormously popular, and not just in France. Much of his work (which included a history of the *Norman Conquest of England*) was translated into English, and the *Historical Essays* (including the *Récits mérovingiens*), which were first collected together in French in 1840, appeared five years later in an English translation printed in Philadelphia.

Although the first of the articles that make up the *Récits mérovingiens* was not published until 1829, Thierry's model of oppression had already been set out in earlier pieces gathered together in 1827 as the *Lettres sur l'histoire de France.*

---

[59] Thierry, *The Historical Essays*, p. xi.
[60] See the reproductions in A.C. Murray, *Gregory of Tours: the Merovingians* (Peterborough, Canada, 2006). On Laurens as a history painter, see also B. Effros, *Uncovering the Germanic Past: Merovingian archaeology in France 1830–1914* (Oxford, 2012), pp. 329–31.
[61] Lépinay, *Peintures et sculptures du Panthéon*, pp. 17–18.
[62] Lépinay, *Peintures et sculptures du Panthéon*, pp. 40–3; I.N. Wood, 'The Panthéon in Paris: *lieu d'oubli*', in *Vergangenheit und Vergegenwärtigung. Frühes Mittelalter und europäische Erinnerungskultur*, ed. H. Reimitz and B. Zeller (Vienna, 2009), pp. 93–102 (at 99–102).
[63] Wood, 'The Panthéon in Paris: *lieu d'oubli*', p. 100; Effros, *Uncovering the Germanic Past*, pp. 322–35.

The first of these had appeared in the *Censeur Européen* in 1817.[64] Two years later Alessandro Manzoni, who was in Paris at the time, came across Thierry's work. He saw in the story of oppression that Thierry had derived from Scott, and behind him the Anglo-Saxon scholar Sharon Turner, a model that he thought he could apply to Italian history. He did so initially not in a historical novel (the *Promessi Sposi* would come later, in 1828), but in a pair of dramas, *Il conte di Carmagnola* and the *Adelchi*. The latter was concerned with the early Middle Ages.[65] It tells the story of Charlemagne's repudiation of his Italian wife, his invasion of Italy, and the defeat and fall of the last Lombard king, Desiderius. In historical reality Desiderius's son Adelchis managed to escape to Constantinople, where he plotted, without success, to reverse the Lombard defeat. In Manzoni's presentation Adelchi is killed fighting the army of Charles, but only after first realising that the Lombard State was doomed because of its oppression of the indigenous Romans.

Unlike Thierry, Manzoni did alter history to suit his argument, though without the death of Adelchi there would have been no tragedy, and the end would as a result have been less dramatically satisfactory. As Manzoni argued in his essay on the historical novel, which is expansive enough to include both epic and also tragedy, the story had to be paramount.[66] At the same time, as we have seen, Manzoni noted the increasing determination of writers of historical fiction to research their subject matter thoroughly, and this is reflected in the citation of source material, either in the text itself or in footnotes. In the case of the *Adelchi*, Manzoni went one stage further, writing his *Discorso sopra alcuni punti della storia langobardica in Italia*. This is a detailed examination of the evidence for the Lombard settlement in Italy (which ultimately comes down to two sentences in Paul the Deacon).[67] It interprets that material as showing that the settlement amounted to major oppression of the Italian people, who were effectively enslaved – the model is ultimately Thierry's for the treatment of the Gauls by the Franks. The *Discorso* looks at the whole history of Lombard dominance, but above all at the early years of their settlement: the *Adelchi* presents the conclusions of the *Discorso* for a literary audience, setting out the picture of oppression largely in two great choral odes, in the speeches of the priest Martin,

---

[64]   Thierry, *The Historical Essays*, pp. 96–7.
[65]   There are numerous editions of both works: there is also an English translation, with useful commentary, in F. B. Deigan, *Alessandro Manzoni's The Count of Carmagnola and Adelchis* (Baltimore, 2004). Wood, *Modern Origins of the Early Middle Ages*, pp. 141–9, and '"Adelchi" and "Attila": the barbarians and the Risorgimento', *Papers of the British School at Rome* 76 (2008), 233–55.
[66]   Bermann, *On the historical novel by Alessandro Manzoni*, p. 72.
[67]   A. Manzoni, *Discorso sopra alcuni punti della storia longobardica in Italia*, ed. I. Becherucci (Milan, 2005); Wood, *Modern Origins of the Early Middle Ages*, pp. 114–19.

who guides Charlemagne's troops, and in Adelchi's final descriptions of the state of Italy under Lombard rule.

Manzoni clearly had a political motive in setting out this interpretation, for the Lombards represent all foreign invaders of Italy, the removal of whom was central to the Risorgimento. Not surprisingly the interpretation offered by the *Discorso* became the dominant reading of the Lombard period, albeit with some modifications, notably at the hands of Carlo Troya and Cesare Balbo.[68]

Equally important for Manzoni (and indeed for Troya) was the idea that the papacy might play a role in the unification of Italy: and indeed papal influence is an important factor in prompting Charlemagne to invade the peninsula in the Adelchi. Hadrian himself makes no appearance, for his representation on stage was not permitted in Italy. He could be, and was, presented on stage in Germany, where Zacharias Werner gave him a central role in his drama *Attila, König der Hunnen* of 1809.[69] Werner, who was for a while seen as the most likely literary successor to Goethe, particularly in the circle of Mme de Staël, wrote a number of historical plays, notably about the Crusades.[70] His works were extremely well researched: the *Attila* shows a remarkable knowledge of all the available sources. In Werner's hands the play becomes a proto-Wagnerian spiritual drama – with its themes of love in death and sacrifice, and its Burgundian (i.e. Gibichung) heroine, anyone reading it must wonder whether Wagner had it in mind as he wrote the libretto for the *Ring*. At the time of writing Werner himself was still a protestant, although his spiritual leanings had already led to a breach with Goethe, and he would become a catholic, and indeed would be the dominant catholic preacher in Vienna at the time of the Congress, when he denounced his earlier theatrical works.[71]

The *Attila* would attract the attention of a number of composers:[72] in particular Verdi saw the opportunity to transform the work into another Risorgimento piece depicting Italy under threat of foreign invasion. Verdi would also add

---

[68] Wood, *Modern Origins of the Early Middle Ages*, p. 115: on Balbo, see also his 'Balbo and the Barbarians' (forthcoming).

[69] Z. Werner, *Attila, Dramatische Werke*, vol. 5 (Bern, 1970). See Wood, '"Adelchi" and "Attila": the barbarians and the Risorgimento', pp. 246–7.

[70] Wood, '"Adelchi" and "Attila"', p. 247, and *Modern Origins of the Early Middle Ages*, pp. 81–4. The dramas on the Crusades, are the two part *Die Söhne des Thais* of 1893–4: *Die Templar auf Cypern*, English translation by E. A. M. Herbert, *The Templars in Cyprus* (London, 1886), and *Kreuzbrüder*, English translation by E. A. M. Herbert, *The Brethren of the Cross* (London, 1892): followed by *Das Kreuz an der Ostsee* of 1806.

[71] Wood, *Modern Origins of the Early Middle Ages*, pp. 82–3:, and '"Adelchi" and "Attila": the barbarians and the Risorgimento', p. 247.

[72] Giuseppe Persiani, *Attila* (1827), Temistocle Solera's *Ildegonda* (1840), Francesco Malipiero's *Ildegonda di Borgogna* (1845). Beethoven's friend Ignaz Seyfried provided incidental music for a production of Werner's play. Wood, *Modern Origins of the Early Middle Ages*, p. 130.

a scene in which hermits fleeing from the sack of Aquileia found Venice – a not-overly subtle allusion to the fact that the work was commissioned by La Fenice: though Verdi's librettists did base the scene on a passage in Sismondi's work on the Italian Republics.[73] And an attempt at verisimilitude was made in the original production (one might remember Manzoni's already-mentioned concern with what was *verosimile*), in that Verdi wanted authentic designs. What this amounted to was sending the designer to the Vatican to look at Raphael's famous fresco of the encounter of Attila and Leo[74] – though in the opera Leo had to be designated simply as an old man.

The issue of the papacy, like that of the Church, was, of course, a bone of contention, and not just because of whether the pope could, or could not, be represented on stage. For Werner, moving as he was towards Catholicism, Leo could unquestionably be a sympathetic, and even heroic figure. Manzoni and Sismondi, however, were very much at loggerheads over the position of the pope, and more generally of Catholicism. Although his study of the Italian Republics was as important in providing historical ammunition for the Risorgimento as was the *Adelchi*,[75] Sismondi had no time either for the papacy or for the Catholic Church, which prompted Manzoni to attack his stance over religion in his *Osservazione sulla morale cattolica*.[76]

Manzoni's stance may have held sway in Italy, but it was challenged strongly by more northerly writers, perhaps most interestingly by Felix Dahn. Dahn's twelve/thirteen-volume *Könige der Germanen*, which came out over the period from 1861 to 1911, is a very precise study which is remarkable for its caution.[77] Dahn knew his sources extraordinarily well. He wrote significant studies of Paul the Deacon and Procopius (he was in the vanguard of those arguing for the authenticity of the *Secret History*), and his analyses of law in his study of kingship are impeccable.[78] Unlike most German contemporaries, and indeed a number of English scholars, in his academic publications he does not overstate the Germanic nature of his information. Occasionally he pauses to say that there must be a Germanic aspect to what he is dealing with, but since he cannot find it

[73] Wood, *Modern Origins of the Early Middle Ages*, pp. 130–1.

[74] *I Copialettere di Giuseppe Verdi*, ed. G. Cesari and A. Luzio (Milan, 1913), p. 441.

[75] I. Porciani, 'Disciplinamento nazionale e modelli domestici', in *Storia d'Italia, Annali 22, Il Risorgimento*, ed. A. M. Banti and P. Ginsborg (Turin, 2007), pp. 97–125 (at p. 102); A. M. Banti, *La nazione del Risorgimento. Parentela, sanità e onore alle origini dell'Italia unita* (Turin, 2006), p. 45.

[76] A. Manzoni, *Osservazioni sulla morale cattolica* (1819), in *Manzoni, Tutte le opere*, ed. M. Martelli and R. Bacchelli, 2 vols. (Florence, 1973), II, 1335–1461

[77] F. Dahn, *Könige der Germanen*, 13 vols. (Leipzig, 1861–1911). It is possible to count the number of volumes in more ways than one.

[78] F. Dahn, *Prokopius von Cäsarea. Ein Beitrag zur Historiographie der Völkerwanderung und des sinkenden Römerthums* (Berlin, 1865), and *Langobardische Studien* (Leipzig, 1876), vol. 1 (only vol. published).

in the sources he has to leave it out.[79] His Germanic enthusiasms, and they were considerable, found a different outlet: in plays, poems, opera libretti and a novel. Of these, the most important is his novel *Ein Kampf um Rom*, which deals with the failure of the Ostrogothic kingdom in Italy. Whether Dahn knew of Collins' depiction of the earlier struggle for Rome, in the time of Alaric, is an interesting question. He could certainly read English, and in any case *Antonina* was translated into German as early as 1850, the very year of its original publication. Dahn's Goths have a good deal in common with those of Collins and Kingsley – though the similarities could easily be derived from their Latin, Greek, and Old Icelandic sources.

Essentially Dahn provides a narrative account of events in the Italian peninsula from the death of Theodoric to the final defeat of the Ostrogoths at *Busta Gallorum*. The narrative largely follows Procopius and Agathias, although love and hate interests are added, while a shadowy senator, Cethegus, who does appear in Procopius (where he is indeed somewhat sinister),[80] becomes the representative of the Italians rejecting both Ostrogothic and Byzantine rule. In addition, there are two rather more bizarre episodes when Vikings turn up: on the second occasion they arrive to take the remaining Goths and their dead leaders to Thule, thus affirming their ultimate association with the Germanic North.

Dahn's novel is certainly a good yarn: good enough to have been made into a film in the 1950s, starring Orson Welles. It is not, however, taken seriously: certainly not as history. Commentators have noted its significance as a *roman-à-clef*, something that Dahn himself makes explicit in his autobiography. As he explained it, Justinian was Napoleon III, Theodora was Eugénie, the Goths were the Austrians, and the scheming Cethegus was Pius IX.[81] First dreamt up in Ravenna in 1858, begun in Munich in 1859, but shelved for much of the 1860s, and only completed in 1874, these parallels, however, became more and more stretched. After all, by 1874 Napoleon and Eugénie were no longer forces to be reckoned with, while the Austrians had been driven out of Italy.

Emphasis on the narrative and on its connections with political events in the 1860s have, I suspect, blinded historians to a more significant aspect of the work,

[79] Dahn, *Könige der Germanen*, vol. 2 (1861), pp. 103, 124; I. N. Wood, 'Early Medieval History and Nineteenth-Century Politics in Dahn's "Ein Kampf um Rom" and Manzoni's "Adelchi"', in *Geschichtsvorstellungen. Bilder, Texte und Begriffe aus dem Mittelalter. Festschrift für Hans-Werner Goetz zum 65. Geburtstag*, ed. S. Patzold, A. Rathmann-Lutz and V. Scior (Vienna, 2012), pp. 535–57 (at p. 546).

[80] Procopius, *History of the Wars*, vii.13, ed. H. B. Dewing, in Procopius, ed. H. B. Dewing, 7 vols. (Cambridge MA, 1914–40), IV, 12. See J. R. Martindale, *Prosopography of the Later Roman Empire*, vol. 2, *A.D. 395–527* (Cambridge, 1980), pp. 281–2, 'Cethegus'.

[81] F. Dahn, *Erinnerungen*, 2nd edn, 4 vols. (Leipzig, 1892), III, 368. See Wood, *Modern Origins of the Early Middle Ages*, p. 194.

which is not just clear from the bizarre role played by the Vikings, but is also closely tied to the representation of the leaders of the Goths as Germanic heroes. This is the Germanic reading of the early Middle Ages that Dahn felt he could not put into his more scholarly work: arguably this is what he thought was the more accurate representation of the early period: we are back with Ranke's *wie es eigentlich gewesen*: with Manzoni's claim that Scott's novels were truer than history: with Sismondi's insistence that he was presenting the conditions of peoples, the relations of inhabitants, and the dominant opinions and domestic habits of the time:[82] with Collins's representation of the spirit of the age:[83] or with Kingsley's 'authentic history'.[84] For Dahn we may suspect that the picture he presented in *Ein Kampf um Rom* was historically more 'true' than the scholarly picture presented in *Die Könige der Germanen*.

Moreover, Dahn's attempt to represent Ostrogothic Italy was carefully executed. Like Sismondi, Dahn spent time to explain the position of the peasantry. The rights of the Ostrogoths over land are carefully established: their treatment of the subject population is the dealt with in more than one episode in the novel. What we see is not oppression, but rather a pattern of justified ownership which caused some, largely unjustified, resentment. It is not hard to see in *Ein Kampf um Rom* the mirror image of Manzoni's *Adelchi*. The Goths are not oppressors: Romans rather than Goths are the trouble makers. Dahn does not claim to be answering Manzoni, and indeed there is no clear citation of the *Adelchi* in his novel. But given his theatrical interests, both as an author and indeed as the son of an actor and an actress, and given his linguistic facility and his love of Italy, it is hard to believe that he did not have the *Adelchi* in mind when constructing *Ein Kampf um Rom*.[85]

The works of literature that I have been considering are rather more complex works than is usually acknowledged – with the exception of the *Adelchi*, whose scholarly credentials are openly proclaimed because of the *Discorso*. But, as we have seen, all these works, even Marmontel's *Bélisaire* and Collins' *Antonina*, were based on a thorough knowledge of the sources – something that Manzoni thought was central to the historical novel, as it had developed by the end of the eighteenth century. The group of works is certainly a rather special one: *Antonina* apart, I have concentrated after all on works of literature written by men who had some claim to be historians: Chateaubriand, Thierry, Manzoni, Sismondi, Kingsley and Dahn. At the same time all of them had axes of one sort or another to grind: Chateaubriand was pushing for a religious revival, Thierry was arguing the case for the Gauls against the Franks, Manzoni, like Verdi, was

---

[82] Sismondi, *Julia Sévéra*, p. 5.
[83] Collins, *Antonina*, p. vii
[84] Kingsley, *Hypatia*, p. 8.
[85] Wood, 'Early Medieval History and Nineteenth-Century Politics in Dahn's "Ein Kampf um Rom" and Manzoni's "Adelchi"'.

promoting the Risorgimento, and Dahn was arguing for Germanic tradition. And to some extent these works were allowing their authors to go beyond the bounds of conventional history, in pushing their precise readings.

Equally important is the impact of these works on the historical imagination, not so much of scholars, although one would be wrong to assume that scholars are immune to such influences, but of the wider public. All these writers were addressing an audience beyond any academic readership. I am aware that to some extent the concept is not entirely valid for the nineteenth century. *Le grand public* might have read Chateaubriand's *Génie du christianisme*: and a sizeable number of people must have read sections of Sismondi's histories, to judge by their print-runs. The publication history of Manzoni's *Discorso*, on the other hand, does not suggest a best seller: nor indeed does that of *Adelchi*, although the choral odes were set to music, and must have been more widely heard. There would seem to have been only one edition of Kingsley's *Alexandria and her schools*, but there were eleven editions of *Hypatia* in the 1880s alone. How many people other than academics ever read Dahn's *Könige der Germanen*? But we have a pretty good idea of the scale of the readership of *Ein Kampf um Rom*. 84,000 copies were printed in the first 18 years of publication: it became even more popular in the run up to the First World War, and in July and August 1914 it was the most popular confirmation present for boys: more popular, that is, than the Bible. By 1938 it had sold 615,000 copies: by 1950, 750,000.[86] These are colossal numbers for the time.

What this must have meant was that the German understanding of the Ostrogothic period in Italy was the image of *Ein Kampf um Rom* – and not that of the relevant volume of the *Könige der Germanen*. So too, the dominant image of the Merovingians in France was that of Thierry's *Récits mérovingiens*. It would appear, however, that Sismondi's *Julia Sévéra* never really took off. As for the history of the persecutions, that was surely dominated not by Gibbon, but by Chateaubriand. And alongside these literary representations there are the images presented to the public through etchings and paintings: Bosse's *Bélisaire*, which actually inspired Marmontel: Laurens's illustrations for the *Récits mérovingiens*: even the designs for Verdi's *Attila*, derived from Raphael's frescoes in the Vatican. The Raphael frescoes would never have been a very good guide to what Attila and the Huns looked like: nor is Bosse's *Bélisaire* to be relied on. But there is rather more to be said for Laurens's illustrations for Thierry's essays. Ranke was clearly right to be suspicious of Walter Scott: nevertheless, these works did make some attempt at achieving verisimilitude. If one believed in the nineteenth century that one could come close to *wie es eigentlich gewesen*, Thierry and Laurens were not a bad place to start.

---

[86] S. Neuhaus, *Literatur und nationale Einheit in Deutschland* (Tübingen, 2002), p. 231.

PART TWO

CONSTRUCTING A EUROPEAN IDENTITY

3

EUROPEAN ETHNICITIES AND EUROPEAN AS AN ETHNICITY: DOES EUROPE HAVE TOO MUCH HISTORY?

Patrick Geary

Until the end of Antiquity, the Roman Empire in the west consisted of provinces whose names and divisions represented large geographical regions bearing little, if any, direct relationship to the various ethnic and linguistic communities that inhabited them: *Pannonia, Noricum, Raetia,* the *Germaniae,* the *Belgicae, Lugdunensis, Aquitania, Tarraconensis, Narbonensis,* etc. While some of these names echoed those of Celtic peoples subdued in the first century or Tacitus's first-century *Germani* (none of whom would have called themselves by that name), ethnic communities as such were not constituent elements of the Roman polity. Rome recognized citizens and non-citizens, and one's ethnic background, if at all remembered, was strictly subordinated to territorial identity and social rank.[1] Heirs of Greek perceptions of barbarians as more a part of the natural world than the world of the *polis,* Romans were prepared to understand those outside the empire (with the exception of the Persians perhaps) as simple biological descent groups, as *gentes* or *ethne, ἔθνη,* stereotypical, quasi eternal races having more in common with species of animals than with the complex and essential constitutional Roman people. However, one could leave one's ethnic identity behind and become Roman – a transformation not from one *gens* to another but a fundamentally different way of being. Proper education, *paideia,* drew aspiring elites of whatever background into deep personal identification with the traditions of Greek and Roman literature, philosophy and values in which

---

[1] On the construction of Roman ethnography see E. Ch. L. van der Vliet, 'The Romans and Us: Strabo's "Geography" and the Construction of Ethnicity', *Mnemosyne*, s. 4, 56 (2003), 257–72. For a general discussion of concepts of ethnicity in Late Antiquity see Walter Pohl, 'Aux origines d'une Europe ethnique: Transformations d'identités entre Antiquité et Moyen Âge', *Annales. Histoire, Sciences Sociales* 60 (2005), 183–208. For a strong argument that ethnicity was a weak category in Antiquity, see E. Gruen, 'Did Ancient Identity Depend on Ethnicity? A Preliminary Probe', *Phoenix* 67 (2013), 1–22.

alternative cultural memories had no place.[2] Roman governance, likewise, ignored ethnicity within its boundaries: *Romanitas* was famously not a question of descent but of law. The *populus Romanus* was understood as constituted not by descent, but by consent, not by culture or by language, but by justice and a concern for the common good. As Cicero in the *De re publica* has Scipio say:

> The *res publica* is the property of the people, but a people is not an assemblage of all persons brought together in just any way, but rather an assemblage of a multitude united by a consensus concerning law and the common good.[3]

This constitutional understanding of the *populus Romanus* was enshrined in the legendary founding of Rome itself. According to Livy, Romulus, seeing that nothing but law could cause the multitude inhabiting his new city to coalesce into one body of a people, he gave them laws.[4] Law, not descent, language, or custom, constituted Romans and the Roman state.

At the end of Antiquity, the conceptual framework of western political power, if not the actual mechanisms of government, had been radically transformed. In place of Roman provinces we find instead *regna* or kingdoms, whose identities expressed ethnic vocabulary: *regnum Francorum, regnum Burgundionum, regnum Wandalorum; regnum Gothorum*.[5] Moreover, the ideology of kingship itself is expressed in generative, biological, rather than constitutional terms. When, for example, the Ostrogothic ruler of Italy Theoderic wrote to the Frankish king Clovis in an attempt to forestall war between Clovis and the Visigothic king Alaric II, Theoderic based his appeal not on justice, law, or the common good, but on the bonds of kinship that should unite both rulers. This kinship, which united the two kings through Theoderic himself, as the head of a family of kings, should bring peace to these rulers' respective peoples. Theoderic terms Alaric *filius noster*, and he claims the same authority over Clovis. He demands that Clovis renounce war 'by the authority of a father and a friend'.[6] As for the peoples that the Clovis and

---

[2] See in particular P. Brown, *Power and Persuasion in Late Antiquity: Towards a Christian Empire* (Madison WI, 1992).

[3] *De re publicae* i.25: 'Est, igitur, inquit Africanus, res publica res populi, populus autem non omnis hominum coetus quoquo modo congregatus, sed coetus multitudinis iuris consensu et utilitatis communione sociatus'.

[4] 'Rebus divinis rite perpetratis vocataque ad concilium multitudine quae coalescere in populi unius corpus nulla re praeterquam legibus poterat, iura dedit'; i.8.

[5] See in particular *Kingdoms of the Empire: The Integration of Barbarians in Late Antiquity*, ed. Walter Pohl (Leiden, 1997) and *Topographies of Power in the Early Middle Ages*, ed. Mayke de Jong and Frans Theuws, with Carine van Rhijn (Leiden 2001). The best general synthesis on the process is Guy Halsall, *Barbarian Migrations and the Roman West 376–568* (Cambridge, 2007).

[6] 'Iure patris vobis interminor et amantis; Cassiodorus, *Variae* iii.4, ed. Theodor Mommsen, MGH Auctores Antiqui 12 (Berlin, 1894), p. 80.

Alaric command, these are *nationes divisae*, but *nationes* characterized not by the *populus* of Roman political tradition but by tribal vocabulary: Clovis and Alaric are *summarum gentium reges*. The language of *gentes*, of *nationes*, long applied to polities outside the Empire, is now the vocabulary with which power within the ancient *limes* is discussed and negotiated. Discourse about authority and governance has taken on a biological character: kings are members of a family of kings and lesser rulers (Clovis, Alaric) must behave as proper sons to their father (Theoderic). The populations they govern are *gentes*, races, and while Theoderic makes no explicit attempt to describe them as unitary descent groups, this will soon follow in such texts as Jordanes' *Getica,* a text composed in Constantinople around the middle of the sixth century that traces the origins of the Goths to a mythic Scandia, and follows the fortunes of this *gens* descending through the generations and kings until their arrival in the Roman empire, their triumphs under Theoderic, and their final defeat by Justinian.[7] This model of the history of a *gens*, organized by rulers and tracing its wanderings across Europe would be later adopted for the Lombards in the *Origo gentis Langobardorum*[8] and the Trojan legend of the Franks reported by the *Liber Historiae Francorum*.[9]

Theoderic's attempt may have been no more successful in evoking the emotional bonds of a 'family of kings' to prevent the Frankish Visigothic war than was the evocation of the common bond among the grand-children of Queen Victoria in preventing the first World War,[10] but this transformation of vocabulary and, with it, this transformation of the modes of thinking about European polities would have a long history, one that is indeed not entirely over. The European polities that emerged in the centuries following Theoderic largely maintained the models and the ideologies already present in his letter. These are the kingdoms of Europe. Rulership was for well over a millennium in the hands of *reges*, and the names and unifying ideologies of their *regna* are derived from the names of peoples, not places: France, England, Hungary, Croatia, Lombardy,

---

[7] Jordanes claims that he is abbreviating a history of the Goths by Cassiodorus who wrote a history in twelve books *De origine actusque Getarum ab olim et usque nunc per generationes regesque descendentem.* Jordanes, *De origine actibusque Getarum*, ed. T. Mommsen MGH AA (Berlin, 1882), p. 53.

[8] *Origo gentis Langobardorum*, ed. G. Waitz, MGH SSRL (Hanover, 1878), pp. 1–6.

[9] *Liber Historiae Francorum*, ed. B. Krusch, MGH SSRM 2 (Hanover, 1888), pp. 241–4. See I. N. Wood, 'Defining the Franks: Frankish origins in early medieval historiography', in *From Roman Provinces to Medieval Kingdoms*, ed. T. F. X. Noble (New York, 2006), pp. 110–19, and H. Reimitz, 'Die Konkurrenz der Ursprünge in der fränkischen Historiographie', *Die Suche nach den Ursprüngen: Von der Bedeutung des frühen Mittelalters*, ed. W. Pohl (Vienna, 2004), pp. 191–210.

[10] On the failure of such royal kinship to impede the outbreak of war, see among others T. Aronson, *Crowns in Conflict: The Triumph and the Tragedy of European Monarchy, 1910–1918* (London, 1986), and Miranda Carter, *The Three Emperors: Three Cousins, Three Empires and the Road to World War One* (London, 2009).

Scotland, Serbia, Deutschland, the list goes on and on. Even the exception proves the rule: The contemporary nation states that do not conform to this pattern such as Italy, Austria, Belgium, or Spain betray by their names their very recent and discontinuous emergence as polities.

Indeed, so deeply engrained is this way of thinking of European kingdoms and nations as the natural form of western political organization and social and cultural cohesion that alternative forms of organization seem deeply problematic. Empires such as the Habsburg, the Ottoman, or the Russian are remembered, a century after their demise, as unnatural and undemocratic because they suppressed the legitimate rights of the peoples (read *gentes*) united within them. Even 'kinder, gentler' multi-ethnic polities seem out of place in twenty-first century Europe: Yugoslavia died a bloody death in the last years of the past century; Czechoslovakia met a non-violent but no less definitive end shortly after emerging from under the Soviet umbrella; and word is still out on Belgium. The European Union, envisioned by many as the beginnings of a United States of Europe, is reeling under the effects of the great recession and the post-2008 fiscal crisis, with ever more nations anxious about the threat to national sovereignty posed by demands of fiscal reform mandated from Brussels, or rather Berlin.[11] Even in Great Britain, Scottish and Welsh nationalists chafe at being joined to something called Great Britain.

If Scotland should eventually secede from Great Britain I do not anticipate the violence that ended Yugoslavia; however, ethnic nationalism on the continent is no laughing matter. From a fringe movement in western European states and a nostalgic movement in the new and re-emerging states of the Soviet empire twenty years ago, it has grown to represent a major force in European politics, particularly since it draws both on myths of past glory and injury as well as on growing xenophobia toward immigrants from North Africa and the Near East.

Thus it is perhaps something of a surprise to look back to the period when these *regna* were in a process of formation and to realize that such forms of political organization were once novel and by no means self-evident. Nor were they the obvious political forms that would follow the break-up of the Western empire. We should remember such polities as the Gallic Empire that existed from 260 to 274 and included much of the West.[12] There could have been other ways for the Empire to end, and the Roman generals of barbarian extraction who took over the pieces might have organized them differently. Why should ethnicity, then or now, have been legitimizing discourse of political performance?

We might blame it on Christianity: 'Go ye therefore, and teach all nations, baptizing them in the name of the Father, and of the Son, and of the Holy

---

[11] Prof. Geary wrote this essay some considerable time before the June 2016 referendum; in the light of the 'leave' vote then his comments seem even more prescient [editors].

[12] J. F. Drinkwater, *The Gallic Empire: Separatism and Continuity in the North-Western Provinces of the Roman Empire, A.D. 260–274* (Stuttgart, 1987).

Ghost' (*Matthew* 28:19). Jesus did not command his disciples to teach all people, understood as individuals. His command was rather to teach all peoples, *panta ta ethne* (πάντα τὰ ἔθνη), *omnes gentes*. In this fundamental, final charge, Jesus affirms the universality of the Christian message, but he simultaneously affirms the organization of humans into *ethne*. The organization of humanity by *ethne* thus seems part of the divine order.[13] Certainly, the model of a nation as a descent group, united by common ancestry and maintaining its distinctiveness from other peoples across time was the model deeply rooted in the modes of thought of first-century Jews. Indeed, as Denise Buell suggests, early Christians used ethnic categories as at once real and mutable in order to advance universalist claims.[14] But as Jeremy Adams pointed out long ago in a much underappreciated study, the ethnic model of nation received by Christianity from second Temple Judaism and found in the appropriated Jewish Scriptures is much more complex and differentiated than one might think at first glance, particularly as developed by the great Latin fathers Augustine and especially Jerome.

For Augustine, as heir of the Roman judicial and political tradition, a *populus* was a constituted and purposeful association, the *populi* par excellence being Israel and, later, the Church itself. As he stated in his *On Genesis against the Manicheans*, 'That *populus* which is spiritually fed by the nourishment of the holy Scriptures and the divine law.'[15]

For Jerome, the translator of the Bible from Hebrew and Greek into the Latin of the fifth century, the people of Israel, the עם (ām) is remarkably similar to the *populus Romanus* in that it is ultimately a constituted body rather than a descent group. From the time that Jerome was in Bethlehem and had acquired a solid knowledge of Hebrew, he consistently translates עם (ām), generally translated in the Septuagint as laos (λαός), as *populus*, particularly when referring to the people of Israel.[16] More generative language, *gentes* or *nationes*, translate the Hebrew goyim (גיים) or the Greek ἔθνη, and was more commonly applied to the non-Israelite other. As Adams concludes, for Augustine and for Jerome,

A *populus* is a group of sentient human beings involved with a law, or with values subject to juridical review. … A *gens* might be as teleological and morally responsible a group as a populus, but with at least equal frequency it could be

---

[13] For a challenging argument of the importance of ethnic discourse in early Christianity see D. Kimber Buell, *Why This New Race? Ethnic Reasoning in Early Christianity* (New York, 2005). But see also the review by Peter Oakes in *The Classical Review*, ns. 56 (2006), 500–2.

[14] Buell, *Why This New Race?*, especially ch. 5, pp. 138–65.

[15] ' … cum ipso populo spiritualiter pascitur sanctarum Scripturarum alimentis et lege divina'; *De Genesi contra Manichaeos* ii.1.40, PL 34, 192–193. J. Adams, *The Populus of Augustine and Jerome: A Study in the Patristic Sense of Community* (New Haven, 1971), p. 40.

[16] Adams, *Populus*, esp. pp. 86–97.

a group unified primarily by genetic origin or language, a society with more beginning and less end.[17]

With these clear distinctions between *populus* and *gens* available to Christian writers as well as to Roman jurists and administrators, it is probably unfair to blame Christianity for the ethnicization of European polities. Given the developed vocabularies of both constituted peoples and biological descent groups available in the Christian political vocabulary, why then should the political vocabulary by which the polity of Europe was imagined choose the latter rather than the former? Is this an ideology brought by the barbarian invaders themselves as they entered the Empire? Perhaps, but one cannot be certain. First, we have no clear evidence of the political vocabulary of barbarian commanders, and the earliest texts that purport to represent their values are highly rhetorical, written by Romans or descendants of barbarians thoroughly educated in Roman tradition. In any event, the vocabulary of *gens*, *populus*, and *natio* become notoriously slippery as used by these early historians. In any event, as a strategy of distinction, a means to maintain separate identities of ruling minority elites within a numerically superior population, such an approach might have much to recommend it.[18] However it is not at all clear that early barbarian kings were all that interested in maintaining such a distinction. The various *reges* who ruled the various divisions of the empire in the West do not seem to have been particularly eager to hold fast to their titles of kings of their specific peoples following their settlement within the empire.

The evidence, analyzed by Andrew Gillett, is at best ambiguous.[19] In some documents emanating from royal chancelleries, kings appear with an ethnic qualifier. In North Africa, Vandal and Moorish kings seem regularly to have included ethnic terminology in their titles. Elsewhere, such terminology appears only in certain documents and under certain circumstances in the Frankish and Lombard kingdoms. Lombard kings and dukes used the title *Rex* or *dux gentis Langobardorum* in some superscriptions, in law codes, and in some letters to other rulers. Some Frankish kings termed themselves *rex Francorum* in some charters or in letters. Kings like Theoderic, the great king of the Ostrogoths who sought to dominate western kingdoms as a father over sons, never terms himself king of the Goths. Most of the time, for most purposes, rulers contented themselves with the absolute title *rex*, without a qualifier that would designate them as kings

---

[17] Ibid., p. 110.

[18] See the now classic volume, *Strategies of Distinction: The Construction of Ethnic Communities, 300–800*, ed. W. Pohl with H. Reimitz (Leiden, 1998), and for a more recent discussion, W. Pohl, 'Aux origines'.

[19] A. Gillett, 'Was Ethnicity Politicized in the Earliest Medieval Kingdoms?', in *On Barbarian Identity: Critical Approaches to Ethnicity in the Early Middle Ages*, ed. A. Gillett (Turnhout, 2002), pp. 85–121.

of a particular people. Actually, this is hardly surprising since their kingdoms included diverse populations – and they claimed authority over them all.

So where does this terminology come from? Perhaps, instead of blaming it on either Christianity or barbarians, the authors of medieval accounts of these peoples must take the blame. The image of barbarian *gentes*, ruled by kings who are kings of peoples, is most developed by historians, more, it would seem, than by the people about whom they wrote. Jordanes, who wrote a history of the Goths, is in this both typical and exemplary.[20] Throughout his *Getica*, the *gens Gothorum* and the *reges Gothorum* are the major actors, as would be expected in a text that, as he says in his preface, traces the origin and actions of the Goths *per generationes regesque descendentia*.[21] Gregory of Tours likewise uses terms such as *of the gens*[22] and *regnum Francorum*.[23]

However, the *gentes* that these rulers lead are anything but the fixed, biological caricatures of Greco-Roman history. For Jordanes, the Goths are indeed a *gens* among others during their wanderings. Yet as the Goths approach Italy and come to power under Theoderic, the language begins to change. Odoacer, the great opponent of Theoderic, is indeed a *rex gentium* who has subjugated the Romans by terror.[24] Theoderic, though, first appears not as a king leading Goths but as a young man of eighteen leading an army of six thousand men drawn *ex populo amatores sibi clientesque* against Babi, king of the Sarmatians.[25] While upon the death of his father he becomes *gentis suæ rex*, this does not seem to Jordanes a public office.[26] It is only after Theoderic has entered Italy and killed Odoacer, at the request of the Emperor Zeno, that he 'laid aside his private dress and the costume of his people and assumed the mantle of royal insignia since now he was the ruler of Goths and of Romans'.[27] Thereafter Theoderic is never termed *rex Gothorum*. In fact, thereafter, in Jordanes' mind at least, Theoderic's

---

[20] Jordanes, *De origine actibusque Getarum*, ed. T. Mommsen, MGH AA 5.1 (Berlin, 1882). Within the enormous literature that has developed on Jordanes and his *Getica* in recent years see above all W. Goffart, *The Narrators of Barbarian History, A.D. 550–880. Jordanes, Gregory of Tours, Bede and Paul the Deacon* (Princeton NJ, 1988); H. Wolfram, 'Origo gentis: the literature of Germanic origins', in *Early Germanic Literature and Culture*, ed. B. Murdoch and M. Read (Rochester NY, 2004), pp. 39–54; and on Jordanes's ethnic terminology, F. Lošek, 'Ethnische und politische Terminologie bei Jordanes und Einhard', in *Typen der Ethnogenese unter besonderer Berücksichtigung der Bayern*, Symposium Zwettl, 1986, ed. H. Wolfram and W. Pohl (Vienna, 1990), pp. 147–52.

[21] MGH AA 5,1, p. 53.

[22] As in *Libri historiarum X*, v.5, ed. B. Krusch and W. Levison, MGH SSRM I (Hanover, 1951) (hereafter *Historiae*), p. 193, where he writes of the *Francorum gens*.

[23] As at *Historiae* vi.24, p. 291; viii.37, p. 405.

[24] *Getica*, 46, p. 120. In Jordanes' *Romana*, Theodoric is likewise called *rex gentium*, p. 45.

[25] *Getica*, 55, p. 131.

[26] *Getica*, 56, p. 132.

[27] '… privatum habitum suæque gentis vestitum seponens, insigne regii amictus, quasi jam Gothorum Romanorumque regnator'; *Getica*, 57, p. 134.

Goths are on the way to merging with their Roman neighbours, a merger which Jordanes thought effected through the marriage of Matasuntha, grand-daughter of Theoderic and Justinian's nephew Germanus.[28] Indeed, this was not the first time that Jordanes assumed that Gothic identity was something that could be put aside. According to him, when Alaric and his Visigoths arrived at the gates of Ravenna in the early fifth century, he was quite prepared for his Visigoths to join with the *populus Romanorum* in such a way that they would be seen as becoming one *gens*.[29]

Gregory of Tours, too, writes of *gens* and *regna,* including *the gens* and *regnum Francorum.* However as Hans-Werner Goetz, and more recently Helmut Reimitz, have shown, Gregory's use of these terms is complex and ideological.[30] Gregory employs the term *gens* primarily for peoples across the Rhine, foreign kingdoms such as that of the Longobards,[31] or military units who together constitute the *exercitus Francorum*.[32] The Franks too are a *gens,* but after the baptism of Clovis, the various groups of *Franci* along with other *gentes* under the rule of Clovis and his successors are merged into one. What appears to be 'ethnic' vocabulary certainly appears in Gregory's writings: he uses such terms as *Franci, gens Francorum,* and *regnum francorum;* occasionally he writes of a geographical *Francia;* he even at one point mentions a *mos Francorum* or Frankish custom.[33] One might be tempted to use his text therefore to draw an image of Frankish identity within the kingdom. However, in reality, this is impossible: Gregory is virtually silent about the origin of the Franks, deliberately erasing whatever may have been common beliefs about origins, migration, and political and social structure. Of Frankish custom, other than a propensity to linger in their cups after a meal until drunk – a topos about barbarians common in Roman history and ethnography – we learn nothing. Very few individuals are specifically identified as *Franci,* and we are never told why they are so designated. The Frankish army, the *exercitus Francorum,* is composed of units identified by other seemingly ethnic labels as much as by *Franci.* Gregory does not even characterize any of the many Merovingian kings who fill his pages as *rex Francorum:* rather, while his kings rule a *regnum Francorum* they are simply identified as *rex,* and as such command all of the peoples in their kingdom. In sum, the apparently ethnic terminology in Gregory is slippery, sparse, and deployed strategically, not categorically. The

---

[28] See Goffart, *Narrators,* pp. 68–75.

[29] *Getica,* 30, p. 97.

[30] Goetz, 'Gens, Kings and Kingdoms: the Franks', in *Regna and Gentes: The Relationship Between Late Antique and Early Medieval Peoples and Kingdoms in the Transformation of the Roman World,* ed. H.-W. Goetz, J. Jarnut and W. Pohl, with the collaboration of S. Kaschke (Leiden, 2002), pp. 307–44.

[31] *Historiae* vi.6, MGH SSRM 1, pp. 272–3.

[32] As in *Historiae* x.3, p. 485.

[33] *Historiae* x.27, p. 520.

matrix into which this terminology can be fitted is not the symbolic system of the social scientist looking to understand Franks as an ethnic group but rather a system within a framework that derives from Gregory's ideological program.[34]

So where, then, are we to look for those fundamental changes that produce a Europe of Nations? A prime suspect is the first European empire since the disappearance of Roman rule, the Carolingians. Under Charlemagne, ethnicity seems to have been instrumentalized as never before, beginning with the king's own title, *Carolus gratia Dei rex Francorum et Langobardorum atque patricius Romanorum.*[35] The recent past was rewritten from a perspective that began to introduce a much more systematic use of ethnic terminology onto a much more complex past. Laws, which had been essentially regional laws, were reformulated not only as regional legal systems but as personal laws that Carolingian elites could carry with them when they colonized conquered regions such as Lombardy. But even here, there were limits. Even as ethnicity became a tool of empire, Frankish identity remained, as it has been since the time of Gregory, much more than an ethnic label, and membership in different peoples could be considered, if not arbitrary, at least malleable. Agobard of Lyons, complaining about the Law of Gundobad, pointed to the complexity of identities within the empire by suggesting that when five people came together they might be governed by five different laws. These were hardly separate ethnicities but rather different legal arrangements that could be manipulated in a court. Paraphrasing Saint Paul, he argued that the separation of 'circumcised and uncircumcised, barbarian and Scythian, Aquitanian and Langobard, Burgundian and Alaman, slave and free' had been abolished by Christ. A similar sentiment was expressed in the tenth century by Regino of Prüm, that *diversae nationes populorum* differ from one another by their 'origin, customs, languages, and laws' (*genere, moribus, lingua, legibus*).[36] This text is often cited as the clearest statement of a medieval model of ethnic differentiation, but while this may be true in one sense, it is to take Regino's statement out of context since he goes on to say that these apparent differences do not really matter for the Christian since all are united in the faith of Christ.

---

[34] On that program see M. Heinzelmann, *Gregory of Tours: History and Society in the Sixth Century*, trans. C. Carroll (Cambridge, 2001).

[35] For recent literature with references to Charlemagne's title see I. Garipzanov, *The Symbolic Language of Authority in the Carolingian World (c.751–877)* (Leiden, 2008), pp. 123–8. The basic study remains H. Wolfram, *Intitulatio: Lateinische Königs- und Fürstentitel bis zum Ende des 8. Jahrhunderts* (Graz, 1967), esp. 219–20.

[36] *Reginonis abbatis Prumiensis chronicon cum continuatione Treverensis*, ed. F. Kurze (MGH SRG 50, Hanover 1890), p. xx: 'Epistula Reginonis ad Hathonem Archiepiscopum Missa, Prefatio Operis Subsequentis: "Nec non et illud sciendum, quod, sicut diversae nationes populorum inter se discrepant genere moribus lingua legibus, ita sancta universalis aecclesia toto orbe terrarum diffusa, quamvis in unitate fidei coniungatur, tamen consuetudinibus aecclesiasticis ab invicem differt"'.

If we want to find the real culprit in the ethnicization of Europe's kingdoms, we must look neither in the Migration period itself nor in the Carolingian Empire. True, a system of *regna* at the end of Antiquity replaced Roman provincial administration and a vocabulary of *ethne* came to dominate discourse, but these kingdoms themselves were not ethnic in any modern sense. Rather we must look to the late eighteenth and especially the nineteenth century when philology and scientific history in the service of romantic nationalism reinterpreted, simplified, and reified the slippery terminology of early medieval sources to create a new and powerful vision of ethnic nations.[37]

In the nineteenth century historically based arguments about nationhood were equally seductive to peoples in search of states and to states in search of peoples. Germans sought a state to embody and extend the unique identity of the German people. France, with a long tradition of state continuity, looked to history to find a people whom the restoration French state could embody.[38] In between were the numerous interest groups, Serbs, Croats, Slovenes, Czechs, Basques, Britons, and others that wanted proof that they, too, had the right to sovereignty, a right based in no small part on the historical claims of the past.

The role of medievalists in this process was essential because they provide a 'scientific' method of combining Indo-European philology and romantic nationalism to rediscover deep histories of aspiring peoples. German scholars led the way, using Germanic philology to project the existence of a Germanic people, recognizable in a common language, into Antiquity even while their contemporaries were trying to call into existence a German state. Such processes were by no means limited to the creation of a German past but could be applied to any corpus of texts or, failing that, 'recovered' oral traditions in any language. Nations and would-be nations employed these tools in their own apparatus of national self-creation, including a corpus of 'monuments of national history' and philologists (many German educated) to elucidate the ancient origins of their nations by tracing their languages back to their first appearance, secure in the knowledge that a people was defined by its language and those who shared a common language shared a common culture and world view.[39]

The philologically based scientific history drafted into the service of nationalism led back ultimately to the period between the third and eleventh

---

[37] On these developments in more detail see P. Geary, *Myth of Nations: the Medieval Origins of Europe* (Princeton, 2002).

[38] See in particular A.-M. Thiesse, *La création des identités nationales: Europe, XVIIIᵉ-XXᵉ siècle* (Paris, 2001).

[39] Among the voluminous literature on the role of scholarship in nineteenth-century nationalist discourse see in particular J. Leerssen, *National Thought in Europe: A Cultural History* (Amsterdam, 2007), and *Editing the Nation's Memory: Textual Scholarship and Nation-Building in Nineteenth-Century Europe*, ed. D. Van Hulle and J. Leersen (Amsterdam, 2008).

centuries and to documents such as those we have just reviewed. Here was to be found the moment of 'primary acquisition' when the ancestors of modern nations, speaking their national language which carried and expressed specific cultural and intellectual modes, first appeared in Europe, conquering once and for all their sacred and immutable territories and often, in so doing, establishing once and for all their natural enemies. Essential in such a vision of nations was its 'scientific', one might well say genetic, nature: ethnic identity was an objective fact of nature, an accident of birth from which one could not escape.

This kind of scientific history, by essentialising and simplifying the sources we have examined above from the early Middle Ages, turned subtle and complex ideologies into objectified identities suited to the demands of nineteenth-century romantic nationalism. Such approaches dissolved distinctions between *populi* and *gentes*, between *laos* and *ethnos*, and took complex myths such as those of the origins of the Langobards and Lombards at face value. Moreover, as peoples and nations became objectified as they never had been in the past, they also became associated in unambiguous ways with specific territories in ways that essentialized peoples and places in extraordinarily powerful, if anachronistic, ways.

After the Second World War such fascination with the medieval origins of particular European nations seemed to go into eclipse. Popular interest in the Middle Ages was largely in the realm of escapist fantasy while questions of economic interdependency, modern technology, and European unity seemed about to make irrelevant these old historical appeals to ethnic nationalism based in a distant past. We were told that nations not so much recovered as were called into being by nineteenth-century intellectuals and politicians; that cherished national origin myths were but 'invented traditions'. The past, in other words, doesn't matter.[40]

But while scholars may scoff, Europe's population remains strongly attached to these traditions of identity based in the distant past but created in the nineteenth century. East and West, populist ideologues have found it convenient to return to prominence old myths of medieval national origins and ancient cultural traditions.

All of these nationalist claims share the common feature of looking at the medieval past and attempting to discover there not only the origins of their peoples but their essences: their claim is that this distant past somehow establishes specific rights in the present and the future.

Largely as a reaction to this nationalist instrumentalization of the medieval past, a new generation of scholars and politicians have been doing just the

---

[40]   The classic expression of this attitude was *The Invention of Tradition*, ed. E. Hobsbawm and T. Ranger (Cambridge, 1983). B. Anderson's *Imagined Communities: Reflections on the Origin and Spread of Nationalism* (London, 1983), distinguishes, however, between imagined and imaginary communities.

opposite, that is, looking to their imaginative constructions of the medieval past to justify not ancient antagonisms but rather European unity. By ambitious educational and scientific projects, Europeans seek to build a European identity to replace national identities. Among these are active programs sponsored by the European community to develop common history textbooks and to support European-wide collaborative research projects that aim to reconcile differing and potentially explosive visions of the past and to create a sense of the unity of European experience.

These are all laudatory goals, but an historian who is sceptical of the nationalist manipulation of the past in order to create division should also be concerned about the European manipulation of the past to create unity. Is it permissible, while rejecting history as a tool of nationalist particularism, for nationalist historians to be just as willing to use the Middle Ages as a tool for European integration? I am particularly concerned because many of these attempts to create a common European identity employ a number of the same techniques as those of nationalist historians. First, once more they look to the past, especially to the Middle Ages, to identify the common essence of European identity. This cannot of course be a common language, but in its place one hears increasingly of a common faith, specifically Christianity, spread throughout Europe between the third and the tenth centuries. Just as ethnic nationalists drew on the ethnic vocabulary of early medieval texts to advance their national vision, these scholars draw on the ecclesiastical visions of a Gregory of Tours, an Agobard, or a Regino to claim a homogeneous Christian identity that will make ethnic variation irrelevant. But such an approach conveniently ignores the often violent nature of conversion, deep conflicts between Orthodox and Roman Christians, even worse violence between Catholic and Reformed Christians, and the recent massive disappearance of all Christianity within a largely secular Europe. Second, there is a tacit assumption that this European culture is static – created once and for all in the distant past and, like the claims of 'primary acquisition', assumes that once this common heritage was in place nothing can or should change it. In a sense, history, claimed as the all-important factor that formed European identity, is for all intents and purposes at an end: The new, common European identity, based on Christianity, whether Latin or Orthodox, and a common culture of the Renaissance and Enlightenment, has now reached a steady state. Those who want to participate in Europe must 'become European' by adopting this identity – the identity itself will not change.

We are already seeing potential problems of this new way of writing and divining Europe's future identity by investigating its past. There is a danger that 'European' may be defined as a new nation, a new people, to be essentialized and opposed to the non-European other. The boundaries of Europe are defined both externally and internally as the boundaries of contemporary Christendom. 'Turkey is not Europe' is the rallying cry of many, and the reason that Turkey is not Europe has nothing to do with its geographical position and everything to do with its religious identity.[41] Within Europe, countries that have prided themselves on their openness to refugees from around the world are prepared for assimilation, but only on their own terms. Immigrants from Eastern Europe or North Africa are expected to adopt the cultural values of their new countries; the idea that their cultures might change the values of Europe is greeted with fear and massive opposition. Just as nineteenth-century nationalists evoked an eternal national identity, so modern Europeanists claim an eternal European identity that all must adopt.

I am not advocating that Turkey should be immediately admitted to the European Union, or that radical religious teachings of whatever stripe should be permitted in the name of political correctness and toleration. But I am concerned, as an historian, that assumptions about contemporary European identity, whether new or old, are based on fundamental misunderstandings of the nature of history. Finding the present and future in the past is never a good idea, particularly because the history of which Europe has too much is a false history: a history that attempts to essentialize and to make an imagined past into a blueprint for the future. Perhaps, in conclusion, we can answer the question posed in our title, 'Does Europe have too much History?' with the response: No, but it does have too many historians.

---

[41] On the changing definition of Europe in the Middle Ages and early modern period see Klaus Oschema, *Bilder von Europa im Mittelalter* (Ostfildern, 2013).

4

A CRISIS OF THE MIDDLE AGES? DECONSTRUCTING AND CONSTRUCTING EUROPEAN IDENTITIES IN A GLOBALIZED WORLD

Michael Borgolte

There can be no doubt that the historian's activity is not going to cease in the foreseeable future, for every new human generation is looking for its origins and its place in an ever-changing world. In Europe, historians are faced with two parallel developments, both of which seem unstoppable, despite some delaying factors: that is Europeanization and globalization. While it may be premature to predict an end of national history, our conception of history is bound to change dramatically, and this change will affect our understanding of the Middle Ages.[1] It is no exaggeration to speak of a crisis of the Middle Ages in our historical consciousness, to the same extent as some scholars have referred to a crisis of our modernity in an age of 'multiple modernities'.

In this context, I should like to distinguish between three ways of telling the history of the Middle Ages. There is, first, the history of medieval Europe as a specific and clearly identifiable entity. Secondly, there is the history of Europe as a diverse body during the Middle Ages; and third there is the history of a millennium or so in which different worlds co-existed, including one that linked Europe to Asia and to North Africa. In the first case, Europe is akin to Latin civilization, the areas under the influence of the Roman-Catholic Church, the Occident or the West. Although these forms of identification have attracted due criticism on part of some historians, they are still the dominant paradigms of medieval history.[2]

---

[1] See M. Borgolte, 'Vor dem Ende der Nationalgeschichten? Chancen und Hindernisse für eine Geschichte Europas im Mittelalter', *Historische Zeitschrift* 272 (2001), 561–96, and 'Europa im Bann des Mittelalters. Wie Geschichte und Gegenwart unserer Lebenswelt die Perspektiven der Mediävistik verändern', *Jahrbuch für Europäische Geschichte* 6 (2005), 17–135, esp. pp. 117–20.

[2] *Multiple Modernities*, ed. S. N. Eisenstadt (2nd edn, New Brunswick, 2005).

In a fairly recent survey, a German historian (Egon Boshof) could still refer without caveat to the uniform culture of the Latin West, which he saw as built on a consensus about fundamental Christian values,[3] while another colleague (Verena Postel) drew a line between the so-called origins of Europe and the present, and emphasized the abiding differences between Europe and the East: 'Europe', she wrote, 'that was the medieval world, as opposed to Byzantium and the Islamic world'.[4] Yet attempts such as these to ascribe an unchanging identity to Europe, which can be traced down to the Middle Ages, are hardly original.[5] Europe has many fathers, it would seem, as it was deemed in some quarters to have been created by the Franks and, more specifically, Charlemagne and the dynasty that bears his name,[6] while by contrast a British historian (Robert Bartlett) has dated the 'Making of Europe' back to the Crusades and the expansion of Latin Christianity during the Central Middle Ages.[7] The thesis of the birth of Europe out of the Middle Ages has, however, been advanced with particular emphasis by none other than the French historian Jacques Le Goff, probably the world's most distinguished medievalist of recent years, who sees the Middle Ages as the most significant legacy of the past for today's and tomorrow's Europe.[8] It is true, as Le Goff concedes, that Europe started as a figure of Greek mythology. Yet, despite her classical origins, Europe was shaped after the end of the Roman Empire, which according to Le Goff was nothing more than a historical aberration and ultimately belonged to the history of the Mediterranean.[9] The Romans were, however, responsible for the division between the Latin West and the Greek

---

[3] E. Boshof, *Europa im 12. Jahrhundert. Auf dem Weg in die Moderne* (Stuttgart 2007), pp. 268, 271. For criticism, M. Borgolte, 'Über den Tag hinaus. Was nach dem Schwerpunktprogramm kommen könnte', in *Hybride Kulturen im mittelalterlichen Europa*, ed. M. Borgolte and B. Schneidmüller (Berlin, 2010), pp. 309–28 (p. 313).

[4] V. Postel, *Die Ursprünge Europas. Migration und Integration im frühen Mittelalter* (Stuttgart, 2004), p. 11; for criticism Borgolte, 'Über den Tag hinaus', p. 313.

[5] See M. Borgolte, 'Perspektiven europäischer Mittelalterhistorie an der Schwelle zum 21. Jahrhundert', in *Das europäische Mittelalter im Spannungsbogen des Vergleichs*, ed. M Borgolte (Berlin 2001), pp. 13–27 (pp. 17–18).

[6] Compare C. Dawson, *The Making of Europe. An Introduction to the History of European Unity* (London 1932); C. Delisle Burns, *The First Europe. A Study of the Establishment of Medieval Christendom, AD 400–800* (London, 1947); *Die Franken – Wegbereiter Europas. Vor 1500 Jahren: König Chlodwig und seine Erbe* (2 vols., Mainz, 1996).

[7] R. Bartlett, *The Making of Europe. Conquest, Colonization and Cultural Change, 950–1350* (London, 1993).

[8] J. Le Goff, *L'Europe est-elle née au Moyen Age* (Paris 2003) [German translation: *Die Geburt Europas im Mittelalter* (Munich, 2004), esp. p. 15]. For criticism of this book, in some detail, see M. Borgolte, 'Kein Platz für Karl. J. Le Goff beschreibt die Geburt Europas aus dem Mittelalter', in the *Frankfurter Allgemeine Zeitung* of 24 March 2004, p. L 17.

[9] J. Le Goff, *Das alte Europa und die Welt der Moderne* (Munich, 1994), p. 9; for what follows, *ibid.*, pp. 9–13. Cf. Borgolte, 'Perspektiven', p. 17.

East, which would eventually gain such significance in Europe's history. This development would be reinforced by Christianity, which Le Goff sees as the most important religious and cultural innovation since the fourth century. The formation of a Latin and a Greek Christianity created a lasting divide between two cultures, a divide that would become entrenched following the creation of political borders. While the Baltic peoples, the Poles, the Czechs, the Slovaks, the Hungarians and the Slovenes were all included into Western Christianity, whose border ran from Scandinavia to Croatia, Russia and Greece were separated from her. Whereas the Greek Church ultimately escaped the domination of the Roman papacy, Latin Christianity was separated from Byzantium and the Orthodox world. This led, according to Le Goff, to the formation of the lavish Byzantine culture, the heiress of the classical Roman world, and the world of Rus, on the one hand, and the West, on the other. The latter was divided into a multitude of realms; it stood under barbarian influence; and it lacked the unifying power of a centre as the dominium over it was disputed between the pope and the emperor. Yet, unlikely as it seems, it would experience an unprecedented economic, political and cultural take-off and expand beyond its boundaries. These developments and, hence, Latin Christianity, were, again according to Le Goff, the defining moment of medieval Europe. Europe took shape through Christianity and the multiple realms into which her body was divided. This unity in diversity thus prefigured the modern 'Europe of the nations'.

This view of the Middle Ages did not simply spring from Jacques Le Goff's Jovian brow; indeed he merely expounded upon, and underlined, a perspective that had a long history of its own and had understandably from the very beginning attracted the critical attention of both the historians of Eastern Europe and the historians of Byzantium. These scholars stressed the shared cultural and religious traditions of Eastern and Western Europe and they even worked out a certain degree of overlap between the political structures of both parts of Europe.[10] In a similar vein, it is easy to show that Le Goff has not thought of the place of Islam in European history in the Middle Ages. What he has to say about this topic is either contradictory or superficial.[11] This is also true of his appreciation of the role of the Jews in medieval Europe.[12] It is therefore not too surprising that some scholars have recently opposed any attempt to equate Europe with a form

---

[10] See especially O. Halecki, *The Limits and Divisions of European History* (London, 1950); cf. Borgolte, 'Perspektiven', p. 18; 'Ostmitteleuropa aus der Sicht des Westens', in *Ostmitteleuropa im 14.–17. Jahrhundert – eine Region oder Region der Regionen?*, ed. M. Dygo, S. Gawlas and H. Grala (Warsaw, 2003), pp. 5–19 (pp. 9–11).

[11] See Le Goff, *Die Geburt Europas im Mittelalter*, pp. 51–2, 107, 251–2, 265–6. For criticism, see M. Borgolte, 'Der europäische Monotheismus und das Problem kultureller Einheit im Mittelalter', in *Festschrift für Aaron Gurjewitsch* [forthcoming], in nn. 27 ff.

[12] Le Goff, *Die Geburt Europas im Mittelalter*, pp. 221–4, cf. pp. 120–2; Borgolte, 'Der europäische Monotheismus', nn. 31–2.

of Christianity, let alone Christianity itself, and have suggested that European history be distinguished from the history of the West.[13]

If a critical tradition can be identified within twentieth-century historiography with regards to the equation of Europe and the West, it is also worth mentioning the role played in this context by a range of smaller disciplines that have historically rejected the exclusive status conferred to Latin sources by mainstream medievalists. Yet it is difficult to overestimate the role played by the European unification process in our reassessment of the medieval past, especially in the years following 1989/1991. While Eastern European states have one after another been joining the European Union, the question of the place of Muslim Turkey in Europe has prompted a heated discussion about Europe's borders and identity. In this context, historians have not tried to draw lessons from the past and to tell politicians what to do in the changed circumstances, but rather they have attempted to reassess history in the light of these new political developments. Whoever has tried to take into account the contribution to European history of different religious groups, such as the Orthodox Christians in the East, the scattered Jewish communities and, last but certainly not least, the Muslims in Spain, Sicily, Southern Italy, Bulgaria, Hungary and eventually also the rest of the Balkan Peninsula – whoever in other words did not confine their interest simply to the Latin West – has had therefore to abandon the illusion of European uniformity. The formula of the unity in diversity of Europe appears as such – a mere formula, that is – once historians have eschewed the idea of a Christian foundation of Europe, and have acknowledged the significant place and influence of that which has long been deemed alien to Europe in her history.

The historiographical and political requirement to think of Europe not as the West, but rather as a geographical entity inhabited by peoples with different cultures, entails the renunciation of any quest for identity on the part of historians. As the French sociologist Edgar Morin put it some twenty-five years ago, thinking about Europe presupposes the ability to acknowledge her inherent complexity. Europe, therefore, is characterized by major differences, and, while those co-exist in a relative small place, they cannot be ignored. Conversely, Europe unites huge contrasts. Morin suggested that scholars abandon the idea of a unified and clearly defined Europe and look not so much for key concepts, but focus instead on the dialectic of contrasting ideas that is characteristic of European culture. This 'dialogical principle', as Morin called it, should be at the core of the historians' approach to European history. They should, in other words, aim to grasp and understand the productive process by which European cultures were able to accommodate their differences as well as the opposition,

---

[13]   F. Cardini, *Europe and Islam*, trans. C. Beamish (Oxford, 2001), p. 11.

competition and complementarity between them.[14] This European non-identity was also the starting point of the British historian Norman Davies's monumental survey of the history of the continent of 1996 – a work to date unmatched in its approach. Difference, as Davies put it, is constitutive of the relationship between all European states – in East and West. While Europe was an idea of the Enlightenment and has never been achieved since, her most distinctive character remains diversity.[15]

Contrary to other parts of the world, Europe has never had a unifying myth of origins, nor does she share a vision of her purpose.[16] However, since her unification is, despite appearances, more advanced now than at any time in her history, European citizens are entitled to ask for new perspectives on her history. Historians who are, for the reasons that I have already mentioned, critical of any approach to European history that privileges a certain idea, or a certain narrative, will find it difficult to respond to this challenge. Their contribution has to be comparative.[17] For only comparative history enables historians to take into account the role of the different cultures and countries in European history, and not to dismiss original contributions on the grounds that they were insignificant in comparison to others that have been deemed more important. By comparing, historians are also seeing diverse cultures in relation to each other. They are, thus, overcoming their specific differences without denying their existence. A comparative history of Europe is bound to discover 'the simultaneity of the non-simultaneous' (in the words of Ernst Bloch), or the similarity of diversity.[18]

This history does not have any message to impart, however, and it is doubtful whether such a situation can be sustained. Yet historians should bear in mind that any European history with a clear message is only one among many possible histories. More to the point, the first and foremost purpose of any history of Europe should be to prompt a debate with other histories of this kind.[19] It is with

---

[14] E. Morin, *Penser l'Europe* (Paris, 1987) [German translation: *Europa denken* (Frankfurt am Main and New York, 1991), p. 19. Cf. M. Borgolte, 'Mediävistik als vergleichende Geschichte Europas', *Mediävistik im 21. Jahrhundert. Stand und Perspektiven der internationalen und interdisziplinären Mittelalterforschung*, ed. H.-W. Goetz and J. Jarnut (Munich, 2003), pp. 313–23 (pp. 320–1).

[15] N. Davies, *Europe. A History* (Oxford and New York, 1996), p. 28; cf. Borgolte, 'Perspektiven', pp. 25–6.

[16] Cf. Davies, *Europe. A History*, pp. 14–15, 35, 45; J. Schmierer, *Mein Name sei Europa. Einigung ohne Mythos und Utopie* (Frankfurt am Main, 1996); W. Schmale, *Scheitert Europa an seinem Mythendefizit?* (Bochum, 1997); M. Borgolte, 'Historie und Mythos', in *Krönungen. Könige in Aachen – Geschichte und Mythos*, 2 vols., *Ausstellungskatalog*, ed. M. Kramp (Aachen and Mainz, 2000), II, 839–46 (p. 845).

[17] Borgolte, 'Mediävistik als vergleichende Geschichte Europas', esp. p. 321.

[18] See M. Borgolte, *Europa entdeckt seine Vielfalt, 1050–1250* (Stuttgart, 2002).

[19] M. Borgolte, 'How Europe Became Diverse: On the Medieval Roots of the Plurality of Values', in *The Cultural Values of Europe*, ed. H. Joas and K. Wiegandt (Liverpool, 2008), pp. 77–114 (pp. 82–3); 'Europäische Geschichten. Modelle und Aufgaben vergleichender

this prerequisite in mind that I suggested, in a recent monograph, that we shift the focus from a Christian to a monotheistic Middle Ages.[20]

From the perspective of the history of religion, the Middle Ages appear as a very specific period. In the immediately preceding classical period, religion was characterized by polytheism.[21] The confines of the classical pantheon were all but precisely defined. While the authorities expected the citizens to fulfil their religious duties, they never interfered with their beliefs. Accordingly, hardly any written record of classical *religio* has survived, let alone any theological treatise establishing a dogma. The Roman pantheon was open to new divinities, which entered a loose association with the Capitoline Triad around Jupiter. While the fate of their state depended on the cult of the gods, the Romans were not particularly interested in imposing their divinities and rites on conquered peoples. On the borders of the empire, Rome's soldiers and public servants met barbarians who too worshipped a multitude of different gods. North of the Alps, they encountered the Celts and the Germans.

These polytheistic religions were successful in integrating vast populations. For they were able to unite scattered local communities with their own rituals within bigger entities, while the local gods were at the same time absorbed into regional or supra-regional pantheons. The last attempt to unify a multi-ethnic realm in Europe by integrating diverse deities into one pantheon was made by Prince Vladimir of Kiev. When he realized that it had failed for want of acceptation by the elite, he changed policy and adopted Christianity in 988. Yet the Christianization of the Rus entailed more than the renunciation of the worship of many gods; it also implied the acceptance by individuals of religious norms that were much more binding than any norm in the theologically neutral context of polytheism.

The Middle Ages therefore marks the end of ancient polytheism and the beginning of the monotheistic period of European history. If ever there was a defining moment for Europe in the Middle Ages, this was it. Yet Europe was not just shaped by one monotheistic religion, but by three of them. While Judaism and Christianity had expanded throughout the Roman Empire and beyond, Islam entered the stage in the seventh and eight centuries. The first monotheists

---

Historiographie', in *Die "Blüte" der Staaten des östlichen Europa im 14. Jahrhundert*, ed. M. Löwener (Wiesbaden, 2004), pp. 303–28.

[20] M. Borgolte, *Christen, Juden, Muselmanen. Die Erben der Antike und der Aufstieg des Abendlandes 300 bis 1400 n. Chr.* (Munich, 2006).

[21] For what follows, see Borgolte, 'How Europe Became Diverse', p. 95–106, citing relevant literature. Cf. also C. Auffarth, *Religiöser Pluralismus im Mittelalter? Besichtigung einer Epoche der europäischen Religionsgeschichte* (Berlin, 2007); *Europäische Religionsgeschichte. Ein mehrfacher Pluralismus*, ed. H. G. Kippenberg, J. Rüpke and K. von Stuckrad, 2 vols. (Göttingen, 2009).

to settle in Europe were the Jews. The presence of a Jewish community in Rome is attested before the birth of Christ. Whether the destruction of the Second Temple by the future emperor Titus prompted a wave of Jewish emigration from the Near East into other provinces of the Roman Empire has been disputed.[22] Spain can be considered the first centre of Jewish religion and culture in Europe and was followed in the third century by Southern France. In the early Middle Ages, large-scale Jewish migration took place as a consequence of the Muslim conquests of Palestine and Spain according to a recurring pattern. Yet Jewish settlements were by no means uniformly spread. Without a state of their own, Jews lived as minorities among Christians or Muslims.

The Christianization of Europe can be traced down to the missions of the Apostle Paul to the Macedonian cities of Philippi and Thessaloniki and the Greek city of Corinth. From the South, Christianity expanded westwards, mostly through the conversion of polytheistic populations. This movement came to a close with the conversion of Lithuania in 1386, but the advance of Christianity had already stalled during the thirteenth century along its eastern borders, in Lapland, Cumania and on the banks of the river Volga, following the invasions of the Mongols, a religiously multifarious or even indifferent people. This extended timeframe as well as the failures that accompanied this process hint at a strong resistance paired with inconsistent support on the part of the Christian bishops and missionaries.

When the Muslims first touched Europe, they hardly encountered any polytheistic population, but only Christians and Jews. Before they crossed the Strait of Gibraltar from North Africa in 711, they had already conquered Damascus, Jerusalem, Antioch and Egypt, starting from the Arabian Peninsula, yet they had failed to take Constantinople. In Western Europe, the Arabs and Berbers were able to destroy, in a wink so to speak, the Christian realm of the Visigoths and occupy nearly the whole of the Iberian Peninsula up to the Pyrenees (only a little later, they also conquered Sicily). The Asturias, however, resisted the Muslim conquest. From there, a movement to re-conquer the lost territories would eventually start. The Reconquista was to last for centuries. But the military victory of 1212 at Las Navas de Tolosa was a turning point; for Muslim Spain would soon be confined to the Kingdom of Granada. At more or less the same time, the Saracens in Sicily, whose position had earlier been weakened by the Normans, were expelled or forced to convert by the Emperor Frederick II and Charles II of Anjou. During the late Middle Ages, Muslims nonetheless made significant gains in South East Europe. While the realm of the Volga Bulgarians, who had adopted Islam in the tenth century, had been destroyed

---

[22] S. Sand, *Die Erfindung des jüdischen Volkes. Israels Gründungsmythos auf dem Prüfstand* (Berlin, 2010), esp. pp. 199–201; for a critical analysis of a new inquiry into the origins, see now M. Toch, 'The Jews – Medieval Era', in *Encyclopedia of Global Human Migration*, ed. I. Ness, M. Borgolte and others, 5 vols. (Oxford, 2013).

by the Mongols, the Great Khan, whose empire encompassed a large part of the Christian Rus, converted to Islam. Yet the advances of the Muslim Turks at the expense of Byzantium and in the Balkans were more significant. With the fall of Constantinople in 1453, the Ottoman Empire replaced the Christian Byzantine Empire. Despite the capture of Granada in 1492, Islam was able to re-assert its position in Europe until the end of the Middle Ages and beyond, even if it did so in areas which were different from the ones that it dominated in the early Middle Ages.

The monotheistic creeds were thus an unending source of conflict, even where Christians, Jews and Muslims did not co-exist or meet each other. For orthodoxy had to be asserted within each of the three monotheistic religions. It is therefore hardly surprising that schisms and heresies from the outset played an important role within them. Yet it would be misleading to assume that religious differences necessarily led to conflicts, let alone to wars of extermination.[23] It is striking that none of the three monotheistic religions disappeared from Europe; on the contrary they tolerated each other both legally and practically. The three monotheistic religions' fight against their own heretics and apostates is altogether a different story, as is their common hostility to so-called paganism, which disappeared as an official religion. Since their members all believed in one God, who had created heaven and earth, they could hardly be indifferent to each other, as polytheists had been. They rather had to be able to talk to each other, in a manner that was controversial to be sure, but which was also characterized by mutual respect. While monotheism thus favoured Europe's cohesiveness, it also, at the same time, threatened it through religious hostility. It is this tension between the shared belief in one God and the never realized claim to uniformity which gave medieval Europe her specific character.[24] Medievalists have started drawing some conclusions from this fact. The history of medieval Europe has, in particular, been interpreted as an unceasing process of cultural integration and disintegration fuelled by religious differences.[25]

If medieval Europe did not have a uniform culture, it is tempting to look for an identity that was shaped by the contact and interplay of different cultures. It may be argued that her dynamism was the result of the unceasing conflicts fuelled by

---

[23] Borgolte, 'How Europe Became Diverse', pp. 100–1, 106 ff, which is in dispute with the thesis of J. Assmann; M. Borgolte, 'A single God for Europe. What the advent of Judaism, Christianity and Islam meant for the history of Europe', in *The Plurality of Europe. Identities and Spaces*, ed. W. Eberhard and C. Lübke (Leipzig, 2009), pp. 541–50.

[24] Cf. Borgolte, 'Der europäische Monotheismus und das Problem kultureller Einheit im Mittelalter'.

[25] *Integration und Desintegration der Kulturen im europäischen Mittelalter*, ed. M. Borgolte, J. Dücker, M. Müllerburg and B. Schneidmüller (Berlin, 2011); *Mittelalter im Labor. Die Mediävistik testet Wege zu einer transkulturellen Europawissenschaft*, ed. M. Borgolte, J. Schiel, B. Schneidmüller and A. Seitz (Berlin, 2008); *Hybride Kulturen*, ed. Borgolte and Schneidmüller.

religious differences. However, a number of objections can and should be made to this thesis.[26] For not only medieval Europe, but North Africa and the Near East too, were shaped by multiple monotheisms. Monotheistic religions were no less dominant there than in Europe, yet Islam and not Christianity was the most important of them. It was only on the banks of the Indus, further eastwards, that the attraction of monotheism was countered by Hinduism and Buddhism, neither of which was ever seriously threatened by Islam, let alone Christianity. It would therefore be more appropriate to speak of a monotheistic world, stretching from the Atlantic to the Arabian Sea, rather than from a monotheistic Europe.[27] Yet even medieval Europe was not uniformly monotheistic, as polytheists, dualists and probably also atheists co-existed with Jews, Christians and Muslims.[28] Finally, it ought to be said that it would be simplistic to draw cultures from religion alone and ascribe them to specific geographical areas.

As has become apparent, the difficulty with a comprehensive history of medieval Europe is in large part due to the absence of clear-cut borders to the East. Even nowadays, the question whether Russia and Turkey belong to Europe or not — geographically, economically, politically and culturally — remains unresolved.[29] Yet globalization is precisely the process by which borders lose significance. Globalization, rightly understood, does not merely designate a form of universal inter-connectedness of people and areas, but it also entails the loosening of geographical borders. Political and geographical boundaries necessarily lose significance when networks of communication and trade span over the entire globe. In the same way in which people in Germany and Europe are called to reassess their place in a changing world, historians should seize the opportunity to think of the Middle Ages in light of the globalization process of our time.

A global history in the age of globalization has to place the relationship and interaction of peoples, cultures and religions at its core. Its purpose cannot be simply to study and compare the history of civilizations, as has recently been

---

[26] See especially Borgolte, 'Über den Tag hinaus', pp. 319–20.

[27] M. Borgolte, 'Juden, Christen und Muslime im Mittelalter', in *Albertus Magnus und der Ursprung der Universitätsidee. Die Begegnung der Wissenschaftskulturen im 13. Jahrhundert und die Entdeckung des Konzepts der Bildung durch Wissenschaft*, ed. L. Honnefelder (Berlin, 2011), pp. 27–48, 423–37.

[28] 'Heathen' and dualists were both, in my opinion, very constructed identifications; see Borgolte, *Christen, Juden, Muselmanen*, esp. pp. 212–42. About atheists, see P. Dinzelbacher, *Unglaube im 'Zeitalter des Glaubens'. Atheismus und Skeptizismus im Mittelalter* (Badenweiler, 2009), and for a pioneering new study, D. Weltecke, '*Der Narr spricht: Es ist kein Gott.' Atheismus, Unglauben und Glaubenszweifel vom 12. Jahrhundert bis zur Neuzeit* (Frankfurt and New York, 2010).

[29] Borgolte, 'How Europe Became Diverse', pp. 85–6.

done. [30] On the contrary, one should be reluctant to identify large cultural entities in terms such as 'Western Christianity' or 'the Islamic World from Spain to Iran', as this kind of identification rests on an ontological assumption, while cultures are imagined identities. Neither should global history be confounded with traditional 'world history'. Its ambition is not to write an all-encompassing history of the world, nor even to concentrate on large-scale studies. It is, rather, to focus on cultural contacts and interactions at the local or regional level. Global history considers any historical context in which cultures met or in which, more to the point, autochthonous populations encountered foreigners. Yet it also requires situating such a context in the greater scheme of things. Global histories of the Middle Ages are thus not only interested in cross-cultural contacts, but also, and even more so, in transcultural networks.

A global history of the period between 500 and 1500 is still wanting, despite attempts to fill this gap. We may only just have an idea of the place of Europe, and of Germany, in this history.[31] The first significant development that we have to consider while contemplating the prospect of a global history of the Middle Ages is that it marks the final stage of the spreading of the human species over the world.[32] While *homo sapiens* had slowly radiated to continental land masses and islands near their shores, it was not until the Middle Ages that the most remote islands were reached thank to the progress of the navigation technique. This process can be observed in the Pacific as well as the North Atlantic Oceans. Starting in 600, the Polynesians spread from West to East until they settled in New Zealand, the last of the world's big areas to be populated, around 1280, as evidenced by the radiocarbon dating of rat-gnawed seeds and the bones of the omnivorous Pacific rat.[33] A thriving trading network is attested for South East

---

[30] For what follows, with reference to the wider literature: M. Borgolte, 'Mittelalter in der größeren Welt. Eine europäische Kultur in globaler Perspektive', *Historische Zeitschrift* 295 (2012), 35–61; 'Über europäische und globale Geschichte des Mittelalters. Historiographie im Zeichen globaler Entgrenzung', in *Die Aktualität der Vormoderne. Epochenentwürfe und europäische Identitäten*, ed. S. Patzold and K. Ridder [forthcoming]; 'Migrationen als transkulturelle Verflechtungen im mittelalterlichen Europa. Ein neuer Pflug für alte Forschungsfelder', *Historische Zeitschrift* 289 (2009), 261–85.

[31] For German-language research, see T. Ertl, *Alle Wege führten nach Rom. Italien als Zentrum der mittelalterlichen Welt* (Ostfildern, 2010); *Seide, Pfeffer und Kanonen. Globalisierung im Mittelalter* (Darmstadt, 2008); *Weltdeutungen und Weltreligionen, 600 bis 1500*, ed. J. Fried and E.-D. Hehl (Darmstadt, 2010); *Globalgeschichte. Die Welt 1000–2000*, ed. P. Feldbauer, B. Hausberger and J.-P. Lehners (Vienna, 2008–2009); also *Die Welt 1250–1500*, ed. T. Ertl and M. Limberger (Vienna, 2009). For a later period, *Globalgeschichte 1450–1620. Anfänge und Perspektiven*, ed. F. Edelmayer, P. Feldbauer and M. Wakounig (Vienna, 2002). Cf. in English, *The Oxford Handbook of World History*, ed. J. H. Bentley (Oxford, 2011).

[32] M. Borgolte, 'Medieval period – a survey', in *Encyclopedia of Global Human Migration*.

[33] J. W. Wilmshurst, A. J. Anderson, T. F. G. Higham and T. H. Worthy, 'Dating the late prehistoric dispersal of Polynesians to New Zealand using the commensal Pacific rat',

Polynesia for the period 1000–1450, but this did not, for example, include Easter Island, which lies 2,000 kilometres away from the nearest other settlement. There, a group of perhaps 15,000 people at the most was able to survive in complete isolation between the first settlement of the island and its discovery by the Europeans in 1772.[34]

At more or less the same time as Polynesians settled on Easter Island, Iceland and Greenland were settled by Celts, and above all Norwegians, that is, a Germanic people.[35] Shortly after the turn of the first millennium, Europeans tried to settle in North America, but were expelled by Amerindians. The Vikings were not, however, the first people to settle in Greenland. Indigenous Americans, the so-called Dorset people, had settled on the world's biggest island as early as 800 BC, and they developed a culture that would last for more than a thousand years. Whether the Vikings met the Dorset people remains open. Around 1400, it was their turn to abandon Greenland, from where they had traded with Norway and the rest of Europe for generations. They may have been driven out by the Inuit. Historians are keen to stress that with the encounter between the Vikings from the East and the Amerindians from the West world migrations had come full circle.[36] Such a view ignores, however, the unstable character of both the early settlements in Greenland and Newfoundland and the transcontinental contacts. While the dispersal of modern humans across the world terminated in the Middle Ages, it would be misleading to assimilate this development to a form of proto-globalization, because for this to be the case it would surely have entailed the creation of a worldwide communication network.

The different worlds of the medieval millennium were separated from each other in more than one respect. Not even the communication networks within them are well known. Mobility in the Americas was ultimately hampered by the lack of pack and draft animals such as oxen, camels and horses, even though the techniques of the wheel and the chariot were known. The so-called Hopewell Tradition in the North East of the modern USA had developed a common network of trade routes, now known as the Hopewell Exchange System.[37] The

ed. by P. V. Kirch, in www. Pnas.org / content / 105 / 22 / 7676.full (accessed 9 October 2010); see also P. Bellwood and E. Dizon, 'Austronesian cultural origins. Out of Taiwan, via the Batanes Islands, and onwards to Western Polynesia', in *Past Human Migrations in East Asia. Matching Archaeology, Linguistics and Genetics*, ed. A. Sanchez-Mazas, R. Blench, M. D. Ross, I. Peiros and M. Lin (London and New York, 2008), pp. 23–39.

[34] J. Diamond, *How Societies Choose to Fall or Survive* (New York 2005); [German translation, *Kollaps. Warum Gesellschaften überleben oder untergehen* (Frankfurt am Main, 2006, 2010), pp. 103–153].

[35] *Ibid.*, pp. 266–347.

[36] A. Jockenhövel, 'Ausblick', in *Grundlagen der globalen Welt. Vom Beginn bis 1200 v. Christus*, ed. A. Jockenhövel (Darmstadt, 2009), pp. 460–72 (pp. 468–70).

[37] B. M. Fagan, *Ancient North America: the Archaeology of a Continent* (London, 1991), pp. 369–84.

Mississippian Culture of the central and late Middle Ages shows many traits, such as the maize-based agriculture and the development of cities, which may have been inspired from Mesoamerica.[38] The Incas of South America built a dense network of roads with a total length of 24,000 kilometres, but this was limited to administrative, military and diplomatic uses, while long-distance traders relied, as in the case of the Maya and the Aztecs, on a maritime exchange system.[39]

We know even less about communication networks south of the Sahel zone. The extent to which the spread of the Bantu languages from Cameroon over millennia is a reliable indicator of human migrations across the area is disputed.[40]

Large-scale communication networks can only be observed for the Middle Ages in those continents that understood themselves as part of the *oikoumené*, that is, Asia, Europe and Africa.[41] The Latin *mappae mundi* drew them as separated from each other by waters: the Mediterranean between Europe and Africa, and the Don and the Nile between them and Asia. These waters never constituted insurmountable hurdles, contrary to the Ocean, which seemed to enclose the three land masses and was seen to separate them from the inhospitable world or from a fourth continent inhabited by monsters.[42] As a matter of fact, the smallest

---

[38] Fagan, *Ancient North America*, pp. 385–406; W. Arens and H.-M. Braun, *Die Indianer Nordamerikas. Geschichte, Kultur, Religion* (Munich, 2004), pp. 16–17; S. Schroeder, 'Die Inbesitznahme von Gebieten und die Entdeckung der Ungleichheit in frühen amerikanischen Indianergesellschaften', in *Die Ursprünge der modernen Welt. Geschichte im wissenschaftlichen Vergleich*, ed. J. A. Robinson and K. Wiegandt (Frankfurt am Main, 2008), pp. 375–430 (pp. 407–21).

[39] T. N. D'Altroy, *The Incas* (Oxford, 2002), pp. 242–6; N. Davies, *The Incas*, 2nd edn (Boulder CA, 2007), pp. 140–2, 177–9; N. Grube, 'Die Kulturen des Alten Amerika', in *Grundlagen der globalen Welt*, ed. Jockenhövel, pp. 412–41; C. Julien, *Die Inka. Geschichte, Kultur, Religion*, 4th edn (Munich 2007); B. Riese, *Die Maya. Geschichte, Kultur, Religion*, 6th edn (Munich, 2006); H. J. Prem, *Die Azteken. Geschichte, Kultur, Religion*, 4th edn (Munich, 2006); D. Webster, 'Vom Ge- und Missbrauch der alten Maya', in *Die Ursprünge der modernen Welt*, ed. Robinson and Wiegandt, pp. 255–326.

[40] M. H. Eggert, 'Bantu-,Wanderungen' im subsaharischen Afrika: Zur Anatomie eines sprach- und kulturgeschichtlichen Phänomens', in *Das europäische Mittelalter im Geflecht der Welt. Integrative und desintegrative Effekte von Migrationen*, ed. M. Borgolte, J. Dücker, P. Predatsch and B. Schneidmüller (Amsterdam, 2012), pp. 193–216.

[41] The following comes almost *verbatim* from M. Borgolte, 'Kommunikation – Handel, Kunst und Wissenstausch', in *Weltdeutungen und Weltreligionen*, ed. Fried and Hehl, pp. 17–56, 469–70 (at pp. 18–19).

[42] J. Block Friedman, *The Monstrous Races in Medieval Art and Thought* (Cambridge MA and London, 1981); A.-D. von den Brincken, *Fines Terrae. Die Ende der Erde und der vierte Kontinent auf mittelalterlichen Weltkarten* (Hanover, 1992); M. Münkler, '*Monstra* und *mappae mundi*. Die monströsen Völker des Erdrands auf mittelalterlichen Weltkarten', in *Text – Bild – Karte. Kartographie der Vormoderne*, ed. J. Glauser and C. Kiening (Freiburg, 2007), pp. 149–173; A.-D. von den Brincken, *Studien zur Universalkartographie des Mittelalters*, ed. T. Szabó (Göttingen, 2008); M. Borgolte, 'Christliche und muslimische Repräsentationen der Welt. Ein Versuch in transdisziplinärer Mediävistik', in Berlin-

of the three oceans, the Indian Ocean, was the best known at the end of the Middle Ages. The Atlantic was, if at all, being crossed on a regular basis in the North East only, while the most active sea route of the Pacific Ocean, which is bigger than the Atlantic and the Indian Oceans put together, ran on its Sino-Japanese fringe.[43]

The three connected land masses of the Middle Ages were tied to each other through a network of East-West routes between China and Western Europe. While long-distance trade took place on land, the bulk of trade used the sea routes connecting the northern Antipodes through the Mediterranean and the Indian Ocean.[44] Coastal cities, which became important stations on these trade routes, connected the long-distance trade with the hinterland by water and road. Alongside the goods and people, new ideas, technical innovations and works of art from abroad could be taken on board. Whilst differences of religion and life-style could not prevent the quest for knowledge, curiosity about the unknown, and the pursuit of wealth, pleasure or profit – these could only be hampered by power and violence.

The region where the continents met, that is, the Black Sea and the Levant, was the axis around which the medieval world revolved. Accordingly, whoever controlled the passages between the Mediterranean and the Indian Ocean – Mesopotamia and the Persian Gulf in the East and the Nile and the Red Sea in the West – held a crucial strategic position. The Persians, Alexander the Great and the Romans had all successively understood this before 'in the early eight century the Muslims acquired a core position from where they were able to link the two major economic units of the Mediterranean and the Indian Ocean'.[45] Until late into the eleventh century, the Muslims controlled all the important trade routes on land and on sea. Western traders played an increasingly important role when the Italian coastal cities of Amalfi, Venice, Genoa and Pisa pushed into the Eastern Mediterranean and established colonies as far afield as the shores of the Black Sea.[46] The rise of the Mongol Empire in the thirteenth century, an empire which would eventually stretch from China in the East to Europe and the Near East in the West, reinforced the position of the Italian merchants who were now able to participate in the Central Asian exchange system. After the

Brandenburgische Akademie der Wissenschaften. Berichte und Abhandlungen 14 (Berlin, 2008), pp. 89–147 (at pp. 132 ff); and most recently T. Lester, *The Fourth Part of the World* (New York, 2009).

[43] R. F. Buschmann, *Oceans in World History* (Boston, 2007).

[44] X. Liu and L. Norene Shaffer, *Connections across Eurasia. Transportation, Communication, and Cultural Exchange on the Silk Roads* (Boston, 2007).

[45] A. Wink, *Al-Hind. The Making of the Indo-Islamic World*, i, *Early Medieval India and the Expansion of Islam, 7th–11th Centuries* (Boston and Leiden, 2002), p. 10.

[46] *Mediterraner Kolonialismus. Expansion und Kulturaustausch im Mittelalter*, ed. P. Feldbauer, G. Liedl and J. Morrissey (Essen, 2005); M. Mitterauer and J. Morrissey, *Pisa. Seemacht und Kulturmetropole* (Essen, 2007).

mid-fourteenth century, however, access to the Far East was blocked for Western Europeans.[47]

The boldest approach to the global history of the Middle Ages has been taken by the American sociologist and historian Janet Abu-Lughod (1928–2013), on the basis of commercial history. As early as 1989, she argued that a world-system which had developed between 1250 and 1350 facilitated commercial and cultural exchange in an area reaching from North West Europe to China. She thus contested the common assumption that such a world-system had not existed before the era of discovery from the sixteenth century onwards. According to Abu-Lughod, a series of isolated regional economic systems became linked between the mid-thirteenth and the mid-fourteenth centuries, and formed a chain of interlocked regions.[48] We should, therefore, not think of merchants travelling all the way from the Atlantic to the China Sea, but rather imagine a series of hubs through which their goods transited. Abu-Lughod distinguished three cultures, the East Asian, the Arabic and the Western, and no less than eight economic subsystems. The European sub-system was structured around the Champagne Fairs, the Flemish cities of Bruges and Ghent and the maritime republics of Italy, primarily Genoa and Venice. This sub-system became interlocked with the Mediterranean sub-system during the twelfth century. Germany only took a marginal position in this world-system. It was connected through Cologne, where Flemish ships docked, and through the Alpine passes, which were used more intensively from the fourteenth century onwards by Venetian merchants. Anyway, it would be misleading to conceive of a system connecting all people and areas – a claim which is generally associated with our current globalization. The thirteenth-century world-system consisted, rather, of spots of long-distance trade in an ocean of regional and local trade. The exchange between these spots was relatively limited and the network they formed was still very thin. The most striking point, according to Abu-Lughod, was, however, that this system was balanced between East and West, and that any of its parts might have become dominant.[49] The medieval world-system could thus have led to an era of Chinese hegemony, which would have hampered the rise of Europe in the early modern period. It was precisely the 'worldwide' connectivity of the first world-system that prevented it from lasting, and from influencing modernity. For the Black Death pandemic that caused its collapse in the mid-fourteenth century spread along the very routes that had established it in the first place.

---

[47] F. Schmieder, 'Nomaden zwischen Asien, Europa und dem Mittleren Osten', in *Weltdeutungen und Weltreligionen*, ed. Fried and Hehl, pp. 179–202 (pp. 189 ff).

[48] J. L. Abu-Lughod, *Before European Hegemony. The World System A. D. 1250–1350* (New York and Oxford, 1989); J. L. Abu-Lughod, 'Das Weltsystem im 13. Jahrhundert. Sackgasse oder Wegweiser?', in *Mediterraner Kolonialismus*, ed. Feldbauer, Liedl and Morrissey, pp. 131–56.

[49] Abu-Lughod, 'Das Weltsystem im 13. Jahrhundert', p. 133.

Historians have only just begun to embark on a global history of the Middle Ages. Yet it has hopefully become apparent that this new history is changing the way we look at the past. Europe seems to have been at the margin of the *oikoumené*, leaning as it was against the Atlantic, which her navigators only tentatively explored, while looking out towards the East – an East that was controlled by either Muslim or Asian traders. Even the Mediterranean had lost the overall significance that it had had in the classical period. Nothing prefigured Europe's hegemony over the world, nor was the West's later domination set in stone.

However important a history of medieval globalization, or a global history of the Middle Ages, may appear, we should not forget that this is only one of many possible 'histories' of the Middle Ages. We may now be about to experience the end of the globalization hype, and to rediscover that, as beings of flesh and blood as well as people endowed with reason and feelings, the biggest difference we make is in the environment in which we actually live. A renaissance of neighbourhoods would thus ask for a different kind of historiography. It seems therefore that there can be no end in sight, either for history or for historiography.

PART THREE

NATIONAL HISTORY /
NOTIONS OF MYTH

5

BARBAROSSA'S HEIRS: NATION AND MEDIEVAL HISTORY IN NINETEENTH- AND TWENTIETH-CENTURY GERMANY

Bastian Schlüter

On 26 March 1977 a very important exhibition for German medievalism opened in Stuttgart in south-western Germany. It was entitled 'The Age of the Staufer' (*Die Zeit der Staufer*) and showed many important exhibits from the High Middle Ages. The exhibition was accompanied by scholarly lectures and colloquia, and in many ways it proved to be a showcase for the pertinent disciplines of medieval studies. Moreover, the Stuttgart Staufer exhibition was an extraordinary popular success. While the organisers had hoped for 200,000 visitors, almost 675,000 went to see it. It was evident that objects from a long-gone era had the power to fascinate a lot of people – for this distant era was still a part of their own history and culture. To me, this intertwining of historical remoteness with the sense of belonging to one's own culture seems to be an important reason for the public's enthusiasm for the Middle Ages. One sensually experiences a different world through the exhibits, yet at the same time is aware that this world is by no means so exotic, but belongs to one's own history. Ever since the Stuttgart exhibition, there have been large Middle Ages exhibitions in Germany, almost on a yearly basis, and they have regularly proved a great popular success. But – to return to the beginning of my essay – why was there an exhibition about one of the most famous medieval ruling dynasties in Stuttgart in 1977? Stuttgart is the capital of the German federal state of Baden-Württemberg, and the exhibition project was initiated by the state government. That government clearly saw the purpose of the exhibition as being educational, in the broadest sense. This ambition can be trenchantly summed up in the following thesis: one wanted to compensate for *too little* history with a *great deal* of history. Baden-Württemberg itself had lacked a history – its creation as a federal state had not been without problems, and in 1977 it was only celebrating its twenty-fifth anniversary. Baden-Württemberg had been founded as a federal state as late as 1952, and the people of the two, henceforth united, territories of Baden and Württemberg were not exactly fond of each other. There were quite a few good (modern) historical reasons why the former kingdom of Württemberg and the former grand duchy of Baden should *not* become a united political entity. Nevertheless, unity was achieved, starting a success story which has lasted to the present day. We know that the process of building a political community needs a foundation in order to function. And a common history bringing about unity and building an identity is by no means the worst material for such a foundation.[1] In this respect, however, modern history offered little of value for Baden-Württemberg – and mutual dislike between the component parts hardly aids nation building. This is where the Staufer exhibition, which the state government presented to itself and its constituents for its twenty-fifth anniversary, came into play. Medieval history was used to emphasise a common historical heritage for Baden and Württemberg. The then state prime minister, Hans Filbinger, stated in the preface to the exhibition catalogue: 'once before, many centuries ago, the south-western region was united, during the era of the medieval Swabian-Alemannic tribal duchy … The German duchy of Swabia had at its core a large part of the later states of Baden and Württemberg.'[2] The historical legitimisation required to unite Baden and Württemberg into one state, which could not be derived from modern history, was achieved by reference to the region's medieval history. By appealing to history in this way, the prime minister aligned himself with a well-established tradition, although under somewhat different auspices than before. In nineteenth-century Germany the Staufen dynasty already held an important place in the repertory of historical references that were supposed to help in consolidating current politics. Certain similarities between the nineteenth and twentieth century also arose in the context of a justification that was subject to historical proof. What once had existed in such an important age could not be bad for the present: this is how the 'educational' message of the 1977 exhibition might be described. What existed once upon a time in such a significant period in the Middle Ages must now become a reality once again – it was along these lines that Germans in the nineteenth century thought of the Staufen era. There was a German empire in the Middle Ages that was supposed to have reached the climax of its power and glory under the Staufen emperors.

It is, of course, common knowledge that a German empire of that sort did not exist for most of the nineteenth century. The old Holy Roman Empire had been dissolved by Napoleon in 1806. A German national movement had

[1] Cf. B. Anderson, *Imagined Communties. Reflections on the Origin and Spread of Nationalism*, 2nd edn (London, 1991), and H. Münkler, *Die Deutschen und ihre Mythen* (Berlin 2009).

[2] 'Schon einmal jedoch, viele Jahrhunderte zuvor, ist der südwestdeutsche Raum zusammengefaßt gewesen, in den Zeiten des mittelalterlichen schwäbisch-alemannischen Stammesherzogtums [...]. Das deutsche Herzogtum Schwaben umfaßte in seinem Kern einen Großteil der beiden späteren Länder Baden und Württemberg'; Hans Filbinger, 'Vom Sinn dieser Ausstellung', *Die Zeit der Staufer*, ed. R. Haussherr and C. Väterlein, 5 vols. (Stuttgart, 1977–79), I, v.

developed in the early nineteenth century, in reaction to Napoleon's supremacy in Germany. This national movement wanted first to get rid of Napoleon, and then, immediately afterwards, to found a unified German national state. In alliance with the other European powers, victory over France *was* achieved in 1814, but German hopes for a unified empire quickly subsided. At the Congress of Vienna the German rulers restored the 'monarchic principle' and retained their compartmentalised and independent territories. A historical imagery projected into the present and the future now took the place of a political reality that was, at least in the short-term, impossible. The source of that imagery was first and foremost medieval history, and at its core was an idealised vision of the medieval German empire between the Ottonian and the Staufen eras. Furthermore, the early years of the nineteenth century also saw the rise of historical scholarship and historiography as an influential educational and intellectual discipline. More than a few professional historians were partisans of the national cause in Germany. After the revolution of 1848/1849 had also failed, and once again it had proved impossible to create a unified national state, medieval imperial splendour became a historical mirror for the present day. This concept was above all embodied by *Die Geschichte der deutschen Kaiserzeit* (*The History of the German Imperial Era*) by Wilhelm Giesebrecht (1814–89), which over several decades proved to be the most influential historical study conveying this conception of history to the educated public. The first volume of this work was published in 1855, seven years after the failed revolution. It stated that:

> The imperial age is, moreover, the period when our nation, united in strength, reached its greatest expansion of power, not only freely governing its own fate, but also reigning over other nations – when the Germans counted the most in the world and when the German name was the most resounding. Too often our nation has experienced the sad effects of its inner fragmentation, too gravely it has suffered under the influence of alien powers using Germany's inner division for their own ends, and too long it has been prevented from the uninterrupted development of its rich powers that it should not long for that age of a unified, great, powerful Germany with the strongest desire.[3]

---

[3] 'Ueberdies ist die Kaiserzeit die Periode, in der unser Volk, durch Einheit stark, zu seiner höchsten Machtentfaltung gedieh, wo es nicht allein frei über sein eigenes Schicksal verfügte, sondern auch anderen Völkern gebot, wo der deutsche Mann am Meisten in der Welt galt und der deutsche Name den vollsten Klang hatte. Zu vielfach hat unser Volk die traurigen Folgen seiner inneren Zersplitterung erfahren, zu schwer hat es unter dem Einfluß fremder Mächte, welche die innere Spaltung Deutschlands für ihre Zwecke benutzten, zu leiden gehabt, und zu lange ist es in der ununterbrochenen Entwicklung seiner reichen Kräfte gehindert worden, als daß es nicht mit der heißesten Sehnsucht nach jener Zeit eines einigen, großen, mächtigen Deutschlands zurückverlangen sollte. W. Giesebrecht, *Geschichte der deutschen Kaiserzeit*, 6 vols. (Brunswick, 1855–95), I, vi.

When one looks closer, it is clear that this juxtaposition of the medieval past and the current present had become somewhat more complicated since the early nineteenth century. This combination did not just work along the lines of 'we used to have that once upon a time, and it was good; so now we want it back'. The medieval empire was, rather, imagined as something still existing, but at present disconnected from reality. It was not really there, but somehow it was, only in secret. Here one can see a difference with the late twentieth-century conception of the Staufen era, as revealed by the Baden-Württemberg exhibition of 1977. This difference can be summarised by the catchphrase 'political romanticism', a term explicitly described as a predominantly German concept by Isaiah Berlin in his famous lecture series 'The Roots of Romanticism'.[4] To this political romanticism belongs the transformation of historical-political imageries with a special added value, an overhang that is heavy with meaning or quasi-metaphysical, as it were. History is not only what we associate it with today – particularly in a scholarly context, it is not something that can be reconstructed out of scholarly research. History is also a space of longing, broadly changing in its wealth of images, a space that could take the place of a present which is viewed as misguided. The most famous inhabitant of this 'space of longing' was Emperor Barbarossa, the Staufer Frederick I. There had long been a myth surrounding his name, although it only gained strong momentum in the nineteenth century: that the emperor is sitting fast asleep in the Kyffhäuser mountain, awaiting the return of his empire. Once that empire is restored, he will wake up, lead his retainers out of the mountain and once again take up the rule that was interrupted by his falling sleep. Thus it was suggested that, 'the emperor is not dead, he is only sleeping'. This was the version of the Barbarossa myth that in the nineteenth century became part of the national-political debate. It was, in fact, a myth that had developed in a completely different context, and its original subject was not Frederick I, but his grandson Frederick II. Such a 'romanticised' recourse to history, in which the past had not passed, but survived in a secret world sealed off from crude reality, would be preserved in Germany well into the twentieth century.[5] I will come back to this point later.

Shortly after the publication of the first volume of Wilhelm Giesebrecht's *History of the German Imperial Era*, to which I have referred above, a quarrel broke out between historians who reacted in different ways to Giesebrecht's interpretation. This controversy, in which the two principal protagonists were the Munich historian Heinrich von Sybel (1817–95) and his Innsbruck colleague Julius Ficker (1826–1902), showed clearly how much the interpretation of medieval

---

4   I. Berlin, *The Roots of Romanticism* [1965], ed. H. Hardy (London, 1999).
5   Cf. K. Schreiner, 'Friedrich Barbarossa – Herr der Welt, Zeuge der Wahrheit, die Verkörperung nationaler Macht und Herrlichkeit', *Die Zeit der Staufer*, V, 521–79.

history was by then instrumentalised for daily politics.[6] By the 1850s and 1860s, people were no longer primarily interested in disputing whether Germany had to be *unified*. That it would be unified was obvious to everyone. But what was still open to debate was *to whom* this soon-to-be united new empire should belong. Should the second German empire have its centre in the north, with protestant Prussia as its unequivocal leader? Or should catholic Austria, with its Habsburg dynasty, also, and as a matter of course, be a part of it? Although based at this time in Munich, Heinrich von Sybel was a Prussian, and strongly in favour of a 'small German solution' (*kleindeutsche Lösung*). Yet he did not say this outright, and with a clear reference to the present. As a historian, he took a detour via medieval history. First, he accused Wilhelm Giesebrecht of dealing much too favourably with the medieval emperors from Otto I when it came to their policies towards Italy. To sum it up in a somewhat popular way – instead of concerning themselves so much with Italy and the South, they should rather have expanded their rule in the centre, in the North and, most of all, in the east of Europe. This reference to Eastern Europe is especially important, because in the middle of the nineteenth century Sybel was thus one of the pioneers of a school of political thought in Germany that was to have fatal consequences in the twentieth century. The political right developed the ideology of a German *Lebensraum*, the German claim to areas of settlement in Eastern Europe, and justified this with reference to the expansion of the medieval empire in the east. This reasoning also entered into Nazi ideology, and it was used to justify German conquests in the east during World War II. Code names for political and military actions by Nazi Germany also made direct reference to medieval history. Austria's *Anschluss* (annexation) in 1938 was called *Unternehmen Otto* (Operation Otto), with reference to Otto the Great. The Russian campaign that started in June 1941 had the code name *Unternehmen Barbarossa* (Operation Barbarossa). Finally, the mass murder of the Jewish population in the occupied territories received the euphemistic title *Programm Heinrich* – an indication of SS leader Heinrich Himmler's adoration of King Henry I. After all, the Ottonians, as the founders of German rule in Europe, were very highly regarded by the Nazis' historical propaganda. It is needless to say that this utilisation of the medieval past had nothing to do with historical accuracy, but was rather the justification of criminal actions by means of a supposedly historical legitimisation.[7] You

---

[6] Cf. T. Brechenmacher, 'Wieviel Gegenwart verträgt historisches Urteilen? Die Kontroverse zwischen Heinrich von Sybel und Julius Ficker über die Bewertung der Kaiserpolitik des Mittelalters (1859–1862)', *Historisierung und gesellschaftlicher Wandel in Deutschland im 19. Jahrhundert*, ed. U. Muhlack (Berlin, 2003), pp. 87–112.

[7] Cf. W. Wippermann, *Der 'deutsche Drang nach Osten'. Ideologie und Wirklichkeit eines politischen Schlagwortes* (Darmstadt, 1981), and Gordon Wolnik, *Mittelalter und NS-Propaganda. Mittelalterbilder in den Print-, Ton- und Bildmedien des Dritten Reiches* (Münster, 2004).

may have noticed that I am speeding a little through the ages – this is just to show you even more concisely what continuities between medieval images of the nineteenth and twentieth centuries existed in Germany. But let me return once more to the nineteenth century. The historian Heinrich von Sybel utilised a recourse to medieval politics in order to reinforce historically a current German policy aiming at a new 'small German' empire under Prussian dominance. The Catholic historian Julius Ficker, who taught in Austria, reacted to Sybel's interpretation from a 'great German' (*großdeutsche*) perspective and came to Giesebrecht's defence. He accused Sybel of not having viable historical proof for his nationalist usurpation of medieval politics, and he pointed to the universalist tradition of the empire. Ficker did make his points more moderately, and by and large with sounder scholarship than Sybel, but the position he adopted clearly related to the present as well as to the past. Ficker also put the case for a unified second German empire, but for him this was only conceivable with the inclusion of Austria. Be that as it may, in the course of the nineteenth century, history had become an accepted authority for the interpretation of contemporary political controversies. And the word of academic historical scholars, who generally counted themselves among the middle-class national movement, carried quite some weight in the political debates in the years around 1860.

Yet it was not the members of the middle-class national movement, whether their perspective was that of 'small Germany' or 'great Germany', who would become the protagonists of the empire's unification. At the same time as Sybel's and Ficker's quarrel, a politician ascended to the highest governmental office who would shape German history in the second half of the nineteenth century as no other would: Otto von Bismarck, who became Prussian prime minister in 1862. After three wars, expressly described as 'wars of unification', Bismarck founded the second German empire 'from above', that is, without the participation of the middle-class national movement. Prussia was by far the most powerful state of the new empire, and its king was offered the honour of becoming the emperor. At first there was some effort made not simply to imitate the traditions of the medieval empire. Thus the new emperor was only called 'German emperor', and not 'emperor of the German empire'. However, at the Prussian court there was the influential party of the 'Neo-Ghibellines', whose highest-ranking representative was the crown prince.[8] These 'Neo-Ghibellines' were great admirers of the medieval empire, and tried hard to mirror in the new German empire the glamour of centuries long gone. A kind of historic marketing took place that was in particular intended to emphasise the connection with the glorious Staufer. We should keep the Barbarossa myth, which was common knowledge in nineteenth-century Germany, in mind: Barbarossa sitting in the

---

[8] Cf. F. L. Müller, *Our Fritz. Emperor Frederick III and the Political Culture of Imperial Germany* (Cambridge MA, 2011), pp. 87–104.

Kyffhäuser mountain, not dead, but only waiting for the lost empire to return. Now, in 1871, another empire had been founded, and the hope which the myth expressed had thus come true. Yet, as was to be expected, Barbarossa did not return in person to take up the dominion of the new empire. Indeed he passed the torch to 'Barbablanca', as the new German emperor William I was called by his followers. The direction of impact of this historical propaganda was obvious – the empire's unfulfilled history with its great emperors from Charlemagne via the Ottonians and the Salians, all the way to the idolised Staufer, had now found its glorious conclusion in the reign of Barbablanca, in the *kleindeutsche* empire under Prussian leadership. Naturally, this utilisation of medieval history for the legitimisation of the new empire was not welcomed by all Germans. It was rejected especially in parts of southern Germany and in Catholic circles, and there understandably seen as brash and impudent. I will return to these counter-movements a bit later. But first, I will briefly mention two monuments which illustrate and very clearly represent the 'invention of tradition' that I have just described.[9] During the period when the new empire was founded, the famous *Kaiserpfalz* (imperial palace) in Goslar, the origins of which date back to *c*. 1000, was restored. Following this restoration, the historical painter Hermann Wislicenus was commissioned to paint the ceilings and walls of Goslar's Aula Regis, starting in 1877. Here Wislicenus achieved a kind of historical synthesis of the Middle Ages and the present to celebrate the new emperor. There are scenes from medieval imperial history beginning with Charlemagne, and (naturally) featuring prominent representations of the Staufen emperors Frederick I and Frederick II. All these portrayals finally culminate in a mural painting entitled 'the Apotheosis of Imperial Rule', showing the new emperor William I among his family and other important persons of the recent past. [See Fig. 2, in the essay by Leerssen, Chapter 6 in this volume.] So we find the usurpation of history in a painting in the hall of the *Kaiserpfalz*: the aim and the final culmination of a great medieval history was the restoration of a German emperor in 1871. Interestingly enough, the portrayal of earlier history in the Kaiserpfalz ends with Charles V and, of course, with Martin Luther at the Diet of Worms in 1521, also a milestone for Protestant Prussia. Further, early modern imperial history was not required as a historical echo chamber.[10]

The second and indeed even more impressive example of this politically-inspired medievalism is the Kyffhäuser monument, which was commissioned after the death of William I in 1888. On its base we see the portrayal of the awakening emperor Barbarossa (Fig. 1). Right above it there is an impressively dynamic equestrian statue of the recently deceased William. Here also

[9]   Cf. *The Invention of Tradition*, ed. E. Hobsbawm and T. Ranger (Cambridge, 1983).
[10] Cf. M. Arndt, *Die Goslarer Kaiserpfalz als Nationaldenkmal. Eine ikonographische Untersuchung* (Hildesheim, 1976).

Figure 1. The Kyffhäuser monument; the statue of Frederick Barbarossa (Photo by Diane Milburn)

Figure 2. The Kyffhäuser monument: William I and Barbarossa (Photo by Diane Milburn)

Barbablanca is portrayed as the great, and virtually direct, successor of the great Barbarossa. (Fig. 2) Once again, legitimisation of power and imperial rule was conducted with the reference to medieval history.[11]

History and politics, history and nation: these were the coordinates that helped medieval images in gaining their effectiveness in the nineteenth century. This effectiveness was considerable and would last well into the twentieth century. We can only perceive the historical culture in a double perspective as that culture developed in the nineteenth century in Western societies, and especially concisely in Germany. On the one hand there is the establishment of historical scholarly disciplines that rationalise history, critically edit sources and traditions, and interpret them according to academic standards. On the other hand the historical knowledge thus found is immediately processed into new myths and tales, and history fulfils a function relating to the present. Or, in the famous words of Max Weber, history is disenchanted in the course of scholarship and at the same time serves for enchantment, because from history comes the glue that keeps communities together and founds nations. In Germany, a good example for this concept is the Song of the Nibelungs. This Middle High German epic, dating from around 1200, with its theme reaching back to the earlier age of Germanic migration, was seen by its early commentators in the eighteenth and nineteenth centuries as a German national epic. The heroism and warlike elements that it featured were taken as expressions of specifically German characteristics. In 1870, when Germany went to war with France, the philologist Karl Simrock stated that:

> This is the poetry of battleground and tent, this can be used to conjure up armies, when it is necessary to fight back against the ravagers of the empire, the murderous Gallic incendiaries, and Roman insolence.[12]

Simrock's interpretation paved the way for a line of reasoning that would be taken up time and again in the future. In the early twentieth century the phrase *Nibelungentreue* (Nibelung loyalty), coined by chancellor Bernhard von Bülow before World War I, was known all over Germany. He used it to describe the relationship between the allies Austria and Germany, and how they should go to war together. This phrase then took up a life of its own, and was considered

---

[11] Cf. C. G. Kaul, *Friedrich Barbarossa im Kyffhäuser. Bilder eines nationalen Mythos im 19. Jahrhundert* (Cologne, 2007).

[12] 'Das ist Feld- und Zeltpoesie, damit kann man Armeen aus der Erde stampfen, wenn es den Verwüstern des Reichs, den gallischen Mordbrennern, der römischen Anmaßung zu wehren gilt'; quoted in Otfrid Ehrismann, *Nibelungenlied. Epoche – Werk – Wirkung*, 2nd edn (Munich, 2002), p. 181, cf. K. von See, 'Das Nibelungenlied – ein Nationalepos?', in *Die Nibelungen. Sage – Epos – Mythos*, ed. J. Heinzle, K. Klein and U. Obhof (Wiesbaden, 2003), pp. 309–43.

to be a German character trait. *Nibelungentreue* was the readiness to devote oneself to the common national cause while discarding individual interests and unconditionally going into battle, even when everything seemed hopeless. Germans would follow their Führer with a similar kind of *Nibelungentreue* in World War II.

In the last part of this essay I would like to emphasise a somewhat different aspect of German medieval images, one which is generally less well-known than the quasi 'official' national and legitimatory recourses to medieval history that have been discussed above. For that, let us take a short look at a meeting in Oxford in 1934. The German medievalist Ernst Kantorowicz was invited there as a guest lecturer after the Nazis had effectively forced him out of his professorship in Frankfurt because he was Jewish.[13] Since the 1920s Kantorowicz had been a member of the circle of Stefan George, the charismatic German poet. Many of its members were historians or scholars of related subjects, and they created a special kind of historiography, heavily indebted to George's aestheticism. Ernst Kantorowicz was not a medievalist by training, but from 1922 onwards had immersed himself in Staufen history, and in 1927 he published his celebrated biography of Frederick II. This book was an immediate popular success, and was translated into English as early as 1931, although it triggered a lively, and by no means entirely favourable, discussion among professional German historians.[14] But let us return to Oxford in 1934. Kantorowicz's host, the classical scholar Maurice Bowra, mentions some conversations with the historian from that time: 'at Oxford Ernst still reflected George's teaching. He was liable to talk about a thing called "secret Germany", which, though meaningful enough in German, lacked substance in English.'[15] What was the meaning of this 'secret Germany' (*Das Geheime Deutschland*)? This interesting concept was part of the core of historical reflection in George's circle. Kantorowicz referred to it in the preface to his biography of Frederick II, and it was indeed the subject of the first of his last, abortive, lecture series in Frankfurt in November 1933.[16] Since a medievalist like Ernst Kantorowicz talked about it explicitly enough to make his English host curious about it, it is worth having a look at the medieval roots

---

[13] Kantorowicz did not formally resign his chair until November 1934, but his attempts to teach a course the previous autumn had been completely disrupted by SA picketing, and he had been forced to ask for leave of absence. Robert E. Lerner, '"Meritorious academic service": Kantorowicz and Frankfurt', in *Ernst Kantorowicz. Erträge der Doppeltagung Institute for Advanced Study, Princeton, Johann Wolfgang Goethe-Universität, Frankfurt*, ed. R. L. Benson and J. Fried (Stuttgart, 1997), pp. 29–32.

[14] Cf. E. Grünewald, *Ernst Kantorowicz und Stefan George. Beiträge zur Biographie des Historikers bis zum Jahre 1938 und zu seinem Jugendwerk "Kaiser Friedrich der Zweite"* (Wiesbaden, 1982).

[15] C. M. Bowra, *Memories 1898–1939*, 3rd edn (London 1967), p. 290.

[16] Text in *Ernst Kantorowicz*, ed. Benson and Fried, pp. 77–30.

of this talk about a 'secret Germany'.[17] I have already discussed the myth of Barbarossa and the significant role that this played in the 'political romanticism' of nineteenth-century Germany. As long as the empire is not united and medieval imperial glory is not restored, Barbarossa will sit in his mountain and wait. Yet the empire was united in 1871 – and Barbablanca, William I, had appeared. However, this clever historical utilisation of the medieval emperor by the new ruling house of Hohenzollern was not to all Germans' liking. Among the critics were the members of Stefan George's circle. There it was known as a matter of course that the notion of the waiting emperor, an emperor between absence and presence, who simultaneously lives and does not live, had not in fact originated with Frederick I, but rather with his grandson Frederick II. *Vivit et non vivit* – in the thirteenth century this prophecy of the Erythraean Sibyl had linked itself to the emperor, whose death in 1250 had made him at one and at the same time a present and an absent emperor in contemporary political propaganda. In Germany this myth of the emperor had continued through the following centuries, and had only switched to Barbarossa about 1500.[18] Yet for Stefan George and his followers, it was Frederick II who was the great mythical emperor of the Middle Ages, the one who was dead and yet not dead, *vivit et non vivit*. For them he represented a Germany that had not found its realisation in the foundation of the empire in 1871. He was the emperor of a different Germany that existed in myth, but not in reality: the emperor of a 'secret Germany'. But what did this other, this secret Germany look like? It was a counter-vision to the North German-Prussian second empire, and, after 1919, also a counter-vision to the despised democracy of the Weimar Republic. In his biography Kantorowicz describes Frederick II as a 'Roman German' (*Römischer Deutscher*).[19] 'For the first time this stranger, this Roman of Swabian blood, embodied that European-German personage whom men had dreamed of, who combined the triple culture of Europe: the cultures of the Church, of the east and the Ancients'.[20] As scholars have repeatedly pointed out, Kantorowicz's biography describes the emperor as a brutal ruler and equally brutal founder of the state. However, at the same time there are the characterisations that I have just quoted. For Kantorowicz, the medieval emperor stands for a Southern and European Germany, for a universal

[17] Cf. Ulrich Raulff, '"In unterirdischer Verborgenheit". Das geheime Deutschland – Mythogenese und Myzel', in *Geschichtsbilder im George-Kreis. Wege zur Wissenschaft*, ed. Barbara Schlieben, Olaf Schneider and Kerstin Schulmeyer (Göttingen, 2004), pp. 93–115.

[18] Peter Munz, *Frederick Barbarossa. A Study in Medieval Politics* (London, 1969), pp. 3–22.

[19] E. Kantorowicz: *Kaiser Friedrich der Zweite* [1927], 2nd edn (Berlin, 1928), p. 375 [*Frederick the Second 1194–1250*, trans. E. O. Lorimer (London, 1931), p. 409].

[20] 'Denn erstmals war in diesem Fremden, dem Römer schwäbischen Bluts, jenes erträumte europäisch-deutsche Menschenbild verkörpert, in welchem Europas dreifache Bildungswelt sich schloß: Antike Orient und Kirche...', ibid., p. 355 [translation from *Frederick the Second*, p. 387].

European world in which antiquity and the Middle Ages, as well as Christian and Eastern elements, come together in a synthesis: 'in those times Germany as an empire was really the symbol and embodiment of the great concept of a Roman Empire embracing all peoples and races of the world'.[21] Here Kantorowicz calls upon the vision of another 'secret Germany' hidden in history; but in retrospect one is tempted to say that this counter-image came a little late in 1927, as the triumphant medievalism of the second empire was long overcome and had itself become history with the founding of the Weimar Republic. Even today it is disputed whether Kantorowicz's heroic Staufer emperor was also supposed to be an antidote to the 'emperor-less' democracy of Weimar. All the same, in the biography there is this image that I have emphasized above, an image of a European-universal German empire in the thirteenth century – an image which is clearly directed against the nationalistically-instrumentalised use of medieval myths from the nineteenth century onwards. After times had changed and conditions in Germany had become a threat to Kantorowicz himself, he called upon the historical mindscape of a universal 'Roman' Germany once more. Here another medieval emperor moved alongside the legendary Staufer – it was Otto III, who in the nineteenth century was seen as a particularly 'un-German' emperor. Indeed, he was branded a traitor to the German cause by nationally inclined historians because of his programme of a *Renovatio Imperii Romanorum*.[22] In 1935 Ernst Kantorowicz called upon the Ottonian as his witness. In a radio lecture that was broadcast at night, a means which still allowed oppositional voices to be heard in a media which had otherwise been brought into line by the regime, the historian pointed out: 'For once before Germany has been "Roman", that is, universal and worldly' – which, according to Kantorowicz, took place under the same emperor who was 'especially accused of romanising the Germans [...] the young Saxon emperor Otto III, "the miracle of the world" who could happily tell his friend and teacher: "Ours, ours is the Roman empire" [...].' Under this emperor would lie the beginnings 'of becoming Roman, of the Germans' becoming universal, something of which people are today ashamed [...].'[23] Two years after the Nazis came to power, Kantorowicz posed a different

[21] 'Damals war Deutschland als 'Imperium' wirklich Gleichnis und Abbild der großen Idee des alle Völker und Stämme der Welt einenden Römerreiches...', ibid., p. 353 [*Frederick the Second*, pp. 384–5].
[22] Cf. G. Althoff, *Otto III*, trans. P. G. Jestice (University Park PA, 2003).
[23] The complete passage reads: 'Denn einmal schon ist auch Deutschland "römisch", das heißt: universal und welthaltig gewesen. Ist es danach zu verwundern, daß der erste Versuch zur Errichtung eines Deutschen Papsttums sich herschreibt von demjenigen Kaiser, dem man besonders gern die Verrömerung der Deutschen vorwirft, von dem jungen Sachsenkaiser Otto III., dem 'Wunder der Welt', der beglückt seinem Lehrer und Freunde vermelden konnte: 'Unser, unser ist das Römische Reich'? Fängt wirklich mit diesem Kaiser das Römischwerden, das Universalwerden der Deutschen an, wessen man sich heute schämt, dann ist es nur folgerichtig, daß man zu seiner Zeit

medieval Germany as a contrast to the brutal Germany of the present. It was a universal Germany, something that had now become impossible, but which was present to those who were aware of it and bound to it as a historical counter-world under the name 'secret Germany'. This 'oppositional Middle Ages', as it were, could not accomplish much in 1930s Germany. The 'Roman' German emperor Otto III had no reputation then – medieval emperors were only utilised by the Nazis when they could be shown as conquerors, mainly of Eastern Europe. Ernst Kantorowicz had to leave Germany in 1938. By way of England he emigrated to America, where, as you know, he wrote further important studies of medieval political thought, most famously *The King's Two Bodies*.

In this essay I have attempted to give some insight on the legitimatory, but also on the oppositional medieval images in modern German history. I will conclude with a literary recommendation, and I will also briefly return to Otto III. It was not only the medievalist Ernst Kantorowicz who invoked the prematurely-deceased emperor and made him the ancestor of a different Germany. A prominent literary interpreter of history also assigned that role to the emperor. I am referring to Thomas Mann, whose novel *Doctor Faustus*, published in 1947, is among the earliest attempts to make the path of German history towards the Nazi catastrophe comprehensible. Writing in his American exile, Mann interpreted German history in literary-allegorical shape. He dates the start of a problematic German path to the very end of the Middle Ages, in the sixteenth century – embodied by the eponymous character of Doctor Faust. Yet Thomas Mann did not only see German history as a wrong way, leading towards fascism. He also described a different, a good Germany – in his opinion this was realised in the Middle Ages, before the Faustian fall of man in German history that began in the sixteenth century.[24] In his 1945 lecture *Germany and the Germans*, Mann ascribed a 'fundamental universalism and cosmopolitanism' to the Germans of the Middle Ages. Both of these were 'a spiritual accessory of their ancient supranational realm, the Holy Roman Empire of German Nation'.[25] In *Doctor Faustus*, the author also describes Otto III as a representative of a Germany that had not become entangled in nationalism like the present one, but was universal and cosmopolitan. However, Mann did not make the emperor a part of a pathetic 'secret Germany', but rather shows him as a ruler beset by doubt, at odds with his 'Germanness'.

---

auch erstmals einem Deutschen [that is Pope Gregory V, BS] auf dem Stuhle Petri begegnet'; Ernst H. Kantorowicz, 'Deutsches Papsttum' [1933/1935], *Tumult – Schriften zur Verkehrswissenschaft* 16 (1992), 15.

[24] Cf. B. Schlüter, 'Ein rechtes Kind des 19. Jahrhunderts? Thomas Mann und die Bilder vom Mittelalter', *Thomas Mann Jahrbuch* 25 (2012), 41–57.

[25] Thomas Mann, *Germany and the Germans* (Washington, 1945), p. 14.

Kaiser Otto III, [grandson] of Adelheid and [son] of Theophano, who called himself Emperor of the Romans, also Saxonicus; the latter not because he wanted to be Saxon but in the sense on which Scipio called himself Africanus, because he had conquered the Saxons. He was driven out of his beloved Rome and died in misery in the year 1002; his remains were brought to Germany [...] – not at all what he would have relished himself, for he was a prize specimen of German self-contempt and had been all his life ashamed of being German.[26]

Ashamed of being German – that was the very opposite of what official Germany wanted in the 1930s and 1940s. For the expatriate Thomas Mann the suffering emperor was the historical symbol of a different Germany. And in this shape Otto III was also a historical mirror image of the German Thomas Mann, who, looking towards Europe, in turn suffered shamefacedly from his Germanness.

Translation: Ernst-Georg Richter

.

---

[26] Thomas Mann, *Doctor Faustus. The Life of the German Composer Adrian Leverkühn. As told by a Friend*, trans. H. T. Lowe-Porter (New York, 1948), pp. 35–6. A historically incorrect version, 'son of Adelheid and consort of Theophano', is to be found in the early editions of the novel and also in the translation of Lowe-Porter.

6

ONCE UPON A TIME IN GERMANY: MEDIEVALISM, ACADEMIC ROMANTICISM AND NATIONALISM

Joep Leerssen

This essay studies the medievalist and legendary iconography of the murals in the twelfth-century Goslar *Kaiserpfalz* (which was restored and decorated between 1867 and 1897) to explore the political, literary and pictorial themes that instilled the Wilhelminian Empire with the mystique of the medieval Holy Roman Empire.[1] I analyse the murals (by Hermann Wislicenus, 1825–1899) as a vortex of Romantic Nationalism, bringing together attitudes and ideologies from the fields of politics, the literary imagination, and academic history-painting.[2]

Restorations

By the time the city of Goslar became part of the newly constituted kingdom of Hanover in 1814, its major landmark, the twelfth- and thirteenth-century Imperial palace (*Kaiserpfalz*) had become badly dilapidated. After its glory days under the Salian and Staufen dynasties, it had been destroyed by fire in 1289, and lost its imperial status between 1300 and 1550. In 1802 the remains of the collapsed palatine church were sold. Shortly after, in 1865, the palace itself suffered a wall

---

[1]   In this essay I follow in the footsteps of the benchmark study by M. Arndt, *Die Goslarer Kaiserpfalz als Nationaldenkmal: Eine ikonographische Untersuchung* (Hildesheim, 1976), of which I have made grateful use throughout.
[2]   On the multi-media expressions of Romantic Nationalism, I rely largely upon, without in every instance giving explicit references to, the great body of expertise assembled by many authors in the *Encyclopedia of Romantic Nationalism in Europe*, ed. J. Leerssen, Study Platform on Interlocking Nationalisms (Amsterdam, 2015), online at http://romanticnationalism.net, hereafter referred to as ERNiE. A great many cultural expressions of Romantic Nationalism, textual and visual, are documented in the repertory of historical materials that is also online at ERNiE, and so marked in the source references.

collapse. To the sensitive Romantic eye, it presented a picturesque icon of the ruin into which the ancient medieval empire had fallen.

By 1865, however, the impending collapse of the *Kaiserpfalz* triggered a conservationist response among the Goslar citizens; a petition was addressed by the city to the central court of Hanover for funds to restore the palace. The request was, however, ill-timed, for the entire kingdom of Hanover was itself doomed. In the Austro-Prussian War of 1866 the king of Hanover, George V, sided against his mighty, encroaching neighbour Prussia. Prussia's rapid victory in that brief war meant that, along with other hapless opponents such as the Free City of Frankfurt, Hanover was annexed and brought under the rule of Berlin. The deposed King George V fled to Paris, from where he would continue asserting the sovereignty of Hanover and of his dynastic house: a token 'Welf Legion' was maintained for that purpose, invoking, in the teeth of the Hohenzollern usurpation, the dynasty's august ancestral name of Welf (Guelph).[3]

That gesture, full of powerless pathos, indicates to what extent Romantic historicism had become entrenched in the dynastic self-awareness of Europe's monarchs – a significant, but often overlooked, conduit from the sphere of cultural self-reflection to that of political action. Since the French Revolution, many rulers had been ousted from their thrones, breaking the dynastic continuity which was considered the very manifestation of the divine right of kings. Following the fall of Napoleon, many of these rulers had had their realms restored to them, but with diminished charisma, and often with the new instrument of a written constitution hemming in their arbitrary power – something which was to create tensions over the next decades, with kings abrogating constitutions and the people protesting or revolting against such autocratic encroachments. (Ernest Augustus, the father of George V, had, for example, suspended the constitution of Hanover in 1837.)[4] The notion of "Restoration" was in the air; it not only applied,

---

[3] On the aftermath of the annexation: S. A. Stehlin, *Bismarck and the Guelph Problem 1866–1890: A Study in Particularist Opposition to National Unity* (The Hague, 1973). The political events of these decades, and the history of Prussian expansionism culminating in the *Reichsgründung* of 1871, have generated an overwhelming amount of historical literature, starting with the almost-contemporary official Prussian accounts by Sybel and Treitschke. In the face of that information overkill, there is an admirably concise survey by S. Berger, *Inventing the Nation: Germany* (London, 2004). What I synthesize in the following pages has profited in particular from M. Hewitson, *Nationalism in Germany, 1848–1866: Revolutionary Nation* (Basingstoke, 2010); T. Nipperdey, *Deutsche Geschichte, 1800–1866: Bürgerwelt und starker Staat* (Munich, 1973); and L. Rieners, *Bismarck gründet das Reich, 1864–1871* (Munich, 1965). The culture-historical background is admirably surveyed in the outstanding essay collection by G. Hess, *Panorama und Denkmal: Studien zum Bildgedächtnis des 19. Jahrhunderts* (Würzburg, 2011).

[4] He was the younger brother of Queen Victoria, who, as a woman, could not succeed to the Hanoverian kingship because of the Salic succession rules in effect there. Between 1714 and 1837, Hanover had been in a personal union with the United Kingdom. Ernest Augustus's 1837 suspension of the Hanoverian constitution sparked the protest by

culturally, to the repairs made to ramshackle buildings, but also, politically, to the rule of kings.

Meanwhile, the citizens of Goslar seemed to react to the Prussian takeover in a coolly pragmatic way. They redirected their application to the new Hohenzollern powers in Berlin, and immediately, in 1867, obtained funds for the restoration. Work was begun in 1868 and concluded, a decade later, in 1879.

One is habitually inclined to see the Prussian state as a dour, unimaginative military-bureaucratic apparatus: the very opposite of the Romantic. When in 1848, national enthusiasm had inspired a delegation from the Frankfurt Parliament to offer the German imperial crown to the Prussian king, it was bluntly refused. Instead Bismarck set out on his long and intricate programme to unify Germany under Prussian leadership with 'blood and iron' rather than with romance and enthusiasm. That does not mean, however, that Prussia was impervious to the ambient spirit of Romantic nationalism and national historicism; and especially outside its Brandenburg heartland, Prussia indeed undertook a good number of restorations of medieval buildings and landmarks. The most famous of these is, of course, the cathedral of Cologne, left unfinished since 1473, and first restored (1815–1842) and then completed (1842–1880) under Prussian rule. In addition, there was the remarkable restoration of the Marienburg, the former headquarters of the Teutonic Knights (in what is now Malbork in Poland). Since the margraves of Brandenburg owed their royal status in the first instance to their Polish-Prussian possessions (located outside of the Holy Roman Empire proper, and originally established by the Teutonic Order), this was symbolically the originary *Stammschloss* of the Hohenzollerns' royalty; its restoration was first mooted in 1803 and carried out between 1815 and 1848. In both cases, the Prussian authorities responded unhesitatingly to a public awareness campaign carried forward by Romantic intellectuals such as Joseph Görres and Max von Schenkendorf.[5] Goslar fits this pattern to a T.

seven professors at the University of Göttingen, the Grimm Brothers among them, who were, notoriously, dismissed and expelled from the kingdom as a result.

[5]   Visual and textual documentation on both cases is online at ERNiE. The restoration of the Marienburg became a hot issue in public opinion after an album of prints depicting the castle's dilapidated state had been published in 1799; Max von Schenckendorf, later a leading patriotic poet of the anti-Napoleonic wars, published an essay calling for its restoration in 1803. The restoration and completion of Cologne Cathedral was urged by Catholic Rhineland intellectuals like Joseph Görres. The ideological motivation here was multifunctional. It was a way for the recently installed Prussian monarchs to make themselves popular with their new Rhineland subjects; it was a sign of enduring German power on a river long coveted by France for its eastern frontier, and as such a counterweight against that other landmark of German Gothic, French-ruled Strasbourg Cathedral; and, last but not least, it was a historicist signal that the new Germany could pick up where the medieval Reich had left off. In both restoration projects the German Romantic poet Joseph von Eichendorff, a Catholic nobleman in

What is more, in the decade that it took to restore the imperial palace at Goslar, the mother of all political restorations took place: a new German Empire was established in 1871, when the Prussian king was acclaimed by all German princes as their emperor. It was the final fulfillment of Bismarck's policy and came hot on the heels of its triumphal culmination: the victory over France in the 1870–71 war. Hence the fact that the imperial proclamation took place in Versailles – not just to humiliate the vanquished enemy, but also to provide a neutral meeting ground for all the German princes (who might have considered a journey to Berlin too submissive altogether).

Thus, when Wilhelm I came to inspect the progress of the repair works at Goslar in 1875, he did so in a new capacity: not just as king of Prussia, but also as German Emperor. That this dignity was not just a newly conquered title of power, but the restoration of a pre-existing imperial dignity, which had lapsed under Napoleonic pressure in 1806, was the generally accepted view of things. The attempt by the 1848 Frankfurt Parliament to unite the German lands under an imperial crown has already been mentioned. The Prussian Crown Prince in his diary of the 1870–71 campaign looked forward to the end of the 'interregnum'; and many a poet (notoriously Emanuel Geibel, in his Schleswig-Holstein sonnets of 1846, and again in his *Deutschlands Beruf* of 1861) had grieved over the emperor-shaped hole in German politics since 1806.[6]

Uncannily, then, both in its ruination and in its restoration, the Goslar *Kaiserpfalz* and the German *Kaiserreich* marched in tandem; and this synchronicity did not go unnoticed.

Undoing the past's undoings: The end of the Holy Roman Empire and the beginning of Romantic historicism

What had happened in 1806? Napoleon had conquered a number of German lands along the Rhine which formally formed part of, and fell under the 'feudal' protection of, the Holy Roman Empire. Ramshackle though it was, fully a thousand years after Charlemagne that empire still provided, at least vestigially, a common constitutional framework under its supreme Habsburg liegelord in his Vienna residence. To indemnify the princes who had lost their lands to Napoleon, a reshuffle of the Reich's feudal governance was undertaken in 1803, which proved to be more than the decrepit imperial structure could take. In particular, with the archdioceses of Cologne, Mainz and Trier having been stripped of their electoral status, the Habsburgs looked set to lose their Catholic

---

the Prussian civil service, played an active role. Cf. H. Boockmann, *Die Marienburg im 19. Jahrhundert* (Vienna 1982); H. Knapp, *Das Schloß Marienburg in Preussen: Quellen und Materialien zur Baugeschichte seit 1456* (Lüneburg 1990); *Religion, Kunst, Vaterland: Der Kölner Dom im 19. Jahrhundert*, ed. O. Dann (Cologne 1983).

[6] Online at ERNiE.

majority in the imperial electoral college. In addition, Napoleon now had imperial ambitions himself; and in an avalanche of upheavals and battles, the last Holy Roman Emperor, Francis II, dissolved the empire, freed the German princes from their liege-ties, and took for himself the substitute title of 'Emperor of Austria' (reverting numerically to the style of Francis I).

This dynastic and symbolic gesture, coming as it did in the welter of cascading crises between the Battles of Austerlitz and Jena, and not long after Napoleon's own imperial coronation, has not usually been considered materially important among historians. It merely confirmed, symbolically, what was already a reality on the ground: the impotence of the Imperial constitution, the centennial shift in power balance away from Vienna. But in its cultural impact its importance should not be underestimated. There was nothing trivial about the disappearance, after a track record of fully a millennium, of a state which united the patchwork quilt north of the Alps under the common appellation 'German'. The old empire's historical traces suffused the public spaces of all Free Imperial cities, and its symbolic charisma was far, far stronger than its actual power. Its loss was felt as a crisis for the German nation. For that was how the Holy Roman Empire specified itself: as being *Das Heilige Römische Reich deutscher Nation*. And the German nation responded, mainly through its intellectuals. Immediately following the end of empire in 1806, the lexicographer Campe (in his dictionary of 1807) stated that the German language was now all that maintained the continued presence in world history of something that could go by the name of 'German'. Similarly, the philologist von der Hagen published his seminal edition of the *Nibelungenlied*, with a firebrand foreword exhorting the nation to heed the stalwart, death-defying example of its ancestors;[7] and Fichte held his landmark public lectures in Berlin in 1808 which he called by that pregnant title: *Reden an die deutsche Nation.*[8]

---

[7] Online at ERNiE.

[8] Launched by Friedrich Meinecke's classic *Weltbürgertum und Nationalstaat* (Munich and Berlin, 1908), the conceptual division between the German *Staatsnation* and the German *Kulturnation* has been a powerful analytical and rhetorical presence – and challenge – in the writing of nineteenth-century German history. Like all such oppositions, it needs to be taken under the proviso that whatever value it has is heuristic. This proviso is especially necessary because Meinecke, himself a German national chauvinist, went much further: he muddied his own waters by advancing a master narrative about the *Kulturnation*'s deep-rooted need to incorporate itself into a *Staatsnation*. That being said, the heuristic opposition, it seems to me, has a more direct basis in historical reality if one sees the developments of 1806 as a crisis where the German intelligentsia, dismayed at the disappearance of its overarching imperial state-constitution, felt that it was thrown back on its inner cultural traditions. In 1806, the cultivation of the *Kulturnation* gained force, alongside a nostalgically restorative *Reichsidee*, in response to the loss of its original *Staatsnation*, the Holy Roman Empire. Thus, *pace* Meinecke, I would suggest that the crisis of 1806 did not so much shock the, as yet state-divided, German intellectuals out of their cosmopolitanism, as that the

What is more, the crisis of 1806 gave rise, almost immediately, to a myth. It was first propounded by the Rhineland Romantic Johann Joseph Görres (he who has been noted as urging, in 1814, the restoration of Cologne Cathedral). Görres published, in Heidelberg in 1807, an edition of early-modern German chapbooks, a textual genre which had been considered infra dig by the august classicist standards of the Enlightenment, but which was appreciated by the new Romantic generation for its vernacular authenticity. *Die teutschen Volksbücher* was prefaced by a dedication to his fellow-Romantic Clemens Brentano, author of fairy tales and compiler of an anthology of folk poems, and that dedication itself took the form of an allegorical wonder-tale, a *Märchen*. The author described how a dream-quest takes him into an underground cavern where the shades of all the ancient, legendary heroes of older German history are assembled: from Siegfried and Charlemagne to Duke Ernst of Swabia. The presiding spirit is the old Emperor Frederick Barbarossa, about whom the main body of the *Teutschen Volksbücher* contains, in fact, a legend: that the emperor did not die on the Crusade, but is rather dwelling in suspended animation in a cavern under the Kyffhäuser Mountain, where his red beard is growing around, or even through, the table at which he sits biding his time. One day he will return and restore his empire.[9]

The theme is familiar: that of the *rex absconditus*, or *rex quondam atque futurus*, which we know from its well-known application to King Arthur. In applying it to Barbarossa in 1807, however, Görres gave the legend a highly political and specifically allegorical meaning. His essay on popular culture (appended to the *Teutschen Volksbücher*) evokes the long decline of Germany, and indeed Europe, after the chivalric period. High-minded ideals were forgotten in the wars of religion and the rise of new types of governance (here Görres betrays his incipient reactionary Catholicism, which was to become extreme in subsequent years). The only vestigial memory of the heroic, chivalric glories of the Middle Ages were those which were kept alive, in debased form but with admirable moral fidelity, by the common people in their hero-tales and chapbooks. And it is from this demotic archive, the bargain basement, as it were, of the High Middle Ages, that the memory of erstwhile glory must now be retrieved.[10]

disappearance of their shared imperial *Staat* paved the way for the *Kulturnation*'s self-assertion, and its dreams of restoration. Cf. also W. Burgdorf, *Ein Weltbild verliert seine Welt: Der Untergang des Alten Reiches und die Generation von 1806* (Munich, 2006); D. Langewiesche, 'Zum Überleben des Alten Reiches im 19. Jahrhundert: Die Tradition des "zusammengesetzten Staates"', in *Das Jahr 1806 im europäischen Kontext: Balance, Hegemonie und politische Kulturen*, ed. A. Klinger, H. Hahn and G. Schmidt (Cologne, 2008), pp. 123–34.

[9] Full German text online at ERNiE.

[10] The notion of the collectively remembered past as an archive has been given fresh analytical traction in memory studies, following Aleida Assmann's identification of an 'archival memory', in her *Erinnerungsräume: Formen und Wandlungen des kulturellen*

Such an agenda suffused the authors of Heidelberg Romanticism: Görres with his edition of chapbooks, Arnim and Brentano's anthology of folksongs, and the Grimm Brothers with their fairy tales and German legends. All wanted to retrieve from the collective memory of the common people a sense of an authentic German identity, following the collapse of the German *Reich* and the moral bankruptcy of the German aristocracy.[11] That is also the allegorical dream-quest with which Görres's book opens: in the underground cavern of the collective popular memories, the shades of the mighty nobles of yore can even now be encountered. And the central figure among them is that cavern-bound Barbarossa, now a folktale figure, once an emperor, awaiting his re-emergence.

In the next few years the Barbarossa myth exploded into German culture.[12] The first follow-through to Görres was given by the Grimm Brothers. They published, hot on the heels of their immensely successful folk- and fairy-tales (*Kinder- und Hausmärchen*, 1812–15), two volumes of *Deutsche Sagen* (1816–18), folk legends with particular location-references. Prominent among these was the legend evoking Barbarossa in his underground waiting room in the Kyffhäuser mountain (midway between Goslar and Weimar).[13] The Grimms' wording,

---

Gedächtnisses (Munich, 1999). As a symbolical or allegorical evocation, especially in their huge, awe-inspiring unordered state, archives are part of the 'historical sublime' which Ann Rigney has identified in Romantic historicism, from Michelet to Carlyle: A. Rigney, *Imperfect Histories: The Elusive Past and the Legacy of Romantic Historicism* (Ithaca NY, 2001). To this can be added that the years since the secularization of monasteries (in Revolutionary France and in the reshuffled Holy Roman Empire) had involved a huge transfer of monastic libraries into new state or court libraries, and that these decades are characterized by a damburst of archival discoveries of old texts – giving rise to the Romantic trope of the 'manuscript found in an attic'. An 1811 open letter by Görres on discoveries in the Vatican Library is online at ERNiE. And cf. also *Free Access to the Past: Romanticism, Cultural Heritage and the Nation*, ed. L. Jensen, J. Leerssen and M. Mathijsen (Leiden, 2009); and *Editing the Nation's Memory: Textual Scholarship and Nation-building in 19th-century Europe*, ed. D. van Hulle and J. Leerssen (Amsterdam, 2008).

[11] P. Fritzsche, *Stranded in the Present: Modern Time and the Melancholy of History* (Cambridge MA, 2004).

[12] The massive and admirably thorough study by Camilla Kaul, *Friedrich Barbarossa im Kyffhäuser: Bilder eines nationalen Mythos im 19. Jahrhundert*, 2 vols. (Cologne, 2007) is the definitive account. Briefer and more popularizing, but also instructive is the chapter in H. Münkler, *Die Deutschen und ihre Mythen* (Reinbek, 2009).

[13] Myth, fairytale, folktale, legend, *Märchen*, *Sage*: a phraseological clarification is necessary, in particular to emphasize that the distinction between *Märchen* and *Sage* is far less important than the one between their accustomed English analogues, Fairy-Tale and Saga. The operative etymons in both words refer to their oral transmission (*Mär*, message, rumour; *sagen*, to say). *Märchen* means "brief hearsay-tale" (the hearsay provenance suggesting elements of wonder or magic); what the Grimms presented as wonder tales taken from oral folk practice, such as 'Sleeping Beauty', was specified as *Kinder- und Hausmärchen*, 'brief hearsay-tales for children and the domestic sphere'. The

though faux-naïve in its folksy diction, already hints at the overtly allegorical meaning of an as-yet-unfulfilled restoration of the empire.

> *Frederick Redbeard on the Kyffhäuser:* Many legends are current about this emperor. He is believed not to have died, but to be alive until the second coming, since no true emperor has arisen after him. Until then he sits hidden in the Kyffhäuser Mountain, and when he emerges, he will hang his shield on a withered tree, and that will cause the tree to [become] green, and better times will come. [...] His beard has grown long, some say through the stone table, others say around the table, to the effect that the beard must grow to curl around the table three times before he awakens, but until now it has only completed two turns. [...] Also a shepherd, who had piped a tune that the emperor liked, was led into the mountain by a dwarf, and the emperor arose and asked: 'Are the ravens still flying around the mountain?' And as the shepherd confirmed this, he exclaimed: 'Then I shall have to sleep for another hundred years.'[14]

The appositeness of this tale for Germany's post-1806 situation was lost on no one, and thereby the legend of Barbarossa was turned into a myth, an endlessly recyclable icon of the need for a reawakening of the old empire. The later (post-1815) trajectory of that myth through the century, notably in the poetry of the Romantic nationalist Friedrich Rückert, culminates in the monstrous Kyffhäuser

usual English rendering as 'fairy tale' is slightly askew, since the *Märchen* protagonists, for all that they encounter magical situations, are usually human, and (although there are plenty of witches, ghosts and dwarfs) elves or fairies are rarely involved. The German *Sage*, for its part, means something very different (unless it is specified as *Heldensage*, heroic tale) from its Scandinavian or English homonyms. It is closer to the notion of "legend", although the latter term, certainly in German, is almost invariably of a pious Christian nature and deals with miraculous incidents in saints' lives. What the Grimm Brothers presented as *Deutsche Sagen* were ancient folk anecdotes and beliefs about specific places and endowing these with heroic or supernatural associations; besides the Barbarossa-Kyffhäuser *Sage*, one can think of the Lorelei on her high cliff overlooking the Rhine. In these pages, I refer to the Barbarossa-Kyffhäuser *Sage* variously as a myth or a legend, depending on whether I am discussing its power to illuminate historical reality with supernatural symbolism (which is what myths do), or its supernaturalism inherited from an ancient transmission-history (which is what characterizes legends).

[14] My translation here is slightly condensed. The original is online at Project Gutenberg, <http://gutenberg.spiegel.de/buch/br-753/13>. It is an established fact that the Grimms in successive redactions of their *Märchen* imposed a homely diction on their source material, such as Romantics would expect to be used in the quaint speech of untaught rustics. I can neither assert nor exclude the possibility that they followed this procedure in the *Deutsche Sagen*, or that certain elements (the greening of the tree, the ravens preventing a return) are highlighted or even interpolated by the Grimms as political allegories with a topical-contemporary meaning. The discussion in Kaul, *Friedrich Barbarossa im Kyffhäuser,* pp. 84–5, is inconclusive in this regard.

monument, built between 1890 and 1896 on the mountain of that name. The bloated, towering edifice shows at the base, in stone relief, the waiting emperor at his stone table; above him, in bronze, there is an equestrian statue of Wilhelm I, King of Prussia and German Emperor, in whose honour the monument was erected.[15]

This ham-fisted allegorical twinning of the Once and Present Emperors emerged almost as soon as the Franco-Prussian War was fought and the Second Reich was established. The professor-poet Felix Dahn had seen the war as a call to arms for all mythical heroes slumbering in their subterranean halls,[16] and accordingly hailed the Prussian monarch as Barbablanca, playing on Wilhelm's white beard and establishing a verbal echo with the medieval Redbeard. In this cultural construction, the proclamation of Wilhelm at Versailles was not just picking up where 1806 had left off – it also restored a far older, medieval *Reichsidee*. That made sense both poetically and politically. North of the Alps, the bereavement of 1806 involved the disappearance of the *Reich* as an institution unifying the German nation, rather than any traumatized loyalty to the Vienna Habsburgs. Nor could Wilhelm's imperial dignity be projected as a reconnection with the last Holy Roman Emperor, for that succession was already taken – Francis's grandson Franz Joseph, emperor of Austria, was still wearing the Habsburg imperial crown in Vienna. The best legitimization of the new empire in historical terms was, therefore, a poetical, allegorical and mythical one, invoking the Staufen dynasty, the chivalric High Middle Ages, and the legendary figure of Barbarossa.

This symbolic sense of restored continuity was consolidated by the fact that Wilhelm ticked all the boxes required for a returning 'True Emperor'. As the triumphalist German enthusiasts post-1871 saw it, he restored unity to the hitherto divided German lands – the Habsburg elephant in the German room was once again studiously ignored. In addition, Bismarck's *Kulturkampf* (his German-nationalist showdown with Ultramontanism, conducted with slogans such as *Nach Canossa gehen wir nicht!*) consciously evoked the memory of the medieval struggle between emperor and papacy, and was seen as a modern re-match for the medieval Investiture Controversy.[17] Finally, the Prussian

---

[15] Rückert's verse and the Kyffhäuser monument are both online at ERNiE.

[16] 'To arms, comrades, arise! The time has come, ye heroes all, awaken! Many thousands of hours did you sit in the dark mountain hall; you dreamt of deep wounds and slept one and all. Now grab your spears and shields, and gird your helmet and axe, and go forth to the grim, wild and mortal battle!' (from 'Juli 1870'). The original, as well as Dahn's lengthy, bilingually Latin/German praise poem *Macte Imperator / Heil dem Kaiser,* which coined the Barbablanca trope, is online at ERNiE.

[17] In 1077, Henry IV, excommunicated by pope Gregory VII, had to do penance at the Tuscan castle of Canossa before being readmitted to full Church membership. The episode was a bitter *lieu de mémoire*, evoked in a poem by Heinrich Heine (1839) and a painting by Eduard Schwoiser (1862). On the eighth centenary of the 1077 humiliation,

annexation of Alsace-Lorraine had brought the long-estranged and much-regretted city of Strasbourg back home into the Reich, and driven France well back from the banks of the Upper Rhine. All the versifiers hailed the new empire with the mythical tropes that the German tree was greening, and the ravens of discord had flown from the Kyffhäuser. Barbarossa *redivivus* was now reigning as Barbablanca.

Murals for the Goslar *Kaisersaal*: Hermann Wislicenus and Academic Romanticism

Even more than in the Kyffhäuser monument or in the poetic effusions of nationalist versifiers like Dahn, the mythical restoration of the Hohenstaufen Empire in the Second Reich was given expression in the newly restored Goslar Imperial palace. Following the completion of the building repairs, an extensive mural decoration project was carried out between 1879 and 1897 in the manor's central hall, the *Kaisersaal*. The painter in charge was Hermann Wislicenus (1825–1899), at that time director of the renowned art academy of Düsseldorf.[18]

Wislicenus, his project, his pictorial technique and stylistic register, all came from a very specific painterly tradition which by the 1880s existed alongside, and in conservative defiance of, a rapidly evolving avant-gardism. The earliest vogue of revolutionary innovations had already come and gone: the *Salon des refusés*, the Barbizon school, the Pre-Raphaelite Brotherhood. It was already a decade and a half since Monet and Cézanne had revolutionized settings and styles with their loosely brushed open-air paintings. In the year after Prussia's triumph of 1871, something called Impressionism had emerged in France. The *fin-de-siècle* was, as it were, already knocking on the door. Amidst all this experiment and innovation, art historians tend to overlook the stubborn persistence of the officially endorsed, 'academic' arts in these decades. Academic art was what true artists at the time were moving away from – indeed it has become a byword for technically accomplished but thematically conformist kitsch – the art of complacency. But it was from this old-school academic tradition that the elites and especially the state institutions of the pre-1914 period still drew the official, monumental art with which they embellished public spaces: the commemorative statues and, indeed, the murals that were part of the decoration of public buildings.

a defiant 'Canossa column' (*Canossasäule*) was erected near Bad Harzburg. Column, poem and painting are online at ERNiE.

[18] A biographical sketch and a section of his notes and statements are given in Arndt, *Die Goslarer Kaiserpfalz als Nationaldenkmal*. On the Düsseldorf Academy: F. Saarschmidt, *Zur Geschichte der Düsseldorfer Kunst, insbesondere im XIX. Jahrhundert* (Düsseldorf, 1902); online at <http://nbn-resolving.de/urn:nbn:de:hbz:061:1-14648>.

Wislicenus was a belated representative of the 'official' art of the nineteenth century, which itself was the product of the art academies that had been established in Europe from the late seventeenth century onward[19] In these academies, which were the national institutionalizations of what in previous centuries had been the studios of individual masters, painters were trained in an increasingly standardized and codified set of classical accomplishments: drawing and brush techniques, the art of perspective, the anatomy of the human body and of animals, the proper rendering of different textures, from fur to glass – all the skills, in short, that lent verisimilitude to their representations. The academies had also established a hierarchy of genres, which ranged from the still life, portrait, and landscape, to culminate in the most prestigious and challenging of them all – the sublime and complex genre of history-painting.

Within these national academies, catering as they did for Europe's post-1789 states and monarchies, history-painting as a genre had undergone a nationalising transformation. Whereas originally the topics were invariably drawn from biblical sources or classical antiquity, after 1790 they were increasingly also drawn from medieval or modern history; and very soon, that began to mean the nation's own history. As a result, in the nineteenth century, academic history painting shows a mix of persisting biblical/classical topics, for example the Roman scenes of Lawrence Alma-Tadema, and scenes from the nation's own history.[20] We can identify, then, a tradition of Romantic, national historicism within the academic tradition: Academic Romanticism.

---

[19] The European prototypes are the papal Accademia di San Luca (Rome, 1593) and the Académie royale de peinture et de sculpture (Paris, 1648). Academies were then established at Antwerp in 1664: Berlin in 1696: at Vienna in 1725: Stockholm in 1735; Madrid in 1744; Copenhagen in 1754; Saint Petersburg in 1757; Dresden in 1764; the Royal Academy in London in 1768; Düsseldorf and Munich in 1773; and Kraków in 1818.

[20] It should be mentioned in passing that Northern-European leaders mentioned by Roman authors could occasionally be included in the historical repertoire even before 1750, for example Rembrandt's painting of the Batavian tribal insurgent leader Civilis. There was also a minor tradition of French or English Romantic history-painters depicting scenes from the English or Italian past. Joan of Arc, crusading knights and the two doomed young Princes in the Tower of London were themes with a transnational appeal, for instance with Paul Delaroche; see S. Bann, *Paul Delaroche: History Painted* (London, 1997), or in the French *troubadour* style, which flourished in the early decades after 1800 (F. Pupil, *Le Style Troubadour ou la nostalgie du bon vieux temps* (Nancy, 1985)). Similarly, in the 1820s, paintings overtly propagandizing the cause of national freedom often used the cause of contemporary Greece as a coded disguise to signify the aspirations of all European nations – the continuity of Delacroix's philhellenic paintings to his French-patriotic 'Liberty leading the People' is telling. But, even while taking all these caveats into account, the overall gravitation between 1810 and 1850, across Europe, is unmistakably towards themes from painters' own national past.

A proper survey of this tradition has yet to be written. Preliminary data gathering and analysis indicates its intriguing overlaps with military painting, Orientalism, genre painting, and landscape, and its nodal academies (with a surprising prominence for Antwerp and, indeed, Düsseldorf).[21]

Hermann Wislicenus's position in Academic Romanticism was anchored in his training with Julius Schnorr von Carolsfeld at the Dresden Academy (1844–1853) and with Peter von Cornelius in Rome (1853). Cornelius had himself directed the Düsseldorf Academy between 1819 and 1824, and as such was Wislicenus's indirect precursor there. And both names, Schnorr and Cornelius, tie Wislicenus in with the Nazarene tradition, which indeed dominates most of Academic Romanticism in Germany.

Nazarenes was the nickname of a group of Romantically dissident art students at the Vienna Art Academy, who, upon failing to obtain re-enrolment when the institution was downsized in 1809, moved to Rome to set up a joint studio there. In Rome they followed their anti-classicist, medievalising taste, and emulated the clear simplicity of late-medieval and early-Renaissance forms, which, they felt, expressed sincerely-felt inspiration – rather than merely showing off technical accomplishment. In particular, they tried their hand at the art of the fresco, undertaking much-noted projects at Rome's Casa Bartholdy (1815–17) and Casa Massimo (1817–19). In the process, they re-launched a fresco-derived clarity and simplicity of outline and colour (*disegno* and *colorito*), which was to remain influential in religious art for more than a century. As many of them were recalled to the German lands to teach at academies like Munich, Dresden and, in Cornelius's case, Düsseldorf, they introduced into these institutions the Nazarene style (clear outlines, bright colours), the themes (historicist genre painting) and indeed the medium of the fresco/mural. Upon his appointment at Düsseldorf in 1819, Cornelius explicitly expressed the ambition to make it a centre for a revived art of the mural.[22]

Later on in the century, many of the most prestigious public commissions were (as Cornelius had hoped upon his appointment at Düsseldorf), precisely for murals. Mural decorations were in great demand for both palaces and government buildings, be they restored medieval, or newly-built neo-Gothic. This in turn bolstered the Düsseldorf/Nazarene style, which, having been inspired by fresco painting in the first place, was well suited to mural display with bright colours set in clearly marked contours. The trend was

---

[21] 3,000 history-paintings from the tradition of Academic Romanticism, dated between 1760 and 1930, are now online at ERNiE, and covered in the encyclopaedic articles and the network analysis of the artists' training filiations.

[22] *Die Nazarener*, ed. H. Dorra and K. Gallwitz (Frankfurt, 1977); F. Büttner, 'Peter Cornelius in Düsseldorf', in *Die Düsseldorfer Malerschule*, ed. W. von Kalnein (Mainz, 1979), pp. 48–55; F. Büttner, *Peter Cornelius: Fresken und Freskenprojekte*, 2 vols. (Wiesbaden, 1980–99).

not merely German: Delaroche's *Hémicycle* for the École des Beaux-arts, Jules Lenepveu's Joan of Arc cycle in the Panthéon, Henri Leys's historical murals for Antwerp City Hall, Johann Sandberg's Gustav Vasa cycle in Uppsala Cathedral, Georg Sturm's canvas-mounted wall paintings for the entrance hall of the Amsterdam Rijksmuseum, Daniel Maclise's murals for the Westminster Parliament buildings and Ford Madox Brown's Pre-Raphaelite celebrations of craftsmanship and labour for Manchester Town Hall: the pattern is well established all over Europe. But it was in Germany that we see a concentration of historicist mural paintings, invariably with a national-medievalist nature: Cornelius's cycle of Bavarian history-topics at the Munich Hofgarten; Julius Schnorr von Carolsfeld's Nibelungen murals in the Munich *Residenz* palace; Alfred Rethel's Charlemagne murals for the city hall of Aachen; Moritz von Schwind's *Minnesänger* and Saint Elizabeth murals for the restored Wartburg Castle at Eisenach; Carl von Piloty's work for the Munich City Hall and the Neue Pinakothek, and so on.[23]

This great European tradition of the nineteenth-century mural, for all that it was closely allied with the official shaping, decoration, and iconographic branding of the public sphere, was, ironically, a dead end in the history of art. But the converse also holds true: for all that Romantic-Academic murals were a dead end in the artistic development of the nineteenth century, they still played an important role in the national design and branding of Europe's public spaces. And it is here that Wislicenus's decoration of Goslar's Imperial Hall offers a unique historical source, illustrating (literally so) the *mentalité* and *imaginaire* of German political romanticism.[24]

---

[23] All these are online at ERNiE. A. L. Arnold, 'Poetische Momente der Weltgeschichte: Die Wandbilder im Schloss Hohenschwangau' (doctoral thesis; Munich, Ludwig-Maximilians-Universität, 2006). *Großer Auftritt: Piloty und die Historienmalerei*, ed. R. Baumstark and F. Büttner (Munich, n.d.). J. Fekete, *Carl von Häberlin (1832–1911) und die Stuttgarter Historienmaler seiner Zeit* (Sigmaringen, 1986). *Mythen der Nationen: Ein europäisches Panorama*, ed. M. Flacke, 2nd edn (Munich, 2001); K. Koetschau, *Alfred Rethels Kunst vor dem Hintergrund der Historienmalerei seiner Zeit* (Düsseldorf, 1929). *Kunst/Geschichte: Zwischen historischer Reflexion und ästhetischer Distanz*, ed. G. Pochat and B. Hagenlocher-Wagner (Graz, 2000); B. Rommé, *Moritz von Schwind – Fresken und Wandbilder* (Ostfildern-Ruit, 1996); H.-T. Wappenschmidt, 'Nibelungenlied und Historienmalerei im 19. Jahrhundert: Wege der Identitätsfindung', in *Die Nibelungen: Ein deutscher Wahn, ein deutscher Alptraum: Studien und Dokumente zur Rezeption des Nibelungenstoffs im 19. und 20. Jahrhundert*, ed. J. Heinzle and A. Waldschmidt (Frankfurt, 1991), pp. 219–50; F. Zelger, *Heldenstreit und Heldentot: Schweizerische Historienmalerei im 19. Jahrhundert* (Zürich, 1973).

[24] Besides the few illustrations of Wislicenus's Goslar murals accompanying this article, 42 specimens are online at ERNiE. Arndt, *Die Goslarer Kaiserpfalz als Nationaldenkmal*, offers a wealth of visual illustrations, both from the *Kaiserpfalz* and from the ambient iconographic tradition, but only in black-and-white. More generally, on the *imaginaire* of German political Romanticism, see Hess, *Panorama und Denkmal*.

Programme painting: Historical iconography and imperial ideology

The murals in the Imperial Hall (Fig. 1) are not just an array of individual embellishments with scenes chosen for their picturesque value. Between them, the constituent themes represent a conscious selection of historical topics chosen for their meaningfulness as they are concatenated into a specific, deliberately planned historical narrative. Wislicenus elaborated this underlying narrative in a programmatic outline which he submitted to the selection committee, and which gained him the commission, rather than the other painters who tendered entries. The end result is therefore not so much a decorated hall-space as a walk-in graphic novel, setting forth a particular story about Goslar and the Empire. Wislicenus's project is a form of 'programme painting' (telling a story by arranging pictorial images), much as compositions such as Smetana's *Moldau* or Tchaikovsky's *Overture 1812* are 'programme music' (telling a story by arranging melodies).

Wislicenus's programme could not fail to reflect the determining parameters of its origin and gestation: the moment of its production, the training of the painter, the Imperial theme and the Goslar locality. But beyond this 'situational logic', the narrative structures characterizing his programme were a deliberately intended, and consciously, historiographically informed, agenda. Wislicenus planned his paintings so as to concatenate into:

Figure 1. The Goslar Kaisersaal: *west wall (with central allegory) and south wall (with doorway)*

a type of epic on the entire destiny of our imperial history, from Charlemagne to Wilhelm, with special attention to the Middle Ages, a period linked to the history of the *Kaiserpfalz* and reaching from the Saxon emperors, by way of Father Salian house, to the last Staufen.

The medieval empire had since Charlemagne taken on the high mission to be a world power protecting the Catholic Church. This universal task reached far beyond the German lands, supported the spread of Christianity, but became a hindrance for the consolidation of the German nation into its own Reich.

Even so, despite the confusions of prelates and emperors, this commitment held until the world spirit announced the end of the Middle Ages and the dawning of a dynamic new life: the Reformation. Its lights fostered a new dispensation, albeit with many struggles. The power of the German emperors reached its limit in Charles V, and from the spirit of the new ages, slowly and majestically, in spite of the awful Thirty Years' War, the firm bulwark of the Hohenzollerns arose.

Much as secular and spiritual power in the Middle Ages had been joined under Charlemagne, so too the more peaceful religion of the modern period has given rise to a new empire, whose only mission is Kaiser Wilhelm's intended legacy of establishing a major protective power for the reconciliation of Germany's secular and religious divisions.[25]

This visionary mission statement for the revived empire[26] finds its visual expression in the centrepiece on the West wall of the *Kaisersaal*, a huge allegory of Wilhelm I succeeding to a restored Empire (Fig. 2). The imagery is jam-packed with topical, historical and mythical allusions. Wilhelm emerges on a black steed, with the Crown Prince behind him, while the architect of the Restoration, Bismarck, stands beside him in the pose of a master builder, flanked by General von Moltke. On the right, the Hohenzollern family look on, including, as youngster, the future Wilhelm II, while on the left, the assembled German princes signify their approval. (The inclusion in the foreground of Wilhelm's inveterate opponent Ludwig II of Bavaria, who is even made to proffer the Imperial Crown, is a triumph of iconographic decorum over actual fact; and the ousted king of Hanover does not appear.) Before and below the approaching emperor, four allegorical figures stand out: two maidens symbolizing Alsace and Lorraine, now (re)united with the Reich; a river-god symbolizing Father

---

[25] Translated and slightly condensed from the original German, in Arndt, *Die Goslarer Kaiserpfalz*, pp. 112–13 (Appendix 10: 'Erklärungsschrift zum Bildprogramm, die sich im Nachlass fand').

[26] Alongside the term *Reich* when referring to the territorial realm, Wislicenus preferred to use the concept of *Kaisertum*: the status of the imperial institution; the two relate as 'kingdom' relates to 'kingship'.

Figure 2. The Goslar Kaisersaal: *central allegory of the Empire's restoration (west wall)*

Rhine, and a muse-like maiden, holding a book (more on her further on). In the background, the shades of Wilhelm's precursors look down approvingly from on high; emperors including Charlemagne, Barbarossa and Maximilian I, and Hohenzollern ancestors including Queen Louise, the *mater dolorosa* of Prussian patriotism in the Napoleonic wars.[27]

---

[27] Arndt discusses the central allegory in *Die Goslarer Kaiserpfalz*, pp. 61–6. As regards Queen Louise, in addition to Arndt, pp. 82–8, see also *Historische Mythologie der*

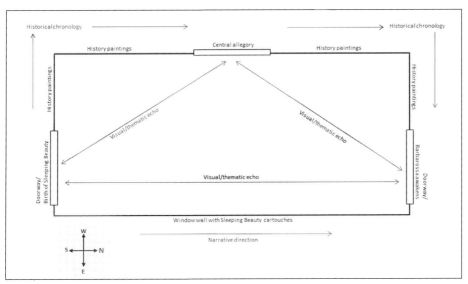

Figure 3. The Goslar Kaisersaal: *ground plan of the Kaisersaal and structure of Wislicenus's programme*

Nothing that could possibly add lustre or meaning has been left out. The mural fairly browbeats the onlooker into submission before the overwhelming doses of figuration and significance – historical, topical and allegorical – that crowd its enormous 50-sq.-metre surface. Even so, it is merely the keystone in the huge narrative arc that fans out from its two sides (Fig. 3). To its left is the period of the empire's beginnings and growth, starting with Charlemagne and culminating in Barbarossa – and hinting at a decline in the scenes representing the frictions between Church and empire. To its right, the moment of crisis when Luther faced Charles V signals the secular decline and spiritual rebirth of the German nation, reaching its climactic crisis in the scene of Queen Louise's deathbed. Key episodes are displayed in large-scale panels, secondary scenes in smaller cartouches, or by way of grisailles. Frequently these evoke the building, decay and reconstruction of the Goslar *Kaiserpfalz* itself: the building becomes part of its own interior design and visual ornamentation. This *mise en abyme* underscores the parallel ups and downs of the building and the *Reich*.

In this epic, the most important reference is without doubt (besides Charlemagne) Barbarossa, who features in a number of the panels and clearly represents the apogee of the Hohenstaufen dynasty and of the medieval empire. Into these scenes Wislicenus cannily weaves a subtle sub-theme: the struggles between the Staufen emperors and the powerful Welf dukes of Bavaria/

Deutschen, 1798–1918, ed. W. Wülfing, K. Bruns and R. Parr (Munich, 1991).

Figure 4. The Goslar Kaisersaal: *Frederic Barbarossa implores Henry the Lion to support his crusade (west wall)*

Saxony. The scenes not only hint at the theme of the internal 'feudal' divisions threatening the strength of the Empire, they are also true to historical fact in that Goslar fell within the power base of these Welf dukes. For after all, this celebration of imperial Prussian power is situated in recently-annexed Hanover... The recent feud between George V, the Welf king of annexed Hanover, and the Hohenzollern Barbablanca becomes yet another confirmation of historical continuity: a latter-day re-enactment of the late twelfth-century struggle between George's ancestor Henry the Lion, the Welf duke of Saxony and Bavaria, and Wilhelm's precursor Barbarossa. Barbarossa's problems with, and eventual ascendancy over, this fractious duke are thematized in a number of panels on the West wall (Fig. 4). Indeed, the theme is already signalled in front of the *Kaiserpfalz* building. The restored manor is guarded by two large equestrian statues of Barbarossa and Wilhelm I, while between them is placed a replica of the Welfs' 'Brunswick Lion' (an iconic twelfth-century bronze statue, originally made to celebrate the power of Henry the Lion.)

Nor does this exhaust the multi-layered complexity of Wislicenus's epic narrative: much could be said about the themes running from panel to panel on the fraught relationship between princes and prelates. There is also a recurrent theme hinting at the perniciousness of the Empire's Mediterranean entanglements, which in the Prussian view addled and weakened the German nature and orientation of the *Reich*. Overcrowded, shrill and bombastic as Wislicenus's paintings are, the artistic equivalent of a Cecil B. DeMille movie, his underlying programme is complex, full of highly recondite historical knowledge and intelligent ways of establishing thematic connections – from painting to painting, and from past to present. The Kaisersaal is a historical echo chamber.

The cleverest thing of all is that in the shock-and-awe execution of this epic programme, with its cast of thousands, the complete absence of the most important imperial dynasty since Barbarossa goes almost unnoticed. With a mere three exceptions, there are no Habsburg emperors whatsoever in the entire evocation of the *Reich*'s eleven hundred year history.[28] The continuity and legitimization of the Hohenzollern emperors as moral successors to Charlemagne and Barbarossa is achieved by writing the Habsburgs, and their four hundred year tenure of the imperial crown, completely out of the picture.

History, myth and fairy-tale: Barbarossa and Sleeping Beauty

The legitimizing continuity between Barbarossa and Barbablanca was established not only by means of an epic narrative programme, but also through the powerful legendary-mythical tropes which have been noted above. Accordingly, Barbarossa features, not only as the historical emperor, crusader and adversary of the Welf dukes, but also as the mythical presence awaiting the healing of history in his Kyffhäuser cavern. One of the two flanking paintings evokes the restoration of the *Reich* in the image of Barbarossa, his beard now white with age (!) emerging from the cavern, sword in hand (Fig. 5). The ravens of discord are seen to fly away, and an eagle is swooping down from the top right. This establishes a visual connection with a similar theme in the central allegory, where another raven is driven away (bottom centre, flanking the allegorical maiden-with-book). Indeed, such elements draw attention to something that certain contemporary critics disliked in the arrangement: its conflation of historical 'real' time and allegorical-legendary timelessness, young Wilhelm II cheek by jowl with personified Alsace and Lorraine, Ludwig II of Bavaria almost rubbing shoulders with Father Rhine.[29]

But this mixture of temporal registers was, we may assume, precisely the point, for Wislicenus goes even a step further. He dovetails the epic story of the *Reich*'s decline and restoration, not just with the legend of Barbarossa's

---

[28] Maximilian I's shade is vaguely present among the celestially onlooking imperial precursors; Charles V is depicted as the man before whom Luther triumphantly vindicates himself, and as the man who has to flee across the Alps from the Protestant princes; that's all. Going by Wislicenus's roll call, the Reich came to an end, not in 1806, but in 1510. Cf. also Arndt, *Die Goslarer Kaiserpfalz*, pp. 54–5.

[29] Cf. Arndt, *Die Goslarer Kaiserpfalz*, pp. 53–7, 116.

Figure 5. The Goslar Kaisersaal: *Barbarossa re-emerges from the Kyffhäuser cavern (north wall)*

underworld exile and re-emergence, but even with the 'once upon a time' of a fairy tale: that of Sleeping Beauty.[30] On the East wall, opposite the historical epic, there are scenes from the Grimm *Märchen*, from Sleeping Beauty's baptism to her wound-by-spindle and comatose slumber, affecting the entire castle and court (Fig. 6). Present-day onlookers may be bemused by the incongruous juxtaposition of epic medievalism and a children's bedtime story. But there is more to the inclusion of Sleeping Beauty than merely a lapse into twee *Gründerzeit* tastelessness.

Märchen and *Sagen* (bearing in mind the conceptual clarification given above in note 13) were for nineteenth-century Germany by no means the anecdotally diverting fantasies that they have since become at the hand of Walt Disney and *Game of Thrones*. For Grimm and Görres, they were the narrative fabric that communicated folk beliefs across the German generations, dimly keeping the memory of ancient belief-systems and epics alive in folk memory. They were vindicated by the Romantics as homely, authentically German, vestiges of what differentiated the nation from France's cold, elitist classicism. They stood, sentimentally, for the 'family values' which the German Romantics felt were fatally lacking in France. And (as the Barbarossa-Kyffhäuser case shows) they were quite capable, for all their humble domesticity, of carrying a heavy freight of political symbolism.

So too with the Sleeping Beauty theme in the Imperial palace, which provides an overt allegory for the inert stasis into which the Reich had fallen after 1500.

---

[30] Cf. Arndt, *Die Goslarer Kaiserpfalz*, pp. 57–60.

Figure 6. *The Goslar* Kaisersaal: *the Reich as Sleeping Beauty; comatose magistracy and army (east wall)*

Figure 7. The Goslar Kaisersaal: *the birth of Sleeping Beauty (south wall)*

As such, Sleeping Beauty is really a replacement narrative for the elided period of Habsburg rule. The theme is introduced on the extreme left-flanking mural on the South wall (Fig. 7), counterpart to the re-emergence of Barbarossa on the North wall, the two bookending, as *Märchen* and *Sagen*, the historical paintings on their narrative line from past to present. 'The Birth of Sleeping Beauty' evokes a fairy-tale atmosphere: a witch in the foreground looks balefully on, while a sprite drifts through the moonlit night towards a castle window. (Such is the intensity of Wislicenus's layering of meanings that the castle silhouette is that of the Wartburg, that most meaningfully German of castles, with its associations with the *Minnesänger*, Tannhäuser and Luther.) From this scene, the various episodes from the tale unfold, set between the windows in the East wall (opposite the history-paintings), and concentrating on the magic sleep which arrests the passage of time in Sleeping Beauty's castle. As in the case of Barbarossa, the political symbolism is made explicit by means of an echo-connection to the central allegory. There, as mentioned earlier, a muse-like maiden reclines next to the Father Rhine figure. She holds a book on whose pages can be read:

> And once the old emperor / emerges from his keep,
> The thorny rose, the German *Reich* / will shoot up in bloom.[31]

The thorny rose overtly signals the German name of Sleeping Beauty (*Dornröschen*) and is used here as an explicit, self-decoding metaphor for the German *Reich*. Clearly, then, the maiden is the spirit of German folk traditions,

---

[31] Und tritt der alte Kaiser / Aus seinem Schloss hervor, / Dann blüht die Dornenrose, / Das deutsche Reich empor.

her book the repository of the nation's *Märchen* and *Sagen.* The echo-connection between this vignette and the Sleeping Beauty painting is further strengthened by the presence, underneath the walls of the fairy-tale castle, of an ancient bard, seated in front of a rose bush (!) next to a stone tablet carrying a carved quatrain. The quatrain complements its counterpart in the central panel.

> The ancient times sank away; / a new Reich arose
> I hear the breeze of springtime / Waft through the German fatherland.[32]

Wislicenus doesn't do subtle. If, in Pierre Nora's words, the essence of a *lieu de mémoire* is to pack a maximum of historical signification into a single historical signifier, then Wislicenus goes one better – he heaps signifiers and yet more signifiers into heaped clusters, so as to drive home a no-holds-barred, all-encompassing, totalizing cultural-historical significance. This 'mode of excess' is both quantitative and qualitative, the relentless bulk matching the unremitting pathos of each scene. The ensemble combines an overkill of size and quantity with an incongruous variety of emotional registers: the intimate endearment of a fairy tale, and the alternating tragic and heroic affects at work in the unremittingly sublime historical scenes. And the late-Nazarene style already points forward, in its brightly-coloured, neatly-delineated, easy-on-the-eye clarity, to what Academic Romanticism would become in the next century: the register of picture postcards, children's book illustrations, devotional effigies, tourist souvenirs and propaganda posters.[33]

The Past is a Magic Mountain

Yet such is Wislicenus's genius that he is capable of reducing all his programme into a single small understated panel situated above the North exit door. This small panel (set into the scene of the emerging Barbarossa, and thus becoming the historical fulfilment to which Barbarossa wakes up) has all the intricacy and logic-defying *mise en abyme* of an M.C. Escher print (Fig. 8)**.** It depicts the most recent episode of all – Wilhelm I's visit to Goslar to inspect the recently completed restoration works. In an open coach, the royal/imperial company is seen driving up to the *Kaiserpfalz*, which is here, once again, depicted inside itself – it is part of the painting, while the painting is part of it. In the bottom left-

---

[32] Die alten Zeiten sanken, / Ein neues Reich entstand: / Ich höre Frühlingswehen / im deutschen Vaterland.

[33] Pierre Nora as quoted by A. Rigney, 'Plenitude, scarcity and the circulation of cultural memory', *Journal of European Studies* 35 (2005), 11–28. I borrow the idea of a 'mode of excess' from what in literary studies is identified as the characteristic of melodrama, as in P. Brooks, *The Melodramatic Imagination: Balzac, Henry James, Melodrama, and the Mode of Excess* (New Haven CT, 1976).

Figure 8. The Goslar Kaisersaal: *history comes full circle (north wall)*

hand corner, cheering figures welcome the emperor. They are dressed, however, in the 'Old German' style popular among the Romantics of 1813: the period celebrated in various panels as the early reassertion of the *Reichsidee*, that of the successful uprising against Napoleon – and, we can add, the gestation period of the historicist nationalism that initiated the Goslar restoration in the first place. The anachronism between the cheering 1813 Romantics and the 1875 emperor on his Goslar visit is resolved by the sprite wafting across the foreground, an echo from the fairy-tale scene-setting painting on the opposite South wall, across the hall. She is holding and turning an hourglass, indicating that, one time-span having run its course, history now revolves into a new era. Meanwhile, in the top-left-hand corner, a woodland scene shows how a handsome prince prepares to waken a maiden, sleeping in a rose bower, with a kiss. Thus, compressed into this small closure-scene, are all four temporalities which are at work in this iconography: the 'once upon a time' of the Sleeping Beauty tale, the 'long awaited prophecy fulfilment'-time of the Barbarossa legend, the historical-evenemential time which this building commemorates and its murals document, and the political actuality of the imperial Prussian regime which the murals celebrate.

The visitor entering into the Goslar *Kaisersaal* through the door underneath this panel is totally immersed in an all-encompassing iconosphere, where all historical periods and even non-historical fantasy-time or epic adventure-time co-exist:[34] taken out of their past tense or out of the subjunctive mode of fiction,

---

[34] As in the discussion by Mikhail Bakhtin, 'Forms of time and chronotope in the novel', in *idem, The Dialogic Imagination: Four Essays*, ed. and trans. C. Emerson and M. Holquist

they share an evolving 'present continuous'. The mutability of narrative is turned into the continuing presence of spectacle; or, to invoke Lessing's famous distinction, the *Nacheinander* ('one thing after another') is transmuted into the *Nebeneinander* ('one thing next to another'). That is what spectacle does, and as Ann Rigney has pointed out, Romantic historians had a knack of hitting the narrative pause-button in order to present the reader with an arresting spectacle-description.[35]

In the nineteenth century there appears to have been an intensified tendency to conflate the registers of historicism and allegory, symbolizing in a single gesture the colourful exoticism of the past and the eternal truths we can learn from it;[36] it makes use of a widespread penchant for total spectator immersion, which also expresses itself in the fashion for panorama-paintings, dioramas and waxworks. It was, in a way, the forerunner of the contemporary appeal for fantasy blockbuster movies in Imax-3D cinemas. Wislicenus's programme turns the Goslar *Kaisersaal* into a space-out-of-time, which is not an object displayed to onlookers, but an ambience of which onlookers themselves become part. Like a Wagnerian *Gesamtkunstwerk*, the *Kaisersaal* immerses its visitors totally, rendering them part of that time-warp, wrapping them into a mythologized German history which Goslar is meant to encapsulate: synecdoche and container of Germany's imperial destiny.

As a political aesthetic, this *imaginaire* follows the prototype that Görres had articulated seventy-five years earlier, when he set his dedicatory *Märchen* to Brentano in a dream-quested cavern populated by Barbarossa and the shades of Germany's medieval heroes. Wislicenus's Goslar counterpoises, in its post-1871 triumphalism, the political trauma of 1806 that had motivated Görres's Romantic historicism.

To read the *Kaisersaal* in terms of Görres's cavern is to see it, indeed, as a *Zauberberg*, a 'magic mountain' where time slows down and stands still. (When Görres's *Märchen* narrator re-emerges he finds that the world has moved on three generations, and that the knowledge he retrieved from Germany's past is of interest only to future generations.) The same motif informs Wagner's *Tannhäuser* (1845), which in turn was to inform Thomas Mann's *Zauberberg* – where Madame Chauchat lures Hans Castorp to remain far beyond his intended visit in the hothouse languor of the Sanatorium). From Kyffhäuser to *Zauberberg*, the

---

(Austin TX, 1981), pp. 84–258.

[35] G. E. Lessing's distinction between the dramatic and the plastic arts as involving, respectively, the *Nacheinander* and the *Nebeneinander*, was made in his *Laokoon* of 1766. The rhetorical alternation between narrative and spectacle is in A. Rigney, *The Rhetoric of Historical Representation: Three Narrative Histories of the French Revolution* (Cambridge, 1990).

[36] Cf. the chapter 'Allegorie und Historismus: Zum Bildgedächtnis des 19. Jahrhunderts', in Hess, *Panorama und Denkmal*, pp. 315–57.

Romantic trope of a subterranean time-bubble links Görres's imagined 'cavern of pastness' to Wislicenus's realization of it in Goslar. It brings together the magical world of folk-beliefs and fairy-tales; the political agenda of restoration, which sees the establishment of a strong state as the retrieval of a lost Golden Age, and the new attitude to the past known as Romantic historicism. In one meaning of the term, historicism is the way in which contemporary readers and spectators are taken out of the here and now and taken on an imaginary journey into the past.[37] Two alternative temporalities are brought together to counterbalance the here and now: the historical past and the power of imagination, historicism and romanticism. And what is taken out of that magic time-warp is the dream of political restoration, cultural revival and national reawakening.

In memoriam Anthony D. Smith (1939–2016)

---

[37]   That is how Jacob Grimm saw the reading of epic; cf. his lecture 'Über das finnische Epos' (1845, relevant excerpt online at ERNiE); cf. J. Leerssen, 'Literary historicism: Romanticism, philologists, and the presence of the past', *Modern language quarterly* 65.2 (2004), 221–43.

7

BETWEEN IDEOLOGY AND TECHNOLOGY: DEPICTING CHARLEMAGNE IN MODERN TIMES[1]

Bernhard Jussen

How do pictures of Charlemagne get into our heads? Charlemagne as a historical figure is a central part of the identification repertoire of the politics of history in the modern age, and particularly in France and Germany. He has survived all the modern ideological upheavals in those two countries, and is just as prominent a figure in historical narratives today as he was two centuries ago. Even if such books – whether textbooks or schoolbooks – are only sparsely illustrated, there is a good chance that Charlemagne nevertheless is shown. In most other European countries, however, he plays a much smaller role.

When comparing images of Charlemagne produced in France and Germany, it is evident how historical politics functions, how in every generation images of figures such as Charlemagne have reflected the respective ideologies and

[1] I would like to thank Allison Brown for her translation and preparation of the English text. The original is 'Bild- und Mediengeschichte. Karl der Große in der Moderne', in *Kaiser und Kalifen: Karl der Große und die Welt des Mittelmeers*, Stiftung Deutsches Historisches Museum (Darmstadt, 2014), pp. 330–49, 381; all illustrations are taken from this article. It takes up aspects of the following three comprehensive essays, sometimes verbatim, and supplements them. B. Jussen, 'Roland', in *Die Welt des Mittelalters. Erinnerungsorte eines Jahrtausends*, ed. J. Fried and O. B. Rader (Munich, 2011), pp. 396–408; 'Bilderhorizonte. Wege zu einer Ikonologie nationaler Rechtfertigungsnarrative', in *Dynamik normativer Ordnungen. Ethnologische und historische Perspektiven*, ed. A. Fahrmeir and A. Warner (Frankfurt, 2013), pp. 79–107; 'Plädoyer für eine Ikonologie der Geschichtswissenschaft. Zur bildlichen Formierung historischen Denkens', in *Reinhart Koselleck. Politische Ikonologie. Perspektiven interdisziplinärer Bildforschung*, ed. H. Locher, Transformationen des Visuellen, Schriftenreihe des Deutschen Dokumentationszentrums für Kunstgeschichte—Bildarchiv Foto Marburg 1 (Munich and Berlin, 2013), pp. 260–279. This last text was translated into English by Tom Lampert: Jussen, 'Toward an Iconology of Medieval Studies: Approaches to Visual Narratives in Modern Scholarship', in *Photo Archives and the Idea of Nation,* ed. C. Caraffa and T. Serena (Berlin: de Gruyter, 2015), pp. 141–65. For the present English text, corresponding passages have been taken from that translation.

conflicts of these two societies: for example the Laicism of the Third Republic, the *Kulturkampf* under Bismarck, Nazism, or the politics of the modern European community. One can also see how state-licensed products (schoolbooks) function in comparison to commercial ones (national histories, trading cards), how new technologies (photography), new business options (inexpensive colour printing), and new market structures (the emergence of photo agencies) influence the selection and circulation of images. The following pages will discuss which developments have left traces in those pictures of Charlemagne that populate our media — the schoolbooks, textbooks, and handbooks from past and present, but also non-scholarly media: the collectible advertising albums, Quartett (Top Trumps) card games, and postcards of past generations.

It should be known from the outset that Charlemagne aroused little interest in the 'great' painters of the Modern Age. In Germany, Julius Schnorr von Carolsfeld (1794–1872), a member of the Nazarene brotherhood, took Charlemagne as a painting subject, but his pictorial ideas attracted meagre widespread interest. Later, in particular, the paintings of Alfred Rethel (1816–59) and Friedrich Kaulbach (1822–1903) stand out from the mass of artists and graphic designers. In France almost the entire repertoire comes from less prominent painters and illustrators. Raphael's Coronation of Charlemagne located in the Stanze in the Vatican did not find many new incarnations as reproductions. Dürer's portrait of Charlemagne was often reproduced in Germany, but it was not considered Frankish enough to have any great influence on the iconography of Charlemagne. Ideas about Charlemagne, or Charles the Great, lived and still live on in the Modern Age, not in the 'great' art world of museums, but at most in less prominent paintings found in smaller auction houses, and especially in genres of small pictures — for example as illustrations in schoolbooks, in collectible picture card albums, and on porcelain.

Justification narratives: Politics of history with Charlemagne

So what images have French historians used to illustrate their chapters on Charlemagne and the Carolingians? A schoolbook by Antoine Bonifacio and Louis Mérieult, published by Hachette in 1952 for the *cours élémentaire*, and with new editions up to 1973, shows in condensed form how the political culture of France had been passing down its image of Charlemagne for generations.[2] It contains no photographic documentation at all and almost no documenting illustrations, using instead, as was customary in the nineteenth century, a rich variety of illustrations in the manner of history paintings. On a double-page spread, we find the highlights of the French pictorial universe on the theme

[2] A. Bonifacio and L. Mérieult, *Histoire de France. Images et récits; Cours* élémentaire, illustrated by Albert Brenet (Paris, 1952), pp. 8–9.

Figure 1. Page of the French schoolbook Bonifacio/Mérieult, Histoire de France. Images et récits; Cours élémentaire, *illustrated by Albert Brenet (Paris, 1952), pp. 8–9; Brunswick, Georg Eckert Institute*

of Charlemagne (Fig. 1): the death of Roland at Roncevaux Pass, an elderly Charlemagne with students at the palace school, and the imperial coronation in Rome. No themes were illustrated more often than these three in French schoolbooks. Even in books with more extensive illustration, only the equestrian statuette in the Louvre and the famous coinage portraying Charlemagne appeared with a similar frequency.

None of these three leading motifs in French schoolbooks was as prominent in Germany. There, until the decline of fictional historical illustrations around 1930, the theme of Charlemagne in Germany assumed pictorial form in depictions of the Saxon mission, or more precisely the destruction of the Irminsul and the baptism of the Saxons, as well as in reproductions of the equestrian statuette in the Louvre and of Aachen Cathedral. None of these motifs was absent in France, but their presence in percentage terms was much greater in Germany. Several other motifs belonged to the repertoire of only one of the countries. In Germany, for instance, these included Dürer's portrait of Charlemagne, depictions of the Palace of Aachen and Charlemagne as the builder, Charlemagne's encounter with Muslim emissaries, and finally the opening of Charlemagne's tomb by Otto

III. By contrast, depictions of Charlemagne with his scholars, as well as of an ageing Charlemagne watching with concern from his window as the ships of the Northmen approached, were largely limited to France.

Charles the Crowned: *Kulturkampf* over the imperial coronation

At first glance it might seem as if the imperial coronation was a transcultural motif with little room for manoeuvre for nationally specific encodings. Yet it is striking that the imperial coronation was depicted in French books almost three times more frequently than in German ones. On closer inspection, it also becomes clear that illustrations of this key scene were used in markedly different ways. In Germany the scene reflected a centre of political conflict, whereas in France it was hardly politically charged at all.

In German historical depictions, the imperial coronation of Charlemagne was consistently a political statement, a reflection of the *Kulturkampf*. Roughly speaking, two pictorial narratives competed in Germany. One variant narrated the imperial coronation as the papal blindsiding of Charlemagne while he was sunk defenceless in prayer. An early example of this is the fresco of Alfred Rethel in Aachen (produced between 1850 and 1860), which depicted the act as a veritable coronation ambush (reproduced in fig. 15). The pope cleverly surprises the ruler from behind with the imperial crown at precisely the moment when Charlemagne, kneeling before Christ on the cross, removes his headpiece. An overwhelmed Charlemagne can only turn with an angry expression from the cross to the pope. Rethel's fresco was repeatedly adopted and his pictorial idea became to a certain degree canonical. The version by Adolf Streckfuß, *Das deutsche Volk: Deutsche Geschichte in Wort und Bild* (1862) may suffice as an early example here (Fig. 2).[3] The illustrator Ludwig Löffler depicted an extremely alarmed Charlemagne who, startled while kneeling at prayer, stares completely unheroically at the impending imperial coronation. Wilhelm Zimmermann's *Illustrierte Geschichte des Deutschen Volkes* (1873) offered a variation of Rethel's interpretation, reduced to the protagonists (Fig. 3).[4]

In contrast to this narrative of the papal ambush on a Charlemagne who had long been imperial and did not need the pope at all, stands the depiction of the imperial coronation as a prearranged and staged hierarchical ritual, with Charlemagne kneeling before the pope, as the scene was still portrayed in the French schoolbook of 1952 (Fig. 1). In Germany an interpretation such as the one by Julius Schnorr von Carolsfeld, which depicted a Charlemagne devoted to the pope, appears to have been acceptable here and there up to the 1860s,

---

[3]   A. Streckfuß, *Das Deutsche Volk. Deutsche Geschichte in Wort und Bild. Ein illustrirtes Hausbuch für Leser aller Stände*, illustrated by Ludwig Löffler (Berlin, 1862), p. 68.

[4]   W. Zimmermann, *Illustrierte Geschichte des Deutschen Volkes* (Stuttgart, 1873), p. 418.

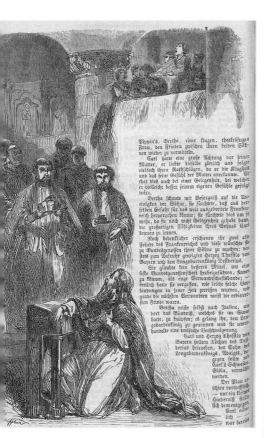

(Left) *Figure 2. Coronation of Charlemagne from Adolf Streckfuß's* Das deutsche Volk, *illustrated by Ludwig Löffler (Berlin, 1862), 68; Frankfurt, Goethe Universität*

(Right) *Figure 3. Coronation of Charlemagne from Wilhelm Zimmermann's* Illustrierte Geschichte des Deutschen Volkes *(Stuttgart, 1873), 418; Frankfurt, Goethe Universität*

for instance in the frontispiece of Karl Heinrich Ludwig Pölitz's *Weltgeschichte für gebildete Leser und Studierende* (World History for Educated Readers and Students) (1820) (Fig. 4).[5]

Later, German illustrators (Figs. 5 and 6) preferred — when this version was used at all — Friedrich Kaulbach's monumental painting of 1861 for the Maximilianeum in Munich.[6] The advantage of Kaulbach's version was that

---

[5] K. H. L. Pölitz, *Die Weltgeschichte für gebildete Leser und Studierende*, 4 vol., 3rd edn (Leipzig, 1820), II, frontispiece.

[6] J. Scherr, *Germania. Zwei Jahrtausende deutschen Lebens* (Stuttgart, 1879), p. 68; Richard Du Moulin-Eckart, *Vom alten Germanien zum neuen Reich. Zwei Jahrtausende deutscher Geschichte* (Stuttgart, Berlin and Leipzig, 1926), p. 64.

Figure 4. Re-engraving of Julius Schnorr von Carolsfeld's painting of the coronation of Charlemagne (1839–40), frontispiece from Karl Heinrich Ludwig Pölitz's Die Weltgeschichte für gebildete Leser und Studierende, *vol. 2 (Leipzig and Frankfurt am Main, 1820); Frankfurt, Goethe Universität*

Charlemagne appears having grown so large that, kneeling proudly and upright (and armed), he is almost as tall as the standing pope who crowns him. Kaulbach's pictorial idea for the theme of the staged imperial coronation harmonized a papal-friendly, Catholic interpretation together with the exigencies of the pictorial representation of a great German. In contrast to Rethel's anti-papal pictorial idea, no earlier variants of Kaulbach's version are known as illustrations. Kaulbach's papal-friendly interpretation appears not to have already been part of the reservoir of German illustrators, and it was not widely disseminated until stock photo agencies first appeared around 1890 (see below).

Illustrators in France were evidently unaware of the German problem with the imperial coronation. Rethel's version of a papal ambush was never used as an illustration in France. The illustration in the French schoolbook of 1952 (Fig. 1) is symptomatic of the indifference to this question. It appeared self-evident in France that the imperial coronation be depicted as a pre-arranged and choreographed hierarchical act, in which Charlemagne did not even have to be — as in Kaulbach's painting — a proud, and armed, giant. A Charlemagne kneeling submissively with his hands folded was not cause for concern among French historians.

Figure 5.   Re-engraving of a photograph of Friedrich Kaulbach's painting of the coronation of Charlemagne (1861) by Adolf Closs, from Johannes Scherr's Germania. Zwei Jahrtausende deutschen Lebens *(Stuttgart, 1879), p. 68; Frankfurt, Goethe Universität*

Figure 6. Photographic reproduction of Friedrich Kaulbach's painting of the coronation of Charlemagne (1861) from Richard Du Moulin-Eckart's Vom alten Germanien zum neuen Reich *(Stuttgart, Berlin and Leipzig, 1926), p. 64; Frankfurt, Goethe Universität*

As long as German national histories illustrated their arguments with history paintings – and while this practice clearly lost popularity around the turn of the century, the older books continued to be reprinted into the 1920s – they took sides by using one or other of the pictorial versions of the coronation. These traces of the *Kulturkampf* remained animated and widespread into the 1920s in German depictions of the imperial coronation of Charlemagne.

Charles the Laicist: Pioneer of the secular school

While the political conflicts of the *Kulturkampf* were consolidated in late nineteenth-century Germany especially in the image of the imperial coronation, in France it was a different motif that expressed the conflict between the state and the Catholic Church.

As long as history paintings were used for illustrations, about one-tenth of the illustrations on Charlemagne portrayed the theme of *Charlemagne à l'école*, a motif that was very rare in Germany. In France the key words 'Charlemagne' and 'inventor of the school' are so inextricably linked that the thought behind the children's song and the hit song that sold millions was appropriate: indeed the hit song *Sacré Charlemagne* by France Gall is still popular today (*sacré* can mean both 'sacred' and be a mild swearword): Who had this crazy idea / One day to invent school? / It's this *sacré* Charlemagne / *Sacré* Charlemagne / … This son of Pépin the Short / Gives us lots of trouble / And we have a hundred complaints / Against, against, against him…[7]

The historical substance of this pictorial history is just as meagre as that of most of the other images. Roughly seventy years after Charlemagne's death the learned monk Notker the Stammerer told a story, in his *Gesta Caroli Magni*, about Charlemagne founding a school. Supposedly he gave 'a great number of boys chosen not only from the noblest families, but also from middle-class and poor homes', into the care of an Irish teacher from abroad and ordered 'that accommodation suitable for study should be made available'. Later Charlemagne himself ostensibly monitored the success and diligence of the pupils in the school.[8] Notker did not say anything about where exactly the school's 'accommodation suitable for study' was located. This lack of clarity opened the floodgates for the imaginations of nineteenth- and twentieth-century historians. However,

---

[7]   The original French lyrics are: 'Qui a eu cette idée folle / Un jour d'inventer l'école? / C'est ce sacré Charlemagne/ Sacré Charlemagne … Ce fils de Pépin le Bref / Nous donne beaucoup d'ennuis / Et nous avons cent griefs / Contre, contre, contre lui! …'

[8]   Notker Balbulus, *Gesta Karoli Magni Imperatoris* i.3, ed. H. F. Haefele, MGH SRG, n.s 12 (Berlin, 1959), pp. 4–5). Quotation from *Einhard and Notker the Stammerer, Two Lives of Charlemagne*, trans. L. Thorpe (Harmondsworth, 1969), p. 94. There is an older translation online at http://legacy.fordham.edu/halsall/basis/stgall-charlemagne.asp.

Figure 7. Saint Charlemagne,
French postcard from the early
twentieth century. Private collection.

French and German historians lived in totally separate political systems and consequently developed very different ideas.

It is a key element in all French pictures of this episode that the setting is in the palace. Sometimes a monk is depicted as the teacher, but the location is expressly not a religiously one. The definitive message is always the same: Charlemagne did not found a monastic school, but instead a palace school, a secular institution. Charlemagne was thus the founder and patron of the French lay school system. Indeed, a postcard, a chromolithograph from the early twentieth century (Fig. 7), dubs him *Saint Charlemagne* and gives him the title that is generally reserved for St Nicholas: *Patron des écoliers* (patron of schoolchildren). The secularist impulse of the French Third Republic was projected back on to the origins of the French educational system: Charlemagne himself looks after the young pupils who are taught in his palace.

In Germany this pictorial motif was largely absent, and when it was imported into a German national history, it was usually reinterpreted.[9] In Richard Du Moulin-Eckart's *Vom alten Germanien zum neuen Reich: Zwei Jahrtausende deutscher Geschichte* (From Old Germania to the New Reich: Two Millennia of German

---

[9]   A rare example of Charlemagne 'in his palace school' appears in F. Bülau, H. B. C. Brandes, and T. Flathe, *Die deutsche Geschichte in Bildern,* 3 vols. (Dresden, 1862), I, 38.

Figure 8. *Charlemagne in the monastic school, from Richard Du Moulin-Eckart's*
Vom alten Germanien zum neuen Reich *(Stuttgart, 1926), p. 75; Frankfurt, Goethe*
Universität

Figure 9. *Charlemagne in the monastic school, from Johannes Scherr's* Germania,
(Stuttgart, 1879, p. 77); Frankfurt, Goethe Universität

History), published in 1926 (the only edition), text and illustration moved this motif precisely to where the French did not want to have it, namely in a monastery (Fig. 8).[10] This interpretation had already appeared in similar fashion – but with far wider dissemination than in Moulin-Eckart's book – in an illustration in Johannes Scherr's *Germania: Zwei Jahrtausende deutschen Lebens*, which was published in nine editions between *c*. 1876 and 1906 (Fig. 9).[11] German illustrators and authors usually depicted Carolingian schools as monastic institutions. In the current Latin book *Prima*, which was published by the Buchner and Oldenbourg publishing houses and has been in use since 2005, today's pupils are offered a French drawing by the symbolist Maurice Denis (d. 1943), but with a German description: 'Charlemagne visits a monastery school.' The drawing of course does not give any indication of a monastery; it clearly shows the palace, as Charlemagne is sitting on his throne in Aachen. The publisher evidently relied on the German photo agency that offered the picture, which is located in the National Library in Paris, along with this traditional German title.

Charles the 'Feudal' Lord: Roland in France and Germany

By far the most popular motif among French pictures of Charlemagne shows Roland, his dying, loyal paladin (fig. 1). Roland accompanied Charlemagne into the Pyrenees to fight against the Moors. On the way home Charlemagne's soldiers ran into an ambush. With his final ounce of strength, Charlemagne's loyal servant blew his bugle in order to warn his lord and master. This motif serves particularly one aspect of the French memory culture: feudal loyalty, which is what historians have declared to be the core of the so-called 'feudal system'. Every picture of Roland that is depicted in a schoolbook or textbook personifies the idea of the unconditional allegiance of the servant to his lord, until death.

This pictorial motif, too, has no historical basis. Writing more than fifty years after Charlemagne's campaign against the Moors in 778, Einhard in his *The Life of Charlemagne* briefly mentioned the deadly attack of the Moors against Charlemagne's soldiers in the Pyrenees. A certain Roland was listed among the casualties: 'Eggihard, the King's steward; Anselm, Count of the Palace; and Roland, Lord of the March of Brittany, along with a great many others, fell in this engagement.'[12] That is all there is. What makes Roland into a historical, heroic

---

[10] Moulin-Eckhart, *Vom alten Germanien* (Stuttgart, 1926), p. 75.

[11] Scherr, *Germania* (1879), p. 77; a German version was also published in Philadelphia in 1883.

[12] Einhard, *Vita Karoli Magni*, i.9, ed. Oswald Holder-Egger, MGH SRG 25 (Hanover, 1911), p. 12: 'In quo proelio Eggihardus regiae mensae praepositus, Anshelmus comes palatii et Hruodlandus Brittannici limitis praefectus cum aliis conpluribus interficiuntur.' English: *Two Lives of Charlemagne*, trans. Thorpe, p. 64 (slightly adapted).

figure that is suitable for the historical picture is the fantasy of the *Song of Roland* from the late eleventh or early twelfth century, the first, genre-forming novel written in French.

Roland as Charlemagne's faithful paladin is used in France to illustrate a period in which he actually played no role historically. Modern authors of French history books and schoolbooks in the nineteenth and twentieth centuries projected the fantasy of *The Song of Roland*, a courtly novel of the eleventh or twelfth century, retrospectively back to the eighth century, the time of Charlemagne. In the French schoolbook of 1952 that was mentioned earlier (fig. 1) it was among the core stock of Charlemagne images. The great bronze statue showing Charlemagne mounted on a horse and led by his paladins Roland and Oliver, which has stood on the Île de la Cité in front of Notre Dame Cathedral in Paris since the end of the nineteenth century, embodies the undisputed leitmotif of the French iconography of Charlemagne.

In Germany this exemplary scene of the 'feudal system' in the Pyrenees about Charlemagne's loyal servant Roland has hardly ever been a pictorial theme. Roland indeed represented a totally different theme — he belonged to the stock of images of late medieval urban freedom. The Roland of German history books does not die in the Pyrenees and never holds a bugle in his hands.[13] The figure of Roland was, indeed, most popular where an anti-feudal stand was to be taken, standing as a colossal giant before urban town halls. If Roland denotes the 'feudal system' in France, then he does the opposite in Germany: urban space as a legal space without the 'feudal system'. Postcards such as the one reproduced here (fig. 10) show how the Roland figures have become trademarks of their cities. This figure in late medieval cities has completely lost its iconographic references to the original context of the figure in the *Song of Roland* – in particular his relationship to Charlemagne – and largely in the accompanying texts as well.

Image motifs do not stop at national borders. In some media the French motif also made its way into German living rooms. Around 1900 some large-format books with printed graphics were very popular, in which German illustrators worked according to French models. The *Bildersaal deutscher Geschichte* (Picture Hall of German History) of 1890 (with many subsequent editions) and numerous collectible picture cards for advertising purposes are examples of this. The Nuremberg Vereinigte Margarine works pushed the fantasy a bit further in their collectible picture card album of 1952 called *Vermächtnis der Vergangenheit* (Legacy of the Past), and made it clear how devious – and how black! – the Muslim enemies were (fig. 11): only a cowardly attack of a black Moor at Roland's back could defeat this Germanic hero. Fatally wounded in the back by the black Muslim, he slips from his horse, his famous bugle placed effectively in the image.

---

[13] For a more detailed examination of the different uses of Roland in Germany and France see B. Jussen, 'Roland' (2011).

Figure 10. Postcard with the statue of Roland, around 1900. Private collection

Figure 11. Collectible picture card 'Roland's death', from the album Vermächtnis der Vergangenheit *(Legacy of the Past) of the Vereinigte Margarine-Werke, Nuremberg, 1952; Frankfurt am Main, Goethe-Universität*

DER ROLAND (ANNO 1404)

Figure 12. Collectible picture card "Der Roland. Anno 1404" of the Le-Ha-Ve (Lebensmittel-Handels-Vereinigung), Hamburg 1927; Frankfurt am Main, Goethe-Universität

Indeed, many years earlier, in 1908, in the *Helden Album* (Album of Heroes) produced by the Cologne chocolate company Stollwerck, the enemies were black.

German knowledge in the nineteenth and twentieth centuries about Charlemagne's paladin Roland can be deduced through the example of the collectible picture cards distributed for advertising purposes, which were the most important medium for generating world knowledge in the century prior to the age of television.[14] The illustrated front of the cards consolidated the iconography that was relevant for a broad pictorial knowledge, and the back of the cards usually condensed the dominant narrative considerably, owing to limitations of space. The standard motifs were the very similar Roland statues in different cities, the oldest of which – in Bremen (fig. 12) – was of course most often reproduced. A giant can always be recognized, carrying a shield and a raised sword, against a town hall backdrop and on a pedestal, usually in frontal view, and sometimes in semi-profile.

The texts always create a link between Roland and the privileged status of the city, portraying Roland as a symbol of freedom from noble rule and always a thorn in the side of the non-urban lords. High justice, direct imperial rule, sovereignty, urban freedom, freedom from feudal duties, law and justice ('sound state institution'): these were the most important concepts tied to the symbol of Roland. In 1927 the Le-Ha-Ve (Lebensmittel-Handels-Vereinigung, Foodstuff

---

[14] For an overview on the commercial collectible picture cards, see B. Jussen, 'Liebig's Sammelbilder. Weltwissen und Geschichtsvorstellung im Reklamesammelbild', in *Bilderatlas des 20. Jahrhunderts*, ed. G. Paul (Göttingen, 2009), pp. 132–9.

Trading Association) created a larger series of urban views, including a series on Bremen. The picture card called 'Der Roland, Anno 1404' (fig. 12) had the following text on the back:

> *'Roland der Riese am Rathaus zu Bremen'* (Roland the Giant at Bremen town hall) was the expression we learnt at school to illustrate alliteration. The statue with the image of Roland that was erected in 1404 is intended as a monument to urban freedom. It represents a paladin of Charlemagne, a deputy of the German emperor, who in public consciousness was considered a patron of all sound state institutions. Like most Roland statues of cities in the Mark and Lower Saxony, Bremen's Roland also takes its self-evident place in the direct proximity of the town hall. It originally stood with its broad back directly against the wall of the old town hall. An election slogan of the later Prussian kings is engraved on the monument: *'Enen jeden dat syne'* (To each his own).

Generally speaking, what was written on the back of this picture card summarizes what people learned about the giant on northern German town hall squares from other media as well. In the words of a collectible picture card of 1910, Rolands were 'a symbol of the jurisdiction and imperial immediacy'. The image of Roland was, therefore, not to be found in the chapter on Charlemagne, as it was in France, but in the chapter on urban freedom six hundred years later. The German Roland illustrated the late Middle Ages; the French Roland, the early Middle Ages. When occasionally (as in the text of Le-Ha-Ve) a reference is made to Roland's role as a liege man of Charlemagne, it is not about steadfast loyalty, to the death, of the vassal to his lord, but that he was a 'deputy of the German emperor', and as such guaranteed urban freedom.

Charles the Frank: beard or moustache?

'Charles the Great with moustache only!' The illustrator Werner Schicke found this gruff instruction by the author Albert Thümmel on a watercolour painting (figs. 13 and 14), which he used as a model for the collectible picture card he created, titled 'Charlemagne receives the emissaries of Harun al Rashid'. It was supposed to appear in the *Deutsche Geschichte* collectible card album in 1953. This album had a circulation of 295,000, making it the most widely disseminated historical narrative in collectible picture cards in the early Federal Republic of Germany. Thümmel, the author of *Deutsche Geschichte,* was evidently dissatisfied because the illustrator had given Charlemagne a full beard, as appears also in Dürer's portrait, for example, or in almost all French pictures. Thümmel wanted a different Charlemagne, a German one, which is why the king on the collectible cards has been drawn 'with moustache only' (e.g. fig. 18). Thümmel devoted considerable attention to ensure that the tall German emperor appeared in the

*Figure 13 and Figure 14.
Reverse and front of the
watercolour of Charlemagne
receiving the emissaries of
Harun al Rashid; Plochingen,
Verlagsarchiv Siegfried Driess*

right light. Not only did Charlemagne's full beard serve to incite the author's displeasure, but also the stature of Otto I ('Otto too small — he was "of tall stature"') or Barbarossa's physique ('owing to the extraordinary significance of Barbarossa for German tradition, he should by no means appear small and "corpulent"!').

The kings had to be properly prepared 'for German tradition', that is, with a moustache, tall, and not too fat. What had easily been adopted in the illustrations did not become established in the text, despite numerous attempts. In the late eighteenth century the phrase 'Charles the Frank' started appearing in many books as an alternative designation for 'Charles the Great'.[15] Until the Nazi era the phrase 'Charles the Frank' was kept alive by authors who were contemporarily very prominent, such as the poet Friedrich Wilhelm Weber (1813–94), who has today faded into oblivion, and the novelist and nature writer Hermann Löns. Weber's 1878 epic *Dreizehnlinden* (Thirteen Linden Trees) was reprinted more than 200 times and was part of the reading canon of the German bourgeoisie.[16] Here, as in many of Weber's texts, Charlemagne

---

[15] For example, C. L. Woltmann, *Geschichte der europäischen Staaten*, 2 vols. (Berlin, 1797–9), II, 69; L. Flathe, *Geschichte des Mittelalters* (Leipzig, 1839), p. 111; K. Stein, *Die letzten fünfzig Jahre (1789 bis 1839). Ein Taschenbuch auf das Jahr 1840 für Zeitungsleser und Geschichtsfreunde* (Berlin, 1839), p. 2.

[16] It was published in English as: *Elmar: A Drama in Five Acts*, arranged for the stage in German from Friedrich Wilhelm Weber's epic *Dreizehnlinden* (Thirteen Lindens) by

had the epithet 'the Frank': 'Let freedom be the purpose of restraint, / as one binds a vine / so that instead of crawling in the dust / it happily winds upward into the air. / Charles the Frank managed both, / Worthy of both love and hate / he held firmly the cross of the church / yet more firmly still the cross of the sword – / And with hands dyed red / he wielded it against our fathers, / An apostle in a coat of mail / A supplicant sprayed with blood – / To win us over for ourselves / he struck us nearly dead; / Pointing toward the celestial castles / He took from us our earthly meadows – / The vestment with its many folds must serve a hundred purposes: / ambition, avarice, cravings for power, / hatred and vengeance it must cover … .'[17] In the work of Hermann Löns (1866–1914), like Weber a standard in middle-class households up to the Nazi period, Charlemagne was also known as Charles the Frank.[18] When the Nazi newspaper *Der Stürmer* and Heinrich Himmler insisted on this epithet, it meant its ultimate end. Sometimes authors fluctuated between references to Charlemagne as 'Charles the Frank' or 'Charles the Great'. Karl Sievers, who was active as a school textbook author from the late 1920s, published the volume *Karl der Grosse* for the *Geschichte in Erzählungen* (History in Stories) series published by Beltz as of 1930. For the eleventh and twelfth editions, both in 1935, the name was adapted to the new political situation and the book was called *Karl der Franke und die Sachsen*, before it was again renamed (at the latest in the fifteenth edition in 1937) *Karl der Grosse und die Sachsen*. After the war the epithet 'the Frank' disappeared entirely and appears today only in what is issued by right-wing extremist publishing companies.

The ambiguity of the picture of Charlemagne, as it were between a Roman and a Frank, can also be seen in the illustrations. Many presentations of Charlemagne in expressly Frankish dress—and a moustache—can be found especially in the collectible picture cards. Although the counter-image of an elderly, wise Charlemagne in Roman dress and a long, generally white, beard could not be eliminated completely, not least owing to the prominence of Dürer's painting, the ostentatiously Frankish Charlemagne is clearly more

---

Otto Thissen; trans. and pub. by F. J. Dockendorff (La Crosse WI, 1935).

[17] F. W. Weber, *Dreizehnlinden* (Paderborn, 1878, with many later editions), ch. 17. The original text reads: 'Freiheit sei der Zweck des Zwanges, / Wie man eine Rebe bindet, / Daß sie, statt im Staub zu kriechen, / Froh sich in die Lüfte windet. – / Beides schaffte Karl der Franke,/ Liebenswertes, Hassenswertes; / Hielt er fest am Kreuz der Kirche, / Fester doch am Kreuz des Schwertes. – / Und mit rotgefärbten Händen / Schwang er's gegen unsre Väter, / Ein Apostel in der Brünne, / Ein mit Blut bespritzter Beter. – / Uns uns selbst abzugewinnen, / Hat er todwund uns gehauen; / Zeigend nach den Himmelsburgen, / Nahm er uns die Erdenauen. – / Dienen muß der faltenreiche / Kirchenmantel hundert Zwecken: / Ehrsucht, Habsucht, Machtgelüste, / Haß und Rache muß er decken.'

[18] H. Löns, *Da draussen vor dem Tore. Heimatliche Naturbilder* (Hanover, 1911, with many later editions), p. 79.

popular in image production than in verbal characterizations and it lasted longer as well. For the author Albert Thümmel, who did not use the phrase 'Charles the Frank', Charlemagne's full beard was a thorn in his side in the early 1950s. Thus the schoolchildren who collected the *Deutsche Geschichte* collectible picture card series between 1953 and the 1990s through *Sparkasse* (savings banks) and dairy companies, saw a clearly Frankish Charlemagne.

Media: Charlemagne between wood engravings, chromolithography, and photography

Up to now we have discussed only pictures that hardly ever appear in present-day history books, that is, illustrations in the style of history paintings, which are plainly fictional presentations. This kind of illustration rapidly lost in plausibility after 1900, until it largely disappeared by 1930. The connection between this fundamental change in visual representation and the technological state of photography, the corresponding reproduction technology, and the emergence of stock photographic agencies around 1890 is apparent. Within a few decades illustrations in the style of history paintings largely turned into a medium used in children's books, schoolbooks for young pupils (Fig. 1), and short-lived media such as the collectible picture cards used as advertising. In the book market for adults, history books or manuals for national history started turning largely toward a style that appeared to be documentary. Furthermore, with the decline of history painting as a genre, the possibility of providing such visual accompaniment to the text for key episodes in national historiography also disappeared. Most previous pictorial themes were necessarily lost. In the new documentary style historians could no longer employ images to address the imperial coronation of 800, Charlemagne's destruction of the Irminsul, or his siege of Pavia; whether depicting Charlemagne as the laicist, the feudal lord, or the builder. The change from an illustrative to a documentary pictorial style in historical works virtually compelled a re-conceptualization of pictorial narrative patterns. In Germany this occurred precisely during those decades in which the political situation changed dramatically several times.

This transformation of pictorial style had fundamental consequences for the way in which historians were able to create pictorial authority for their historical conceptions, and thus for the position of historical works as part of a politics of history. There was not of course a complete change of pictorial style. On the one hand, there had always been publications in the documentary style; on the other, historians have repeatedly employed, up to the present day, peculiar admixtures of fictional illustration and documentary style.

It should be stated explicitly that the change from an illustrative to a documentary style was in many situations only a change of style, and by no means necessarily led to the introduction of a genuine pictorial document.

Apparently it was sufficient (and often still is) that the object depicted simply be 'old'. Current books on the imperial coronation of Charlemagne no longer employ nineteenth-century history paintings by Kaulbach or Rethel, but instead a late medieval illustration from, for instance, the *Sächsische Weltchronik* or the *Grandes Chronique de France*. This exchange does not accomplish much — an image created 500 years after the event is no more documentary than one created 1500 years later — but it evidently appears to be more documentary or 'authentic'. Even today the use of medieval images from the High and Late Middle Ages to illustrate the Early Middle Ages is widespread. This is what is meant by the phrase 'documentary style'. Apparently many historians feel more comfortable with this procedure than with using history paintings from the nineteenth century, although the former is no more reliable than the latter, and perhaps even less so, because the tensions between image and text are more difficult for many readers to discern.

Charles the Licensed: photography agencies change the supply of images

Prior to the introduction of photography there had occasionally been copyright notices, but references in German national histories to stock photo agencies appeared only around 1890, especially to the Berlin Photographic Society and to Hanfstaengl in Munich. The technology of photographic reproduction and with it a new form for the distribution of pictures – through agencies – quickly led to a reduction in the diversity of images. Rethel's fresco is a good example of this: whereas prior to the emergence of stock photo agencies the anti-papal pictorial idea of the coronation ambush on a defenceless Charlemagne was an idea replayed artistically in different ways (see the variations in Streckfuß and Zimmermann (Figs. 2 and 3)), Theodor Ebner's *Illustrierte Geschichte Deutschlands* (first edition 1887, fifth edition 1906) is an early case of the new form of picture selection with the help of stock agencies. Ebner published the re-engraving of a photographic reproduction of Rethel's imperial coronation (Fig. 15).[19] The reference beneath the reproduction of Rethel's fresco, 'with permission of the Photographic Society in Berlin', points to the role of stock photo agencies in the canonization process.[20] With the emergence of stock photo agencies the anti-papal pictorial idea obtained its authoritative, now technologically reproduced, form in the version of Rethel's fresco.

[19] T. Ebner, *Illustrierte Geschichte Deutschlands* (Stuttgart, 1890 [orig. 1887]), p. 179.
[20] On this still young field of research, see M. Bruhn, *Bildwirtschaft. Verwaltung und Verwertung der Sichtbarkeit* (Weimar, 2003).

Figure 15. Re-engraving of a photographic reproduction of Rethel's coronation, from Theodor Ebner's Illustrierte Geschichte Deutschlands *(Stuttgart, 1890 [orig. 1887]), p. 179; Frankfurt am Main, Goethe Universität*

Charles the Documented: a coin, a horse, a mosaic

When history paintings were no longer used, options for illustrating the period of Charlemagne dwindled dramatically. What remained were ultimately a coin, showing Charlemagne in the style of the aged Roman emperor, and the small equestrian statuette in the Louvre, which can be interpreted – with some degree of generosity yet not without plausibility – as Charlemagne. The third image that is obviously an image of Charlemagne, the Triclinium mosaic in Rome, was for a long time hardly of use in the modern era because it all too clearly adopted the papal perspective. Here Charlemagne's empire was too dependent on the pope.

Did the differences between Germany and France in the use of images to portray Charlemagne disappear with the establishment of the documentary style? If the equestrian statuette or the portrait coinage of Charlemagne became the predominant pictorial formula in both countries for the theme of Charlemagne, how could national differences in images continue to be articulated? Yet even documentary images of the very same object could accentuate completely different arguments in Germany and in France. While the equestrian statuette looks no different in a French book than it does in a German one, *meaning*, as we know, arises through context, and in the case of images in a national history through pictorial context. Since the 1920s in Germany a second monument has regularly appeared in the context of the equestrian statuette of Charlemagne: Widukind's tomb in Enger (in Westphalia in northern Germany).[21] The tomb was not created until the eleventh or twelfth century, so it is totally irrelevant for the time of Charlemagne. The popularity of this tomb in chapters on the Carolingian period is an example of how the documentary style could be used even without actually documenting, and how national differences were preserved, even within the medium of the documentary style.

Richard Suchenwirth's *Deutsche Geschichte*, the most widely disseminated book on German history during the Nazi era (730,000 copies between 1934 and 1942), visualized all of German history from the Bronze Age to Hitler in forty-one plates. The book used two plates for the Carolingian era, Dürer's portrait of Charlemagne, followed by Widukind's tomb.[22] In nineteenth-century works of historical scholarship with documentary illustrations this juxtaposition virtually never appeared. In these books Charlemagne was frequently depicted in several variations – the statuette, Triclinium mosaic, Dürer's portrait – but none of these authors had deemed Widukind's tomb worthy of an illustration. Although the Saxon mission was often depicted in works that employed history paintings, the focus here was not Widukind, but rather the destruction of the Irminsul, religious instruction, or baptism.

The creation of this juxtaposition between Charlemagne and Widukind as the pictorial condensation of the Carolingian era could be passed over by pointing out that these books largely reflected the spirit of the Nazi period, and thus that Charlemagne's uncertain status and Widukind's special place of honour are not surprising. However, this constellation did not disappear with the Nazi era, quite the contrary. Post-war works often repeated it even more aggressively. In Eberhard Orthbandt's widely read historical works, the Widukind tomb and Charlemagne statuette are depicted on opposite pages, equally large and

---

[21] G. Krüger, *Geschichte des Deutschen Volkes. Ein Grundriß* (Leipzig, 1937), plate section after p. 40 (here the photograph of the tombstone is shown together with a drawing from the manuscript of the *Leges Barbarorum*, which depicts Charlemagne with his son Pippin, and a photograph of the imperial throne in the Aachen Cathedral); H. Hagemeyer, *Gestalt und Wandel des Reiches. Ein Bilderatlas zur Deutschen Geschichte*, (Berlin, 1944); here, in the chapter 'Das fränkische Reich', first Widukind's tomb is shown as a full-page illustration (p. 88); several pages later the statuette of Charlemagne (p. 91); a very early picture of the tomb is shown in E. Heyck, *Deutsche Geschichte* (Bielefeld and Leipzig, 1905), p. 199; the equestrian statuette of Charlemagne is shown earlier in three views: Charlemagne's head as a detail (p. 189), and the frontal (p. 190) and profile (p. 191) total view.

[2] R. Suchenwirth, *Deutsche Geschichte. Von der germanischen Vorzeit bis zur Gegenwart* (Leipzig, 1934), plates 5 and 6.

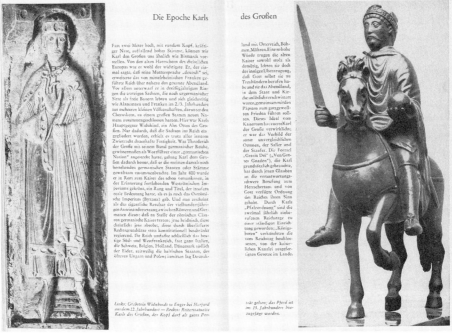

Figure 16. Charlemagne and Widukind, from Eberhard Orthbandt's Illustrierte Deutsche Geschichte *(Munich, 1963); Frankfurt am Main, Goethe Universität*

on equal footing, programmatically framing the chapter title, 'The Epoch of Charlemagne' (*Die Epoche Karls des Großen*) (Fig. 16).[23]

This example can also be used as an occasion to examine the different transformation speeds of text and image. In the 1950s, few German historians (apart perhaps from contemporary historians) appear to have revised – that is, to a certain extent de-Nazified – either their words or their images. Their focus (and apparently that of the Allies as well) was directed at texts. Hardly anyone evidently reflected on when a configuration such as the juxtaposition of Charlemagne and Saxon leader Widukind had emerged and what its message had been.[24] The medium of photography was from the outset tied to a promise of faithful representation, but illustrators and authors quickly found ways to assemble the 'objective' pictures into non-documentary photo series.

---

[23] E. Orthbandt, *Illustrierte deutsche Geschichte* (Munich, 1963, with further editions up to 1966); plates not numbered.

[24] An exception was the emigrant Veit Valentin, whose *Geschichte der Deutschen* (Berlin, 1947) had conspicuously 'de-Nazified' illustrations. After Valentin's death in 1947, the year the book was published, the licensed edition of the book by Knaur publishers (1960) had precisely that nationalist configuration that Valentin had avoided; on this see Jussen, 'Bilderhorizonte' [above, note 1].

Charles the Hybrid: blurring ideologies between schoolbook and collectible picture album

The observations made up to now have referred largely to schoolbooks and to academic and popular history books. National conflicts and political currents can be clearly recognized in their chapters on Charlemagne. In other media, though, the clarity of national image stocks and their messages continually lose their clear-cut character. Collectible picture cards circulated as commercial advertising – prior to television the most influential medium for conveying historical ideas – frequently contained material from other (for example, French) image stocks.

The Dutch cocoa producer Bensdorp made things easy for itself in producing a picture series included for its German customers (Fig. 17). The company had a German text printed on the back of the card, but it used a lithograph for the picture side that had been intended for the domestic market, and included a Dutch caption 'Karel de Groote een School bezoekend'. The motif corresponded

Figure 17. Collectible picture card 'Karel de Groote, een School bezoekend' of the Dutch chocolate company Bensdorp around 1912; Frankfurt am Main, Goethe-Universität

neither to the German nor the French canon of images. The setting portrayed on the collectible picture card is totally free of associations with a monastic context and might have been taken from a French image. The only person on the picture who could be the teacher is the layman at the right margin of the picture. The bishop is an extra who serves no function in the picture. The title, 'Charlemagne visiting a school', is totally unsuitable since it refers neither to a monastic school, as was common in Germany, nor to the palace school, which is what a French audience would have expected. All in all, this high-quality and very popular chromolithograph picture was not easy for German collectors to classify and the author of the text on the reverse side evidently had the same problem, since the encyclopaedia-like text on Charlemagne has nothing at all to do with the scene in the illustration.

It was not only through Dutch cocoa that this motif entered German living rooms. The Cologne chocolate producer Stollwerck also incorporated the motif of 'Charlemagne in the school' into its *Helden-Album* (Hero Album) of 1908 (Fig. 18). Although the picture card itself provided no orientation as to the location of the event, the only figure in the illustration that could possibly have been a teacher was a cleric, as is typical of German illustrations

of this scene. Charlemagne is dressed in ostentatiously Frankish style and – through his moustache – is clearly adapted to the German iconography. In contrast to the Bensdorp illustration, which in the French pictorial tradition shows an elderly man with a long beard sitting in a chair and leaning on his sword, the Stollwerck Hero Album depicts an 'authentic' German hero. The *Berliner Morgenpost* newspaper also depicted the scene in their 52-picture series from 1928 with a clerical teacher and an emphatically Frankish ruler. Although these motifs were somewhat Germanized, the albums for collectors propagated a theme that did not belong to the stock motifs of German historians.

Figure 18. Collectible picture card from the Helden *(Heroes) album of the Cologne chocolate factory Stollwerck, 1908. Frankfurt am Main, Goethe-Universität*

Figure 19. Collectible picture card of the imperial coronation of Charlemagne 800 CE, from the Alles für Deutschland *(Everything for Germany) album of the Yosma company, Bremen 1934; Frankfurt am Main, Goethe-Universität*

The collectible picture card album called *Alles für Deutschland* produced as advertising for the Yosma cigarette brand in 1934 was an album that paid homage to Nazism. It did not, however, use the anti-papal illustration style of the coronation ambush, which might have been expected in a Nazi context, but instead borrowed from the papal-friendly picture type of Kaulbach, which shows a staged, hierarchical ritual (Fig. 19). When after the war the Herba publishing company in Plochingen designed the *Deutsche Geschichte* collectible card album of 1953, making use of widely-available picture stocks, the artist for the coronation of Charlemagne got everything confused (Fig. 20). Apparently he did not understand the intention of the picture he used as his model. While the pope cunningly crowns Charlemagne from behind, as if this were portraying the coronation ambush on an unwitting Charlemagne, like Rethel's design for Aachen's town hall (reproduced in Fig. 15), the scene displays nothing that might otherwise denote an ambush. The scene is set up as a planned ritual, much like Kaulbach's painting for the Maximilianeum in Munich.

The same can be observed of Charlemagne's loyal paladin Roland. Beyond the somewhat disoriented early stages of national historiography, which began at the same time as the age of history paintings, Roland, who dies for his lord

Figure 20. Collectible picture card of the imperial coronation of Charlemagne 800 AD, from the Deutsche Geschichte *(German History) album of the Herba company, Plochingen 1953; Frankfurt am Main, Goethe-Universität*

and master in 'feudal' loyalty, was not a subject for German schoolbooks and history books. When the narrative of Charlemagne's loyal paladin, and of his battle, defeat and death in the Pyrenees, did nevertheless end up in German living rooms and children's rooms, it was through the commercial medium of collectible picture cards. They indeed often portrayed something that had no place in history books.

PART FOUR

LAND AND FRONTIERS

8

REFLECTIONS ON THE FRONTIER IN EARLY MEDIEVAL IBERIA

Richard Hitchcock

My principal concern in this essay is with the north and north-west frontier between al-Andalus and the Christian states in the upper third of the Iberian Peninsula during the tenth century. There are two main reasons for this focus. Firstly, there is a certain amount of material available for this period that is susceptible to analysis and debate, and secondly, the interpretations of this period, including a number by prominent Spanish historians, have given rise to a fierce and inconclusive polemic.

By the beginning of the tenth century, there had been a permanent Muslim presence in Iberia for two hundred years. This state, controlled by a dynasty of Umayyad princes who founded the emirate in Córdoba in 756, was known in Arabic sources as al-Andalus and in Latin chronicles as Spania derived from Hispania which had been the Roman name for this province. It is important to draw attention to the fact that, during the period 756–911, al-Andalus was governed according to the precepts of a conservative tradition in Islam. In essence, this meant that conversion was not compulsory, and that the two religions of Judaism and Christianity were permitted to be practised, subject to certain constraints. Muhammad had made special dispensation in the Qur'ān for the *ahl al-kitāb*, People of the Book, as Jews and Christians were called. Provided they paid an extra annual tax, and that they desisted from blaspheming against Muhammad the Prophet in public places, then they could continue to worship in their synagogues and churches unmolested. Furthermore, for the first two centuries of Islam in the Iberian Peninsula, Islam and Christianity were confined to major cities and towns – which is to say that they were an urban phenomenon. In my view, there is scant substantiable evidence to maintain that Islam was known among the rural population, and the lack of references to, or remains of, churches in the two thirds of the Peninsula that comprised al-Andalus (with less than a handful of exceptions) suggest that Christianity was not prevalent there either. It is beyond the scope of this presentation to discuss this absence

of revealed religions amongst the majority of the population until the tenth
century, but it does have relevance to the subject in hand.

When the armies commanded by Muslims initially overran the Iberian
Peninsula in the aftermath of the invasion in 711, constituent elements broke
off and settled in many different areas. These settlers known in the Arabic
sources as *baladiyyūn*, those who settled in an area or region, may have consisted
principally of Berbers who had been recruited in North Africa, and were
familiar with making a living from the land, through the cultivation of crops,
or the management of cattle. They would have been nominally Islamized in
order to receive the statutory stipend as soldiers, and some may have acquired
Arab names, but their adoption of Islam may well have been restricted to the
obligatory recitation of the *Bismillāh*. What features of Islam that that they may
have acquired under military orders would have been shrugged off when they
were out of contact with Muslim authorities. Many may have been descendants
of the Vandals who had established themselves in North Africa under Gaiseric
in the fifth century, in other words, ethnically European and Latin-speaking.
Their livelihood was subject to the vagaries of the climate more perhaps than
to any other factor. With this in mind, the defeat of the equivalent of a Muslim
platoon by guerrilla forces in a skirmish in an undetermined date in the 720s
in the remote fastnesses of the Cantabrian Mountains (the so-called Battle of
Covadonga) would have caused hardly a ripple.[1] What happened in essence was
that the majority of the Muslim troops were at that time deployed beyond the
Pyrenees from their base much further eastward at Zaragoza. Events north and
west of the river Duero were of little concern.

When eventually the Umayyad emirate became established in 756, there were
three broad frontier areas called in Arabic *thughūr* [singular *thughr*] generally
perceived to be equivalent to English Marches.[2] By the ninth century, the three
were each dependent on a major city in al-Andalus: the *thaghr al-a'lā*, the Upper
March with its capital of Zaragoza; the *thaghr al-awsāt*, the Middle March based on
Toledo; and the *thaghr al-adnā*, the Lower March, going northwards from Mérida.
The Upper March encompassed the Ebro valley and, in the eighth century a
broad swathe of land from Pamplona to Barcelona, reduced, after being attacked
by Northern states in 799 and 801 respectively, to Tudela, Huesca, Zaragoza and
Lérida, still an enormous expanse of land. The distinguishing and ever-present
feature for the Middle and Lower marches was the River Duero, or Douro in
Portugal. When the Umayyads came to acknowledge, at an indeterminate date,

[1] For the invention of this alleged 'triumph' by later chroniclers, P. Linehan, *History and
    the Historians of Medieval Spain* (Oxford, 1993), pp. 101–5.
[2] See, for fuller details, especially on the Upper March, the entry 'al-Thughūr (a.)' by J.
    D. Latham and C. E. Bosworth, in *Encyclopaedia of Islam*, ed. P. Bearman, Th. Banquis,
    C. E. Bosworth, E. Van Donzel and W. P. Heinrichs, 2nd edn (Leiden, 1999), fascicule
    169–74, pp. 446–9 (X, 446, col. 2).

but certainly from the ninth century onwards, that al-Andalus needed to be defended from encroachments from the north, fortresses were constructed with permanent garrisons stationed there. A tenth-century example was Calatalifa [Arabic *qala't al-khalīfa*, the castle of the caliph], so called because the caliph 'Abd ar-Rahmān III (912–961) visited the site in the valley of the river Guadarrama, most probably on his return from Simancas in 939 where his troops were soundly and surprisingly defeated by a combined force of Leonese, Castilians and Navarrese.[3]

To prevent his conquerors from taking advantage of their victory, he would have ordered his return route to be fortified against possible later incursions. Between Toledo which stands on the river Tagus [Tajo] and the Duero lies a forbidding range of mountains, the Sierra de Guadarrama, so that it would only make sense to fortify the far, northern, side if it was feasible to maintain a substantial Muslim presence there. We find, therefore, a fortress just to the south of the Duero at Medinaceli [Arabic *madīna Sālim*, the town of Sālim] – its Arab gate still survives. It has the distinction of being the town (now it is more of a village) where Ibn Abī 'Alī al-Mansūr died in 1002, on his return from his last incursion into the Christian kingdoms. It was endowed with a particular importance by 'Abd ar-Rahmān III, as he centred his strategy for controlling the Middle March there, where it usurped this role from Toledo. When an expedition was planned against the nascent state of Castile or indeed the north-west, this was the town where troops would be gathered, and from which the summer expedition (*aceifa*, from the Arabic *as-sā'if*, summer) would have been launched. We have a notice to this effect by Ibn Hayyān (987–1075), perhaps the foremost historian for that period of al-Andalus, almost certainly quoting an earlier account, who mentions that a spring expedition of 933 went to Galicia from Toledo. 'Abd ar-Rahmān crossed the frontier zone forcing dissidents in the fortresses en route to surrender, and bringing safety and security to the region'.[4] It is instructive to be reminded that armies and campaigns going north from Córdoba would have required roads on which to transport the accoutrements of battle, and that the network put in place when Hispania was a Roman province would have taken them on specific routes. Towns along such routes would be the ones to be fortified. The one exit northwards was to Mérida, the former Roman provincial capital, Emerita Augusta; thence there was a choice: due north skirting the Sierra de Gredos via Salamanca towards Astorga, or eastwards to the south of the Sierra de Guadarrama towards Zaragoza, with a detour south, half way along to Toledo. Medinaceli was on this second route, strategically sited to repel attacks from the North.

3   R. Collins, *Spain: An Oxford Archaeological Guide* (Oxford, 1998), 'Calatalifa'.
4   Ibn Hayyān, de Córdoba, *Crónica del califa 'Abdarrahmān III an-Nāsir entre los años 912 y 942 (al-Muqtabis v)* (Zaragoza, 1981), p. 244.

The principal cities that lie in the so-called 'cuenca del Duero', the Duero river basin, are Zamora, Simancas and Osma; to the south are Ledesma, Salamanca and Segovia; to the north Palencia, León and Burgos. So the older provinces that the basin comprises are those of Burgos, Palencia, León, Valladolid, Zamora, Segovia and Salamanca. There are tributaries to the north and south of the Duero; these originate in mountains, so that some irrigation is assured. The extensive plains between the sierra north of Madrid and the Cantabrian chain are on average about 2500 feet, with areas well adapted to wheat, and also home to sheep, perhaps merinos bought in from North Africa by Berber pastoralists. As the climate is one of extremes, dry and very hot in the summer but exposed to cold winters, there would have been large movements of herds southwards in the winter, irrespective of any notional frontiers. One may infer therefore that the frontier lands were no impediment to the seasonal demands of necessary pasturelands. This entire zone was what constituted the frontier between the kingdom of Asturias and al-Andalus for much of the period up until the tenth century, although control of the northern and southern peripheries could fluctuate enormously depending on the respective extent of political turmoil in either state.

The modern polemic is focused on whether or not the frontier zone was depopulated. The two notable Spanish antagonists in the twentieth century were both highly respected scholars; and indeed both were traditionalists, in that they shared a belief in an 'eternal Spain'. The first, the redoubtable medieval historian Claudio Sánchez-Albornoz (1893–1984), author of *Despoblación y repoblación del valle del Duero* published in Buenos Aires in 1966, had what might be described as a 'take-no-prisoners' approach to Spanish history.[5] He had taken refuge in France at the time of the Civil War in Spain, and later spent forty years in exile in Buenos Aires where he was, for a while, a leader of the Spanish Republican Government in Exile. His thesis was founded on a passage in the Chronicle of Alfonso III (reigned 866–910) relating to the reign of Alfonso I of Asturias (739–757) which has been translated as follows: '[Alfonso] took many cities in battle' (*bellando cepit*) – twenty-nine are listed from Tuy and Lugo in the northwest, Oporto and Braga in present-day Portugal through Astorga and León, taking in Zamora and Salamanca in the south, as far as Miranda de Ebro in the east. 'Killing all the Arabs with the sword, he led the Christians back with him to his country', that is to say to Oviedo and the Cantabrian mountains.[6] In another ninth-century chronicle, referring to the same King Alfonso, the chronicler writes that 'he laid waste to the lands known as the Gothic fields down to the river Duero, and extended the kingdom of the Christians' (*Campos quos dicunt*

5   C. Sánchez-Albornoz, *Despoblación y repoblación del valle del Duero* (Buenos Aires, 1966).
6   K. Baxter Wolf, *Conquerors and Chroniclers in Early Medieval Spain*, translated with notes and introduction (Liverpool, 1990), p. 169. The translation above is that of Wolf.

goticos usque flumen Dorium eremavit et xristianorum regnum extendit). On the basis of these texts and what he believed to be the supporting testimony of some Arabic sources, as well as arguments relating to the repopulation of the area, Sánchez-Albornoz proposed that there was a radical depopulation of the 'Duero River Basin'.[7] I quote his emotionally laden words to give an idea of the passionate intensity of his personal feeling and involvement in the issue. 'I am only sure of the emptying of the area between the Duero and the Cantabrian-Asturian mountains and especially the plains of León and Castile... I am sure. I have written it. I insist on such a firm positive statement.' At the same time he did concede that 'not all the upper meseta was totally depopulated', by which he presumably had in mind the area to the north of the Duero, but here he is not specific.[8] However, in the passage quoted above from Ibn Hayyān, reference is made to the Muslim invaders being a source of joy for the 'dwellers of the Upper and Lower Marches', who were as a consequence of their success able to gather their crops and store their goods. This text seems to demonstrate that the area through which these particular troops passed in 933 was not unoccupied. Sánchez-Albornoz is regarded as the high priest of those who argue that all the cities mentioned were totally deserted, and the adjacent rural areas were a wasteland. He was followed, for example, by Salvador de Moxó who, albeit in a roundabout manner, also adduced evidence from Arabic sources, although these are in fact far from uniform, regarding deserted areas in frontier zones.[9] He insisted on the disappearance of a large majority of the Roman cities in the Duero valley.

The second of the two Spanish antagonists mentioned above, the philologist and historian Ramón Menéndez Pidal (1869–1968), maintained that these texts could be interpreted in a different way, and that the cities were not wholly deserted but were rather subjected to an administrative overhaul. The pivotal issue for him is the interpretation of the word 'poblar'. He argued that it must signify, 'bringing a new politico-administrative organization to a township that is disorganized, amorphous or perhaps dispersed because of the upheaval caused by Muslim domination, however fleeting this may have been'.[10] In other words the word 'poblar' means to organize and not to populate, and he adduces toponymic evidence. If instances of the place-name 'Puebla' or its derivatives can

[7] C. Sánchez-Albornoz, *Spain, An Historical Enigma*, trans. C. J. Dees and D. S. Reher, 2 vols. (Madrid, 1975), II, 636–7. The Spanish version of the latter sentence conveys the author's unshakable conviction. 'Tengo por seguro, he escrito. Insisto en tan tajante afirmación.'

[8] Ibid., II, 630.

[9] S. de Moxó, *Repoblación y sociedad en la España cristiana medieval* (Madrid, 1979), pp. 34–5.

[10] R. Menéndez Pidal, 'Repoblación y tradición en el cuenca del Duero', in *Enciclopedia Lingüística Hispánica* (Madrid, 1960), pp. xxii-lvii, esp. pp. xxxi-xxxvii.

be attested in areas that were known never to have been depopulated, such as Galicia, and northern Asturias, then 'it can be reasonably concluded that the act of 'poblar' in León, or the valley of the Duero does not mean that there was a lack of inhabitants in those territories'. When it comes to the matter of those locations that were 'repopulated' in the late ninth and tenth centuries, Menéndez Pidal's opinion was that 'without doubt they had inhabitants who were there before and had stayed on despite the 'liberating' expeditions of Alfonso in the eighth century'.[11] This is a perfectly tenable theory. Menéndez Pidal was a philologist of vast erudition, who felt that his analysis was watertight. Sánchez-Albornoz was by no means convinced, yet could not bring himself to berate his fellow-scholar, and one held in such high regard, calling his riposte 'a respectful response'. In the case of other historians, even one as eminent as Américo Castro, he was severe in his admonitions.

Now, as a military strategy, the creation of a vast desert between Asturias and al-Andalus, is understandable; it would be a kind of no-man's land to deter invading forces. Notwithstanding this, land that is potentially productive, for arable or pastoral use will always be exploited to a greater or lesser extent. Derek Lomax, in his remarkable book *The Reconquest of Spain*, was sceptical: 'Sánchez-Albornoz has argued that a total desert was created which successfully protected Asturias against Muslim invasions, but this is dubious. Place-names, church dedications and details of landholding in later charters show that some peasants stayed on their farms in the lower Duero valley.'[12]

Calamities may happen to cities, but life in the rural areas goes on, and indeed one can argue that natural disasters such as famine and drought were of greater immediate concern than military campaigns. In this regard Thomas Glick, in his re-analysis of medieval Spain wrote that: 'It is probable that the drought more than the king was responsible for the depopulation of the Duero Valley, where in any case at least scattered nuclei of herding folk must have remained', and this observation highlights two significant factors.[13] The first relates to the enormous impact of climatic conditions which could drastically transform the demography of a region. Villages or hamlets could certainly be abandoned and left deserted in times of drought and other natural disasters, but would be repossessed when circumstances improved. Secondly, the reference to 'herding folk' draws attention to the uses of the land. The immense plateau extending from Zamora to León in the north, and from Valladolid in the east to Burgos in the north, is said to have constituted a kind of no man's land until its repopulation in the time of

---

[11] Ibid., p. xxxvi.

[12] D. W. Lomax, *The Reconquest of Spain* (London, 1978), p. 27. His reference to 'farms' is problematic, I think – certainly not 'farms' in anything like the modern sense. The book is remarkable because of its author's unshakable conviction that the 'Reconquest' was a continuing Christian crusade.

[13] T. F. Glick, *Islamic and Christian Spain in the Early Middle Ages* (Princeton NJ, 1979), p. 45.

Alfonso III; yet it is irrigated by two rivers, the Esla and the Pisuerga, both more than two hundred miles long, whose numerous tributaries extend like tentacles criss-crossing the region. Even allowing for the dramatic seasonal changes of the weather, with extreme heat in the summer months and corresponding cold in the winter, it seems improbable that the water from these rivers should not have had beneficial effects on pasturelands and crops. This whole zone was a far cry from the arid deserts of the Maghrib, the place of origin of some of the settlers. It is more likely, therefore, that there were scattered pockets of inhabitants, villagers or peasants, neither a threat to Muslim expeditionary forces passing through, nor to the designs of Alfonso and his successors, perhaps 'a vast, if incomplete depopulation' in the words of Lomax, although the evidence is at best fragmentary.

One of the many bees in Sánchez-Albornoz's bonnet was his deeply held belief that 'the Reconquest is the key to the history of Spain', an idea he first put in print in 1928, and he was scathing of those with contrary views. For him, the repopulation in the ninth and tenth centuries was the sequel to the 'Reconquest'. This is not a standpoint widely accepted nowadays, though the fact that the two were considered to share a common link is demonstrated by the title of the 1951 book *La reconquista española y la repoblación del país*.[14] What Sánchez-Albornoz perceived as a gradual but massive process of repopulation was part of the inexorable tide of 'Reconquest' with a capital 'R'. Another firm believer in the total depopulation of the area of the Middle March, Fray Justo Pérez de Urbel (1895–1979), refined this view by claiming that it was the monastic community in a general sense which was the means through which repopulation and colonization were achieved.[15] The origins of Castile were an abiding preoccupation for him, and he did not deviate from his view that communities of monks were fundamental in the repopulation of lands secured by Counts from the end of the ninth century onwards. It may be seen, then, that both Pérez de Urbel and Sánchez-Albornoz adopted an uncompromising stance vis-à-vis depopulation to highlight the achievements of the repopulating Christians, be they the counts of nascent Castile, monastic communities or the beneficiaries of Alfonso III's policies.

Ordoño II (850–866) initiated the repopulation of cities that had been left abandoned a hundred years earlier, specifically Tuy, Astorga, León and Amaya.[16] He put walls around them and gates on the high ground. Later on, his successor Alfonso III continued the practice with cities as far south as Zamora and as far west as Burgos. Sánchez-Albornoz's own words sum up his hypothesis: 'the

---

[14] *La reconquista y la repoblación del país* (Zaragoza, 1951). The chapter on the 'Reconquista y repoblación de Castilla y León durante los siglos IX y X', ibid., pp. 127–62, was contributed by Fr. Justo Pérez de Urbel.

[15] J. Pérez de Urbel, *Los monjes españoles en la Edad Media,* 2 vols. (Madrid, 1933), II, 280.

[16] The phrase used is 'deserted from antiquity', Wolf, *Conquerors and Chroniclers*, p. 175.

repopulation made the Duero plains an island of free men in feudal Europe and the new advances in colonization affirmed that common liberty.'[17] The city of Zamora on the northern banks of the Duero constitutes a pertinent example. It had been a Roman city on the direct road between Mérida and Astorga, and was targeted by the kingdom of Asturias and by the Muslims for its strategic position in the frontier zone. In 893, according to Arabic sources, it was occupied, heavily fortified and restored at the instigation of Alfonso III partly by his own people and partly by '*ajam* from Toledo', that is to say, those belonging to the indigenous population who did not speak Arabic. This text has been taken to mean Christians of Toledo, but the word *ajam* does not carry with it any necessary religious affiliation, and therefore does not warrant this interpretation. Much later on in his reign, 'Abd ar-Rahmān III failed in his attempt to recapture Zamora in 939, when he and his army, an amalgam of his own troops and allies of dubious loyalty, were decisively defeated near Simancas, at the battle of Alhandega (Arabic *al-khandaq*, a ditch or trench), by Ramiro II in alliance with the forces of Castile and Navarre. Given the location, the tenure of Zamora was crucial. If it was sufficiently reinforced to withstand forays from the South, then the area northward to León was protected; if the Muslims could hold it, then they had a secure command of that zone of the frontier.

There was, furthermore, significant resettlement in the plains of the upper Duero during the first half of the tenth century. This made political sense for the Christian states of the north. They had consolidated their positions in the ninth century vis-à-vis al-Andalus, notably because of the policies of Alfonso III. He let it be known that possession together with ownership of land was available to any who cared to come and settle. This offer was made from political strength; he knew that support from neighbouring Christian states would be forthcoming if the frontiers were seriously threatened, and that therefore he was powerful enough to withstand Muslim incursions. In other words, it was a pragmatic strategy which had nothing to do with religious motivation. Lomax's statement that 'the Asturian Kings believed themselves to be Visigoths and ... decided to reconquer the south as if receiving property stolen from their ancestors', is not generally accepted nowadays.[18] Religion was seldom a factor in the relations between north and south; not until, that is, the end of the eleventh century and the onset of the Crusades, which epoch was to see a defining change in the history of the Iberian Peninsula. In the tenth century, both sides made inroads into the frontier zones when they were militarily powerful enough to do so. Fortunes had fluctuated over two centuries until Alfonso III's time, when the pendulum shifted in favour of the north owing in large measure to the political disarray in al-Andalus. One should, however, mention that from 912, the date of the accession

---

[17] Sánchez Albornoz, *Spain, an Historical Enigma*, II, 645.
[18] Lomax, *The Reconquest of Spain*, p. 40.

of 'Abd ar-Rahmān III as *amīr*, later, from 929, as caliph, the pendulum swung toward the other quarter, gradually to start with, but subsequently with great momentum, so that by 950, it was as if it were installed. When this occurred, the dominant power throughout the Peninsula was the Islamic state of al-Andalus.

Alfonso's 'repopulation policy' inviting all and sundry to settle may be said to have created a demographic movement akin to the Californian gold rush in the nineteenth century. From the testimony of toponymy which has, though, to be treated with caution owing to the difficulties of assigning invariably accurate and reliable dating to the new place-names, one may observe that immigrants came from all parts of the Peninsula: Gallegos from Galicia, Castellanos from Castile, Coruñeses from La Coruña, for example. What has preoccupied Spanish historians in particular has been the influx from al-Andalus. There is no doubt that a number of immigrants came from the south: place names such as Cordoveses, Toldanos and Mozarves, in a document of 941, testify to this.[19] There are, moreover, numerous Arabic proper names in Latin monastic documents of the ninth and tenth centuries, which have given rise to a number of theories. If one finds, for example, seventeen abbots with Arabic names scattered throughout the region, not to mention presbyters and monks, does not this provide proof positive of the persecution of Christians in al-Andalus? Much has been made of this so-called evidence of the maltreatment of Christians by Muslims, because it provides ballast for the theory that consciousness of religion was at the basis of attitudes between south and north and vice-versa. If there was a 'Reconquest', then surely Muslims and Christians had to be religious foes. Years of mulling over the texts and their significance have led me to contrary conclusions, briefly summarized as follows. If religious persecution was forbidden according to the legal code prevalent in al-Andalus at that time, then that could not account for the emigration, for which there is ample testimony. One might add to this the following thought. If these abbots and the rest came from the small clusters of committed Christians in urban environments, then they would certainly not have been Arabicized. It would have been anathema for them to have adopted Arab nomenclature. The phenomenon of Arabic names in the Latin documents may be explained by a number of other theories. What seems perfectly possible is that those non-Muslim but not necessarily Christian individuals or families, probably resident in cities where they are likely to have acquired Arabic names, were unable to resist the lure of the land and prospects of economic betterment, and so they migrated north. Those who became associated with the foundation of monasteries would have adopted Christianity *in situ*, and this may also have applied to the abbots as well as to other clerics. Land could be occupied through *presura*, the possession of deserted land with the permission of the

---

[19]   R. Menéndez Pidal, *Orígenes del Español. Estado lingüístico de la Península Ibérica hasta el siglo once*, 5th edn (Madrid, 1964), pp. 441–7.

monarch, and with the consequent obligation to cultivate, the policy making sound economic sense for a burgeoning kingdom.[20] However, on a greater scale, land could be made over to monasteries. It seems as though monastic settlers had the pick of the land and were responsible for its profitable organization and exploitation, with perhaps several hundred members of the community employed in different and complementary skills. One may gauge the extent of the prosperity and influence of the monastery of Sahagún for instance, whose church was consecrated in 935 in the presence of the king, Ramiro II, by the fact that it was razed to the ground in one of the summer campaigns of al-Mansūr in 988.[21] By the middle of the tenth century, 'Abd ar-Rahmān's central frontier, that is to say on the Middle March, stretched in a line north of Toledo, but south of the Guadarrama and Gredos sierras. In other words, it had moved from the Duero to the Tajo, with a string of towns such as Coria, Talavera, Máqueda, Madrid and Guadalajara, providing a defensive chain. This information may be gleaned from the fifteenth-century Arab historian, al-Himyarī who, using earlier sources, describes Coria, for example, as 'being a very solid fortress surrounded by a strong wall of ancient construction,' and Talavera, some twenty-five miles from the Guadarrama mountains, as 'being at the [outer] extreme of the Muslim March, and one of the best defended of the big cities'.[22]

There was, however, one notable dissident to the view that Spain, 'eternal Spain', triumphed over Islam owing in large measure to the impetus of the so-called Reconquest. Américo Castro (1885–1972), an exile who later became an American citizen, argued that Spain came into existence through *convivencia*, the mutually beneficial co-existence between Muslims, Jews and Christians. In his view it was nonsense to call people like Seneca in the Roman period, and the indigenous communities of al-Andalus, Spaniards because Spain did not exist at that time. Although he did not dispute the concept of reconquest, albeit with a small 'r', he gave the argument a significant twist: 'the reconquest lasted eight centuries precisely because the Christians did not truly feel themselves to be Spaniards.'[23] I have always insisted that the phrase 'Muslim Spain' is a misnomer, not from a Castrist perspective, but because of the absence of any recognition of what might be termed 'Spanishness' in either early Latin or Arabic accounts. For

---

[20] I. de la Concha, *La 'presura'. La ocupación de tierras en los primeros siglos de la reconquista* (Madrid, 1946), p. 27.

[21] Glick, *Islamic and Christian Spain*, p. 90, attributes the taste for olive oil in Leonese territories, that is to say north of the Duero, and its beneficial impact on the economy to the influx of migrants from the south, but I believe that he is referring to trade, as the upper limit of the cultivation of the olive is generally accepted to have been the Tagus valley.

[22] E. Lévi-Provençal, *La Péninsule Ibérique au Moyen-Age d'après le* Kitāb ar-Rawd al-Mi'tār fī Habar al-Aktār *d'Ibn 'Abd al-Mun'im al-Himayrī* (Leiden, 1938), pp. 198 and 155.

[23] A. Castro, *The Spaniards. An Introduction to their History* (Berkeley CA, 1971), p. 232.

the Muslims, the inhabitants of the north of the Iberian Peninsula were identified by their regional names. The Arabic word for Christians, *naṣārā*, was almost exclusively confined to practising urban Christians. Other terms describing non-Muslims in al-Andalus were religiously neutral, and these, it goes without saying perhaps, were in the vast majority.[24] The real distinction between states was political and not religious or ethnic. Thomas Glick in conjunction with Pi-Sunyer, in an article with a focus on acculturation, wrote that, 'however one may approach it, the central problem of medieval Spain -- the formative period of its national culture – is the meeting and bilateral adjustment of two distinct cultures, Christian and Muslim (in reality, a number of distinct Christian and Islamic sub-cultures)'.[25] There may have been a certain integration of cultures in particular epochs, and in certain areas of the Peninsula, such as the tenth century in the kingdom of León, but it is of paramount important to recognize that to talk of 'medieval Spain', as if it were one period, is misleading. The 'Spain' in this phrase prior to 1085 was al-Andalus. Prior to the capture of Toledo by Alfonso VI of Castile in that year, it was the rulers of al-Andalus who exercised absolute political power. Their control did wax and wane during this period, but the hegemony of the ruling elite, in Córdoba until the Caliphate was declared to be in abeyance in 1031, was by and large unchallenged. The predominant influence emanating from the principal cities was Islamic. The 'adjustment' referred to above took place beyond Andalusi borders where the dominant culture (Islamic) either imposed itself on a pre-existing lifestyle, or filled a void. Although this culture was not eradicated after 1085, and indeed continued to prevail in a number of spheres, notably intellectual and architectural, the foremost influence in the Peninsula thereafter was Christian.

I will bring these reflections to an end: the Middle March in the Iberian Peninsula in the tenth century, the Arabic *thughr al-awsāt*, the area lying between the rivers Duero and Tajo, and the zone north of the Duero had never been a no man's land, despite the asseverations of Sánchez-Albornoz, whose insistence of a total depopulation seems *prima facie* unlikely. The inhabitants of smaller towns and villages would have been subject to the vicissitudes of war, when the forces of one side invaded and triumphed at moments propitious to them. If land and properties were devastated, then it and they would recover. Crops could be sown and herds replenished often within the year, and resilience is a quality which has been attributed to these rural communities. After Alfonso's effective policy of encouraging immigration, the regions north of the Duero were organized through *presura*, and in the ensuing decades, and notably after his disastrous defeat in 939, 'Abd ar-Rahmān maintained a defensive wall north

---

[24] See the useful and informative study of Eva Lapiedra Gutiérrez, *Cómo los musulmanes llamaban a los cristianos hispánicos* (Valencia, 1997).

[25] Thomas F. Glick and Oriol Pi-Sunyer, 'Acculturation as an Explanatory Concept in Spanish History', *Comparative Studies in Society and History* 11 (1969), 136–54 (at p. 138).

of the Tajo but south of the Duero. Throughout the ninth and tenth centuries when either side raided, it was not out of any form of religious motivation. It was simply a recurrence of the age-old practice. If one state reckoned itself to be militarily stronger than its neighbour, then it could not resist the temptation to invade. Neither religion nor indeed nationhood entered into the equation at that time.

This interpretation of events and situations is not intended to be taken to be definitive, and it is indeed possible that it may be regarded as the substitution of one set of theories for another, but it does not, I believe, run counter to the sources, and does reflect and is in accord with my current thinking on Muslim-Christian relations in that particular area at that particular time.

9

GERMANY'S GROWTH TO THE EAST: FROM THE POLABIAN MARCHES TO GERMANIA SLAVICA[1]

Christian Lübke

My essay addresses the general theme of this volume, focusing on a topic that has been given scant attention by German historians and by the general public in Germany. My subject is the Slavonic contribution to German history. While this dimension of German history has not been entirely neglected by modern historiography, the significance of its impact has generally been underestimated in the public discourse. The following example may suffice to illustrate the latter point. In 2007, the German *Land* (province) of Brandenburg, which is strictly speaking a post-reunification creation, decided to commemorate the conquest of the castle of Brandenburg-upon-Havel by Margrave Albert the Bear, who thereafter used the title of margrave of Brandenburg. The regional government of Brandenburg organized a series of events on that occasion, and posters were displayed on which one could read the following text:

> It is our birthday. The *Land* of Brandenburg celebrates the 850th anniversary of its creation. Two documents testify the birth of our Land in 1157. On 11 June 1157, Albert the Bear achieved the conquest of (the castle of) Brandenburg. From 3 October 1157 he would call himself margrave of Brandenburg. 850 years have passed since.

The posters concluded – in English – 'Happy Birthday Brandenburg!'[2]

The only website of the federal government on 'Structural policies and new Länder' flagged the events as follows:

---

[1] I should like to thank the organizers for inviting me to contribute the following reflexions on 'land and frontiers' to this book.

[2] See e.g. <http://www.landtag.brandenburg.de/sixcms/media.php/5701/Folder_Landtag_850.pdf> [accessed 13 September 2016].

The march of Brandenburg is 850 years old – a jubilee worthy of celebration. The commemorations will start on 11 June 2007 with a service for the march and, hence, the *Land* of Brandenburg to be held at Brandenburg Minster.

It would be unfair to accuse the authors of this text of ignoring Brandenburg's Slavonic heritage. The Brandenburg text is, for instance, introduced by a short overview of the *Land*'s history, which reads as follows:

This year's commemorations are an opportunity to engage with the changing history of our Land, from the Slavonic settlements of the sixth century to the first dynasty, the Ascanians, and to the movement of town foundations of the thirteenth century.

The information provided by the federal government's agency was even more precise about the events proceeding (and leading to) 1157. I quote:

Brandenburg was an important Slavic castle and the centre of an extended territory from the tenth century. King Henry I conquered the castle and adjacent territory in 928/29. It is assumed that the first diocese east of the river Elbe was created around 948. The Germans were pushed back following the Slavonic uprising of 983. Yet as the result of a policy of rapprochement and cooperation between Slavs and Germans from the tenth and eleventh centuries, Albert the Bear, the margrave of the northern march, inherited Brandenburg Castle and the Hevelli realm from the last Slavic ruler Pribislav-Henry in 1150. Margrave Albert and Archbishop Wichmann of Magdeburg were able to reconquer the castle on 11 June 1157 after a long siege and a series of bloody wars, paving the way for continuous German domination over the area. 1157 thus marks the beginning of the first stable territory in Brandenburg whose traditions and boundaries have shaped our *Land* to this day. Brandenburg can rightly claim to be one of the oldest German *Länder*.[3]

I should like to make just two remarks about Brandenburg's early history. The text that I have just quoted states that Albert managed to reconquer Brandenburg Castle in 1157, which from now on would remain in German hands, thus marking the beginning of the first stable territory that shaped the traditions and boundaries of modern Brandenburg. It would therefore appear that Brandenburg entered German history in 1157. Conversely, the Slavonic history of Brandenburg, while known, is kept at some distance, and is deemed

---

[3]   See <http://www.bundesregierung.de/Content/DE/Magazine/emags/estructure/006/thema04-850-jahre-mark-brandenburg-ein-besonderes-jubilaeum.html> [accessed 13 September 2016].

to be merely a prehistory, that ultimately does not really belong to the history of the modern German *Land*.

This perspective is one generally shared in Germany, while the alternative interpretation, on which I shall comment a little later, and which I would support, remains largely unknown. This situation is a sequel of the development of German historiography from the middle of the nineteenth century. Engaging with this historiography is thus a precondition for any approach to the history of the relations between Germans and Slavs. For everything that we know about these relations, and the way in which we interpret the primary documentation, are all the result of the 'making of medieval history'; that is the influence of the historical context in which our knowledge of the past is produced on historiography. In this particular case, the historical context was characterized for more than a century by the competition between Slavs and Germans, and more particularly between Germans and Poles. I shall therefore start my paper by looking at German perceptions of the eastern areas of Germany, a collection of territories settled by people who, until quite late in the Middle Ages, undoubtedly spoke a Slavonic language. I would stress that the predominance of the Slavonic languages in eastern Germany is beyond doubt, as this fact tends to be obscured in contemporary Germany by people who make pseudo-scientific claims about the non-Slavonic origin of the inhabitants, especially the Wends.[4] I shall not, however, labour this point any further.

Instead, I should like to emphasize the contrast between the official interpretation of Brandenburg's history, as mentioned earlier, and the alternative interpretation to which I have already alluded. I refer here especially to the pioneering work of Herbert Ludat (1910–1993) as a historian of Eastern Europe. In his 1971 synthesis on *The Land between Elbe and Oder in 1000*, Ludat laid the foundations for most of our knowledge of the early history of Brandenburg, even though his work has not always encountered the interest that it deserves.[5] In 1968, in an article entitled 'The Slavs and the Marches of the Elbe as a problem of European history', Ludat had already addressed the history of that March, the precursor of modern Brandenburg.[6] Yet for Ludat Brandenburg's history was first and foremost a problem of European history, which started early with

---

[4] See the criticism to these positions e.g. W. H. Fritze: 'Slawomanie oder Germanomanie? Bemerkungen zu W. Stellers neuer Lehre von der älteren Bevölkerungsgeschichte Ostdeutschlands', *Jahrbuch für die Geschichte Mittel- und Ostdeutschlands* 9/10 (1961), reproduced in W. H. Fritze, *Frühzeit zwischen Ostsee und Donau. Ausgewählte Beiträge zum geschichtlichen Werden im östlichen Mitteleuropa vom 6. bis zum 13. Jahrhundert*, ed. L. Kuchenbuch and W. Schich (Berlin, 1982), pp. 31–46.

[5] H. Ludat, *An Elbe und Oder um das Jahr 1000. Skizzen zur Politik des Ottonreiches und der slavischen Mächte in Mitteleuropa* (Cologne, 1971).

[6] H. Ludat, 'Elbslaven und Elbmarken', in *Festschrift für Friedrich von Zahn*, ed. W. Schlesinger (Cologne, 1968), pp. 39–49.

the connexions between the main Slavic stronghold of the Havel area and its neighbours. He accordingly saw the history of early modern Brandenburg and its ties with Prussia as the endpoint of a more than one thousand year old history in which the march of Brandenburg and its double capital town Berlin-Cölln would become the centre of the Brandenburg-Prussian monarchy and, eventually, of the German *Kaiserreich* of the nineteenth century. However, this history was not only the history of Germany, or for that matter simply that of Brandenburg or Prussia. In his characteristic attention to Polish historical research, Ludat saw Brandenburg's advance to become the dominant region of German history as a dynamic that would shape the political map of Central Europe for centuries and Polish history, in particular.

Ludat understood that the divergent interpretations of Brandenburg's history by German and Polish historians was a problem to be solved as much as an object of interest in its own right, since Brandenburg was, in his words, a disputed area both at the level of the nation-state and at that of the peoples. The differences between German and Polish approaches were, according to Ludat, due to diverging interpretations of the impact and significance of medieval colonization, on the one hand, and of the nature and achievements of the Prussian state on the other. These disputed developments were responsible, in his opinion, for the concentration of competing political and ethnic interests in the area. After the successive partitions of Poland in the eighteenth century and the failure of the Polish national movement of the nineteenth century, the impulse for modern Polish nationalism based on a strong reflexion of the past did, perhaps not surprisingly, originate there. When, at the beginning of the twentieth century, radical ethnicism gained attraction, Polish intellectual elites came to share two fundamental convictions:

first, that the German expansion towards the East had ultimately been detrimental to Polish interests, and in particular because it led to the loss of the old Piast country between the river Oder and the Baltic Sea, while the negative impact of the Prussian monarchy on Polish state-building was even more disastrous;

second, that the Germans felt confident that they had a mission to fulfil, based on a sense of their cultural superiority and the cultural inferiority of the Slavs.

These misperceptions were the fruits of generations of teaching and experiences in a context dominated by the history of Brandenburg-Prussia. Overcoming them was a daunting task which, as Ludat knew, might take generations, even if historians were willing to address them consequently and durably, and to seek a common solution to them. So far as historians are concerned, it is fair to say that nationally-driven historiography has by and large given way to a more professional and dispassionate approach. Ludat might have been too pessimistic here. Yet while this development was certainly encouraged by the changes in Europe in 1989, an earlier turning-point was perhaps the conference on 'The Slavs of the Elbe region between Germany and Poland', that took place in Poznań in 1980.[7] In his opening statement, the Polish historian Gerard Labuda had endorsed the view of Kazimierz Wachowski, as developed at the beginning of the twentieth century in his classical work on *The Western Slavs* (1902).[8] Back in 1950, Labuda had re-edited Wachowski's work; a third edition was published as recently as 2000. Labuda stressed with Wachowski that the Western Slavs had for centuries played an essential role in the development of the culture and statehood of the Pomeranians, the Poles, and even the Czechs, forming a human wall against German expansion.

In the discussion that followed this lecture, another Polish historian, Benedykt Zientara, dismissed Labuda's and Wachowski's thesis by emphasizing that no evidence could be found in support of the idea that the Western Slavs understood themselves as a protecting wall against the Germans as part of a conscious sense of Slavic solidarity.[9] More recently, most historians have come to share in Zientara's outright refusal to project nationalist images onto the Middle Ages. Another factor in the development of a more informed approach is the work of the Polish-German textbook-committee, which was set up in 1972, and led to the publication, among other textbooks for teachers, of Winfried Schich's and Jerzy Strzelczyk's volume on *The Slavs and Germans between Spree and Havel – The Origins of the March of Brandenburg*.[10]

The picture is, however, less positive if we look at the public debate. Here the misperceptions that Ludat had rightly condemned seem to be particularly resilient. It suffices to recall the formulation according to which Margrave Albert the Bear had reconquered Brandenburg Castle, as this seems to suggest a form of German entitlement to the area. Such a view conceals the importance of the sustained, and not infrequent, military interaction that characterized the relations between German and Slavonic-speaking people in the march of Brandenburg, and beyond it in the marches of the Elbe area over several centuries. The commonalities between both peoples are best expressed by the portmanteau

---

[7] *Slowiańszczyzna połabska między Niemcami a Polska. Materiały z konferencji naukowej zorganizowanej przez Instytut Historii UAM w dniach 28–29 IV 1980 r.*, ed. J. Strzelczyk (Poznań, 1981).

[8] K. Wachowski, *Slowiańszczyzna Zachodnia: studya historyczne* (Warsaw, 1902).

[9] Zientara gave this statement in the discussions during the Polish conference mentioned in footnote 6 which have been summarized by J. Strzelczyk, 'Słowiańszczyzna połabska (Uwagi na marginesie poznańskiej konferencji)', in *Slowiańszczyzna połabska,* pp. 265–99 (here p. 277).

[10] W. Schich and J. Srzelczyk, *Slawen und Deutsche an Havel und Spree. Zu den Anfängen der Mark Brandenburg* (Hanover, 1997).

notion of *Germania Slavica*, which was introduced four decades ago in order to emphasize the integration into one entity of two linguistically, ethnically and culturally distinct communities.[11]

Germania Slavica first reflects the historical process that it describes.[12] The Slavic settlement in the area is attested from the seventh century at the latest. There the Slavs met people who would later perceive themselves as Germans. Starting with Charlemagne, the Frankish, and later Saxon, Empire in the West increasingly influenced the political, social and economic fates of its Slavic neighbours. As the result of the colonization to which I have already alluded, the formerly autonomous Slavic communities east of the Elbe and Saale rivers became a part of an increasingly Germanized East-Frankish/Roman Empire. Yet the idea of a *Germania Slavica* developed against a specific social and political context, which we need to consider in order to be able to understand the circumstances under which German scholars have confronted the Slavic past, and indeed the past of other non-German peoples in Eastern Europe.

Historiographically, the notion goes back to, if not quite medieval chroniclers, most certainly to the scholars of the German Enlightenment. August Ludwig Schlözer (1735–1809), a professor at the University of Göttingen, addressed the influence of Saxon colonization on the Kingdom of Hungary in his history of the Transylvanian Saxons. Schlözer worked out what he saw as the positive outcome of the contacts between peoples that were at different stages of the development of their culture, namely, between the Germans on the one hand, and the Hungarians on the other. The Hungarians had advanced from 'an insignificant Asian horde to a powerful and civilized European nation', as Schlözer found, which prompted him to write: 'Germans, behold, this is your work, be proud of it! As for you, Magyars, don't forget what was done for you, don't forsake your history, and be grateful!' Contrary to appearances, though, Schlözer was free of any negative prejudice against the assumedly culturally inferior Hungarians. Instead he insisted that no prerogative could be drawn from the fact that some people accessed civilization centuries earlier than others; conversely, it was no disgrace to have developed later than other cultures.[13] The kind of objectivity that informed Schlözer's view would soon be lost by German historians.

---

[11] *Struktur und Wandel im Früh- und Hochmittelalter. Eine Bestandsaufnahme aktueller Forschungen zur Germania Slavica*, ed. C. Lübke (Stuttgart, 1998).

[12] Research in such questions is the main subject of 'Germania Slavica' projects; see W. H. Fritze, 'Germania Slavica. Zielsetzung und Arbeitsprogramm einer interdisziplinären Arbeitsgruppe', in *Germania Slavica I*, ed. W. H. Fritze (Berlin, 1980), pp. 11–40; C. Lübke, 'Germania-Slavica-Forschung im Geisteswissenschaftlichen Zentrum Geschichte und Kultur Ostmitteleuropas e.V.: Die Germania Slavica als Bestandteil Ostmitteleuropa', in *Struktur und Wandel im Früh- und Hochmittelalter*, pp. 9–16.

[13] A. L. Schlözer, *Kritische Sammlungen zur Geschichte der Deutschen in Siebenbürgen* (Göttingen, 1795).

As a result of the following Romantic period's interest in the people from below and in smaller nations and peoples, Johann Gottfried Herder (1744–1803) published his famous *Ideas about the Philosophy of History of Mankind,* in which he paid attention to those peoples who had not been able to consolidate their power and win wars. Herder drew a picture of the Slavs as settlers with a developed culture who had suffered the repeated attacks of foreign nations, not least the Germans. Thus the bellicose Franks and Saxons had refused to engage with agriculture and trade, but had, instead, chosen to eradicate the Slavs or to enslave them while the spoils of war had been distributed under the bishops – a fate not dissimilar, as Herder stressed, to that of the Peruvians under Spanish rule.[14]

Garlieb Helwig Merkel (1769–1850) accentuated the opposition between autochthonous self-sufficient societies and the conquerors from the West with particular reference to the population of the Baltic region. Merkel's criticism was aimed, in particular, at the continuance of serfdom in the Russian province of Livonia. The ultimate blame for the fate of the serfs in the Baltic was assigned by Merkel to the domination of the German-Baltic knights following the settlement of the Teutonic Order in the Middle Ages. Not unlike Herder, Merkel emphasized the cultural achievements of the autochthonous population prior to the settlement of the so-called German colonists. He even speculated that the inhabitants of Livonia would have taken a leading role in the development of knowledge as well as at the political level if they had been given the opportunity of a development of their own. The exogenous action thus had not only thoroughly negative effects on the native societies, but it could not by any mean be justified.[15]

The era of Restoration following the Congress of Vienna led to a radical reassessment of the impact of German colonization in the East, in which a new generation of historians who had been trained in a climate dominated by the development of, and enthusiasm for, the national movement after the wars of liberation against Napoleon aimed to assert the role of the dominating German power, Prussia, within European history. The director of the Secret Archive and also professor of the University at Königsberg, Johannes Voigt (1786–1863), was driven, in his *History of Prussia,* by one overriding question: to explain the redemptive and positive contributions of German colonization to the development of freedom and culture on the Baltic shores, since, as he claimed, 'this area was destined from the earliest days to promoting German life, German thought and German customs'.[16]

[14] J. G. Herder, *Ideen zur Philosophie der Geschichte der Menschheit,* ed. Heinz Stolpe, 2 vols. (Berlin, 1965), II, 273–83, 385–92 [first published 1784–91].

[15] G. H. Merkel, *Die Letten, vorzüglich in Liefland am Ende des philosophischen Jahrhunderts, Ein Beitrag zur Völker- und Menschenkunde* (Riga, 1796).

[16] J. Voigt, *Geschichte Preußens von den ältesten Zeiten bis zum Untergange der Herrschaft des Deutschen Ordens,* 9 vols. (Königsberg, 1827–39).

Gustav Adolf Harald Stenzel (1792–1854), historian and chief archivist at Breslau, while focusing on the impact of German colonization on Silesian society in the Middle Ages, took the political instrumentalization of the past one step further. He was aware that the renewed Polish claims on Silesia, which had been assigned to Prussia following the partitions of the eighteenth century, were first and foremost made by the Polish nobility, and so he stressed the historic responsibility of the Polish aristocracy in the progressive enslavement of the peasantry. He contrasted their fate with the development of the immigrants from the West (mostly German peasants) into a strong and economically robust population group.[17]

Soon Stenzel would be given the opportunity to ventilate his opinion in a context that would prove to be of great significance in the appreciation of German colonization. When the first German national parliament convened in the Paulskirche in 1848, the question arose as to whether the former Polish constituencies around Poznań should be allowed to send MPs to Frankfurt. The question of the borders of a future German national state was thus on the agenda. The select committee for international law, which had been asked to work out a solution to this issue, suggested under Stenzel's chairmanship that the German MPs for Poznań and the surrounding area be admitted to the national parliament. The reason given by its members was that the Polish aristocracy had forfeited its, and hence Poland's, right to self-determination, and that German rule was even in the interest of the Polish peasantry.[18]

Loud cheers accompanied the anti-Polish speech of the MP Wilhelm Jordan (1819–1904) when he stated that the rights of the Germans in formerly Polish territories should not been abandoned for naïve sentimentalism. The Germans had secured these rights through conquest, colonization and civilized manners.[19] The theme of the superior character of German culture which Jordan sought and of which he saw some justification in history would be prevalent for more than a century in the public discourse as well as in German historiography.

However, the continuity of Slavic settlements in areas that had for a long time been associated with German identity represented a much bigger challenge than the direct opposition between Germans and Poles. In a context that was

---

[17] G. A. Stenzel, *Geschichte Schlesiens*, i, *Von den ältesten Zeiten bis zum Jahr 1355* (Breslau, 1853) [only volume published].

[18] M. G. Müller and B. Schönemann, *Die "Polendebatte" in der Frankfurter Paulskirche. Darstellung, Lernziele, Materialien* (Braunschweig 1991); B. E. Vick, *Defining Germany: the 1848 Frankfurt Parliamentarians and National Identity* (Cambridge MA, 2002), pp. 151–2, 157–8.

[19] Vick, *Defining Germany*, pp. 134–5, 155–6, 183–4; see also the historiographic survey about the whole topic given by J. Hackmann and C. Lübke, 'Die mittelalterliche Ostsiedlung in der deutschen Geschichtswissenschaft', in *Historiographical Approaches to Medieval Colonization of East Central Europe. A Comparative Analysis against the Background of Other European Inter-Ethnic Colonization Processes in the Middle Ages*, ed. J. M. Piskorski (Boulder CO, 2002), pp. 179–219.

increasingly marked by the claims of the Russian Pan-Slavists on former Slavic territories, which were perceived as a threat to rival German claims, it became common to argue that the Slavic population on German soil had been largely decimated by wars against the Germans. Some scholars even went so far as to deny the existence of Slavic settlements between the Rivers Elbe and Oder.

After the First World War and following the remapping of Eastern Europe at Versailles, political factors played an even more important role than before in the question of the relations between Germans and Slavs in the Middle Ages. This question would be at the core of the so-called *Ostforschung* which defined itself, according to one of its initiators, Hermann Aubin (1885–1969), as a scholarly contribution to negating Polish claims on Eastern Europe, and hence as part of a political strategy that aimed to contain Poland after its re-creation in 1918. In this particular context, the German colonization in the East would be seen as a central achievement of the Germans during the Middle Ages (this was even the subtitle that Karl Hampe (1869–1936) gave to his highly influential work on the 'Migration to the East').[20] Eventually, some historians came to support the view that the East was part of an ethnically and culturally defined German soil (*Volks- und Kulturboden*). According to the Leipzig historian Rudolf Kötzschke (1868–1949), this notion designated the area that belonged to a people, which it possessed, inhabited, dominated, and in which it was rooted; and to which it was entitled because of the long chain of ancestors who had made it inhabitable, and following a historic event which had led to these peoples' settlement there.[21] Whilst Kötzschke intended to work out the extension of German and Slavic settlements in history, its avowed aim was to 'explore the historical continuity of East German settlements to the present and to lay the foundation for a historical justification of German rights over the East'. Shortly before Nazi Germany invaded Poland, the Breslau historian Walter Kuhn (1903–1983) praised the 'vital force inherent in German culture in the East' at a moment in which, according to him, the Germans of the East were engaged in an ethnic struggle.[22] In the same vein, Erich Maschke characterized the Baltic Sea as a 'Germanic sea'.[23] A certain similarity with the vocabulary of contemporary Nazi propaganda concerning the need for *Lebensraum* for Germans in the East can hardly be denied.[24]

[20] K. Hampe, *Der Zug nach dem Osten. Die kolonisatorische Großtat des deutschen Volkes im Mittelalter* (Leipzig, 1921).

[21] See e.g. R. Kötzschke, 'Die deutsche Wiederbesiedlung der ostelbischen Lande', in *Der ostdeutsche Volksboden. Aufsätze zu den Fragen des Ostens*, ed. W. Volz, 2nd edn (Breslau,1926), pp. 152–79.

[22] W. Kuhn, 'Volkstumsbewahrende Kräfte im Deutschtum des Ostens', in *Deutsche Monatshefte in Polen* 6 (16) (1939/49), 1–5.

[23] E. Maschke, *Das Germanische Meer. Geschichte des Ostseeraums* (Berlin, 1935).

[24] See in general M. Burleigh, *Germany Turns Eastwards: A Study of Ostforschung in the Third Reich* (Cambridge, 1988); for Kötzschke, especially pp. 30–1, and for Kuhn, pp. 105–8, and 176–8.

With the end of World War II, yet another reassessment of the period of the German colonization took place. This progressive shift was due to a critical distance to pre-war positions, not just out of shame about the recent events, but also (and this too was the result of the war) to the discovery of extensive archaeological evidence in the destroyed Eastern European cities. This evidence attested to the degree of development of Slavic culture before the settlement of the Germans, for which no written material was available. In Germany, however, this paradigm shift in the analysis was delayed by the continuity of personnel in the historical profession. The *Ostforscher* had been driven out of those parts of Eastern Europe where they had attempted to justify historical claims on the part of the Germans; but they had no particular difficulty in adapting to the context of the Cold War. They were still in the mainstream, and could now exalt German culture as a primary defence line against the communist threat from the East.[25]

Change therefore only happened at a slow pace, and in the specific context of the German partition. In the West, common opinion in the 1950s still maintained that the Germans had brought civilization and progress to the East, so to speak on behalf of the West. The result of this action was the creation of a Western buffer against the East, an Occidental East. On the other hand, GDR propaganda strongly reacted against what it called a 'clerical-imperialist Western ideology'. At the same time, East German historians, for example Ingrid Hagemann, developed a negative approach towards the German colonization, in line with the Marxist interpretation of history, where the emphasis was placed on the role of 'feudal' lords in the Eastern expansion of Germany, and its irruption into the autonomous development of the Slavs east of the Elbe river. The historical role of the Slavs, they argued, had been in containing the rapid expansion of the Frankish and, subsequently German, state into the East. As the result of this decisive action, Polish state-building could take place. The Slavs were also the first to exploit and use the economic resources of the area of the GDR. Finally, according to Hagemann, the importance of Slavic peasants, craftsmen and town-dwellers in the assimilation zone, which would lead to the rapid growth of the agriculture and the cities, could not be overestimated.[26] Eventually, historical analysis of this issue also changed in the Federal Republic, where, under the influence in particular of Walter Schlesinger (1908–1984), the notion of German Eastern colonization gave way first to the concept of movement to the East, before it was replaced by Eastern settlement, and eventually, internal colonization (*Landesausbau*).[27] This last was no

---

[25] Thus Hermann Aubin, who had held the chair of medieval history at Breslau before 1945, was appointed to a similar post at the University of Hamburg 1946–54, and from 1952 was the editor of a new journal, *Zeitschrift für Ostforschung*.

[26] I. Hagemann, 'Die mittelalterliche deutsche Ostexpansion und die Adenauersche Außenpolitik', in *Zeitschrift für Geschichtswissenschaft* 6 (1958), 797–815.

[27] See especially W. Schlesinger, 'Die geschichtliche Stellung der mittelalterlichen deutschen Ostbewegung', *Historische Zeitschrift* 183 (1957), 517–42; 'Die mittelalterliche

longer seen as a predominantly German phenomenon, but rather was imbedded in European history. In this process, Germans and Slavs created a community of settlement and activity. This is the very context in which the notion of *Germania Slavica* was introduced by scholars who were looking for historical evidence for the Slavic preconditions of the colonization of the central Middle Ages. In stark contrast to the *Ostforscher*, this group of scholars was interested in early Slavic history and possessed a good command of Slavonic languages, and they were open to research by Slav scholars. For Wolfgang H. Fritze (1916–1991), who had been a student of Schlesinger, the concept of *Germania Slavica* designated the mutual interaction between Slavic and German ethnic characters in the context of the medieval German East colonization. For Fritze, this notion referred to the historically speaking Eastern German (or, more to the point, Central-Eastern German) *Länder* of Mecklenburg, Pomerania, Western Prussia, Brandenburg, Saxony-Anhalt, Saxony and Silesia. It was tied to the notion of a second wave of ethnic building, the development, that is, of new German tribes in the East with a strong Slavic component during the central Middle Ages. [28]

The entanglement of German and eastern, predominantly Slavic, history in the process of internal colonization of the central Middle Ages prompted a comparison with Eastern European and even other European countries, as has most recently been suggested by the Berlin Eastern European historian Klaus Zernack (b. 1931). For Zernack, *Germania Slavica* merely represents the first stage of the Eastern colonization, which is part of a universal process of acculturation running from the West to the East of Europe, at the end of which stands the Westernization of Eastern Europe. According to this pattern, a series of other colonization areas developed further East, which are also in part characterized by ethnic mixing, such as the *Polonia Polonica*, the *Polonia Ruthenica*, the *Russia Ruthenica* and, finally, the *Russia Fennica*.[29]

Herbert Ludat, to whom I have already alluded, took a slightly different perspective as he paid attention to the Slavic prehistory of the colonization period at the core of the *Germania Slavica*.[30] He was interested in the formation of the Slav nations and their integration into medieval Christianity. Accordingly, he saw the marches of the Elbe region and their Slavonic settlements as crystallization

---

deutsche Ostbewegung und die deutsche Ostforschung', in *Deutsche und europäische Ostsiedlungsbewegung. Referate und Aussprachen der wissenschaftlichen Jahrestagung des Johann-Gottfried-Herder-Forschungsrates vom 7. bis 9. März 1963* (Marburg an der Lahn, 1964), pp. 7–46, reproduced in *Zeitschrift für Ostmitteleuropaforschung* 46 (1997), 427–57; and 'Zur Problematik der Erforschung der deutschen Ostsiedlung', in *Die deutsche Ostsiedlung des Mittelalters als Problem der europäischen Geschichte,* ed. W. Schlesinger (Sigmaringen, 1975), pp. 11–30.

[28] See Fritze, as cited in footnote 11.
[29] Klaus Zernack, *Poland und Russland. Zwei Wege in der europäischen Geschichte* (Berlin, 1994)
[30] Ludat was Professor of East European History at the University of Giessen 1956–78.

points of European history, thus enabling the integration of areas that were beyond what he saw as the cultural watershed of the Rhine and the Danube into the European family as equal members. For Ludat was, like Schlözer almost two centuries before him, convinced that there is no such thing as a chronological prerogative in cultural history.

As early as the 1950s and 1960s, Ludat prompted encounters between German, Czech and Polish historians with an interest in the history of the settlement and political structures of the Western Slavs before the colonization period.[31] This was also the very context in which Eastern German scholars developed the research on the north-western Slavs, albeit with a stronger, and successful, methodical emphasis on the archaeology and toponomastics of settlement. For Eastern German research had a strong focus on the history and culture of the Slavonic tribes within the border of the GDR ('west of the Oder and Neiße rivers', as the textbook on *The Slavs in Germany* has it),[32] as opposed to Schlesinger's Central-European approach and Zernack's macro-historical perspective on the impact of colonization on social and political structures in region of mixed settlement. This choice was aimed at giving a historical legitimacy to the new border between the GDR and Poland after World War II. The textbook on *The Slavs in Germany* was composed in the Central Institute of History and Archaeology, which had been created in 1969. It concludes with the so-called 'feudal' German expansion of the twelfth and thirteenth centuries; that is a historical process at the end of which stood the settlement and economic unity of Germans and Slavs, following Schlesinger's interpretation. Accordingly, no engagement with the settlement of German peasants east of the two rivers was required. Similarly, the focus on the history of the Slavs in the early Middle Ages triggered intensive collaboration with other disciplines such as archaeology and linguistics, especially onomastics, a process which met an increasing echo in the international scholarly community.[33]

Germania Slavica was an equally powerful notion in terms of its ability to combine different approaches to the German-Slavic history of the Middle Ages, from the classical discipline of medieval history, medieval archaeology and onomastics to art history, geography and ethnology. The notion of *Germania Slavica* has eventually also been used outside its context of origin. Danish colleagues talk about the *Dania Slavica* in order to designate their research on the Slavic presence on the Danish islands and the trade between Danes and Slavs from the Elbe region and the Baltic Sea. What has transpired in these new developments is nothing less than a radical transformation of the perception of

---

[31] The presentations of the conferences were published in *Siedlung und Verfassung der Slawen zwischen Elbe, Saale und Oder*, ed. H. Ludat (Gießen, 1960) and *Siedlung und Verfassung Böhmens in der Frühzeit*, ed. F. Graus and H. Ludat (Wiesbaden, 1967).

[32] *Die Slawen in Deutschland*, ed. J. Herrmann (Berlin, 1970, 2nd revised edn 1985).

[33] See especially the series Deutsch-slawische Forschungen zur Namenkunde und Siedlungsgeschichte, vols. 1–40 (Berlin, 1956–2003).

the Slavs in recent research. The negative prejudice against the Wendish pirates, which was coined by Saxo Grammaticus, has, for example, finally been replaced by a factual and objective observation of the evidence.[34]

One hopes that this overview of the historiography has made some of the main aspects of the German expansion to the East apparent. In conclusion, I should like to share with you my own understanding of a historical process that started long before the so-called first creation of Brandenburg. As someone who has embraced and promoted the *Germania Slavica* approach, I am keen to stress that I pay as much attention to the Slavic experience, so far as it can be reconstituted, as to the western perspective of the Frankish-Saxon-German chronicles. The difficulty of this approach arises from the fact that we lack written documents from the Slavs of the Elbe region, but rely instead on information about their neighbours, as well as archaeological evidence, toponomastic analysis and anthropological models. These interdisciplinary tools should be applied to the very first encounters between Slavonic and German-speaking peoples in order to be able to understand the process by which Slavic culture and Slavonic languages were able to spread westwards. The understanding of this process is of particular interest to me as it influenced the perceptions that the different ethnic groups had of each other. In this context, it is worth emphasizing that the Slavs of the Elbe region were not a coherent people, but that they were divided into, or formed, different groups that were partly hostile to each other, such as the Wilzes and the Obotrites in the north.[35] Some of the Slavs moved into German-speaking areas where they were employed on, and integrated into, the Frankish domains, without necessarily giving up their lifestyle or immediately converting to Christianity. Not surprisingly, therefore, it was missionaries who complained about them, notably St Boniface, who even referred to the stench that they were said to emit.[36]

Further east, the Elbe Slavs settled in small units that came under the control of the Frankish margraves. This area west of the rivers Elbe and Saale is clearly identifiable through Slavic toponyms. The rivers Elbe and Saale were the proper borders in the eyes of the Carolingians, which gives me an opportunity to clarify the situation there. *Grenze*, the German word for a border, is actually of Slavonic origin, and is attested in Middle German in the thirteenth century, although not

[34] *Zwischen Reric und Bornhöved: die Beziehungen zwischen den Dänen und ihren slawischen Nachbarn vom 9. bis ins 13. Jahrhundert: Beiträge einer internationalen Konferenz, Leipzig, 4.–6. Dezember 1997*, ed. O. Harck and C. Lübke (Stuttgart, 2001).

[35] See e.g. M. Hellmann, 'Grundsätze der Verfassungsstruktur der Wilzen' and W. H. Fritze, 'Probleme der abodritischen Stammes- und Reichsverfassung und ihrer Entwicklung vom Stammesstaat zum Herrschaftsstaat', both in *in Siedlung und Verfassung der Slawen*, pp. 103–40 and 141–219.

[36] *S. Bonifatii et Lulli epistolae*, ed. M. Tangl, MGH Epistolae Selectae 1, 2nd edn (Berlin, 1955), p. 150 no. 53.

before.[37] It would of course be misleading to conclude from the fact that the Germans used a Slavonic word, and that this word entered their vocabulary relatively late, that they did not have any notion of a border prior to the thirteenth century. If we search, instead, for a designation of the notion of border in the early medieval context in German-speaking areas, things are more complex. We encounter the words *limes* and *finis*, both commonly used in Latin texts and which referred to a dividing line between two areas, pretty much like Slavonic, but also the German *mark* (anglicized as 'march') which already used in the ninth century.

In finibus Danorum is the incipit of the description of the ethnic groups that had settled on the banks of the Danube by the Bavarian geographer of the ninth century.[38] These groups had settled on the northern banks of the Danube (*ad septentrionalem plagam Danubii*). A little further south of the 'frontiers of the Danes', we encounter a border called the *limes Saxoniae*, which was instituted by Charlemagne around 810.[39] We then find mentioned for the first time in the middle of the ninth century a *limes Sorabicus*, which refers to an area rather than a line, and was under the control of a *dux Sorabici limitis*, and which hence alludes to a *mark*.[40] The word *mark*, however, and the designation of the imperial official in command of the area as a margrave (*marchio*) are not attested before the second half of the tenth century, that is, after the integration of the Slavic areas east of the rivers Elbe and Saale into the empire by Otto I.

The location of the marks 'beyond the rivers Elbe and Saale' (*ultra Albiam et Salam*) testifies, in particular in the context of the creation of an archdiocese in Magdeburg, to a conception of borders based on rivers. This border had an ethnic-religious foundation; east of it lived Slavic people who had already been or were waiting to be converted to God (*gens Sclavorum modo ad deum conversa vel convertenda*).[41] An important step towards the conversion of the Slavs of the Elbe and the Baltic areas was taken when the area 'stretching to the Oder' was ceded by the Slavic ruler of Brandenburg Tugumir to Otto I in 940, which would attach yet another river to representations of frontier and border.[42]

[37] I. Reiter, 'Grenze', in *Handwörterbuch zur deutschen Rechtsgeschichte*, 2nd edn (Berlin, 2008, in progress) II, 541–6.
[38] See the edition in E. Herrmann, *Slawisch-germanische Beziehungen im südostdeutschen Raum* (Munich, 1965), pp. 220–1.
[39] *Magistri Adam Bremensis gesta Hammaburgensis ecclesiae pontificum*, ed. B. Schmeidler, MGH SRG 2 (Hanover 1917), ii.18; W. Budesheim, 'Der "Limes saxoniae" nach der Quelle Adams von Bremen, insbesondere in seinem südlichen Abschnitt', in *Zur slawischen Besiedlung zwischen Elbe und Oder*, ed. W. Budesheim (Lauenburg, 1992), pp. 28–43.
[40] *Annales Fuldenses sive annales regni Francorum orientalis*, ad an. 849, ed. F. Kurze, MGH SRG 7 (Hanover, 1891), p. 38.
[41] *Diplomata Ottonis I.*, ed. T. Sickel, MGH Diplomata regum et imperatorum Germaniae 1 (Hanover, 1879–1884), no. 366.
[42] *Widukindi monachi Corbeiensis rerum gestarum Saxonicarum libri tres*, ii.21, ed. P. Hirsch and H.-E. Lohmann, MGH SRG 60 (Hanover 1935), p. 85 [English translation, *Widukind*

There was, however, no clearly-defined linguistic, let alone ethnic, boundary between Slavs and Germans. The situation was, rather, characterized by linguistically and ethnically mixed areas. This was probably also true of the *limes Sorabicus*, to which I have already alluded, since the *dux Sorabici limitis* Thakulf was familiar with the language and the customs of the Slavs.[43] The entanglement between German and Slavic population was possibly the result of the immigration of small Slavic kinship groups. As late as in the tenth century Slavic families (*familiae Sclavorum*) would settle in the area of the middle Elbe and Saale rivers. They had their own villages or dwelt in wards of their own, which means in close contact with their German neighbours, the other families of colonists, *Liten* and servants. We do not, however, have any evidence of a political organization of the Slavs within the boundaries and structures of the Frankish and Ottonian Empire, beyond the level of the kinship group.[44]

While Charlemagne had not intended to expand further east, he had in fact prepared the ground for further intervention beyond the Elbe and Saale rivers. This enabled him effectively to control both the Slavic tribes and the rulers whom he had recognized, especially where a danger arose from the contact between Saxons, Danes, Obotrites and Wilzes. After the shift of the power to Bavaria in the second half of the ninth century, Frankish politics lost sight of the Slavonic tribes of the Elbe and Baltic areas of the north, and focused thereafter on the rise of the Moravians in the south-east.

It was not until the rise of the Saxon Liudolfings, the ancestors of the Ottonian dynasty, that the region between Elbe/Saale and Oder would recover its significance for imperial politics. The later king Henry I had from early on in his time as duke been interested in the territories east of the Saale. This was all the more important as the Hungarians had used this area as a starting point for their military expeditions against the Saxons. Henry's military adventures were eventually successful with a series of victorious expeditions against individual Slavic tribes from 928 and a Slavic army at Lenzen in 929 as well as his victory over the Hungarians at the battle of Riade in 933.[45]

Despite the success of his military strategy in the Slavonic areas, Henry did not really envisage the extension of his rule eastwards beyond the ancient Elbe-Saale-line, although he was ready to send a legation to collect tributes there. By

---

of Corvey, Deeds of the Saxons, by B. S. Bachrach and D. S. Bachrach (Washington, DC, 2014), pp. 81–2]; C. Lübke, *Regesten zur Geschichte der Slaven an Elbe und Oder*, 5 vols. (Berlin, 1984–8), II, no. 66.

[43] See footnote 39.

[44] C. Lübke, 'Slaven und Deutsche um das Jahr 1000', *Mediaevalia historica Bohemica* 3 (1993), 59–90.

[45] *Widukindi monachi Corbeiensis rerum gestarum Saxonicarum*, i.35–6, 38, pp. 48–57 [English trans., *Widukind, Deeds*, pp. 49–57]; Lübke, *Regesten* II, nos. 25–31, 38–9.

contrast, his son Otto I subsequently pursued both the political subordination of the Slavs east of the Elbe and also their conversion. To mention simply ecclesiastical initiatives, this led to the creation of the dioceses of Brandenburg and Havelberg in 948; the archdiocese of Magdeburg as well as a series of additional dioceses such as Merseburg in 968; and finally to the establishment of the diocese of Oldenburg (in Wagria) as a suffragan see of the archdiocese of Hamburg-Bremen. At a political-military level, these measures were complemented by donations of land east of the river Saale, and the institution of margraves whose marches duplicated the ecclesiastical map, while being based on the existing localities of the individual tribes whose income the king had awarded them. This laid the foundation for an irreversible process, or so it might have seemed, which would shift the eastern border of the Frankish Empire substantially, from the Elbe and Saale rivers eastwards as far as the River Oder. This process was, however, interrupted by the Slav uprising of 983 in the area between the middle Elbe River and the Baltic Sea, as a result of which the Elbe would remain as the imperial border for more than a century and a half.[46]

I cannot elaborate any further, as we are running out of space, on the confederation of tribes behind the uprising, the Liutizes. The culture of the Liutizes was characterized by a renaissance of pre-Christian, gentile beliefs and an acephalic political structure without overt leadership. Its resilience in the face of its Christian neighbour state is remarkable.[47] Yet in the middle of the twelfth century the last heathen area of Central Europe finally gave in to this pressure and the gentile religion of the Liutizes disappeared. The surrender of Brandenburg Castle to the hands of Margrave Albert the Bear was only one more step in the conquest of the Slav territories of the Elbe area. This process was not even exclusively German, for the Danes in the north and the Poles in the east also competed for this rich area.

The scramble for the territories and resources of the heathen Slavs of the Elbe and Baltic areas was the result of the transformation of the European economy and society. For, as cities grew, they developed a relationship of complementarity with the countryside, fuelled by an increasingly monetarized economy; and the cultivation and trading of crops, in particular, became increasingly profitable. As a consequence of this transformation, an expansion of arable land took place. During this process, colonists were hired from the West to exploit new arable land, settlements and cities were founded with new statutes, and a series of additional investments into the infrastructure took place. As early as 1108,

[46] For an overview of the events see C. Lübke, 'Die Erweiterung des östlichen Horizonts. Der Eintritt der Slaven in die europäische Geschichte im 10. Jahrhundert', in *Ottonische Neuanfänge*, ed. B. Schneidmüller (Mainz, 2001), pp. 113–26; idem, 'Magdeburg und seine östlichen Nachbarn in der Zeit des heiligen Adalbert', *Bohemia* 40 (1999), 38–53.

[47] C. Lübke, 'The Polabian Alternative: Paganism between Christian kingdoms', in *Europe around the year 1000*, ed. Przemysław Urbanczyk (Warsaw, 2001), pp. 379–89.

ecclesiastical officials from the court of Archbishop Adalgot of Magdeburg tried to mobilize the aristocracy for a crusade against the Slavs of the Elbe region.[48] It was not until the middle of the twelfth century that this movement really got underway. But by the end of this process, according to the chronicler Helmold of Bosau, 'all the country of the Slavs extending towards the Baltic Sea and the Elbe River ... was now, through the grace of God, made, as it were, one colony of the Saxons'.[49] This ethnic shift was made possible by the hiring of about 200,000 people from the West, including Flemish and Dutch peasants, who would settle in around 50,000 holdings and farms, creating a series of new villages stretching along a line from Schwerin southwards to Spandau and Dresden.[50] There, those colonists would be hired who would settle further eastwards according to the *ius theutonicum*, which conferred upon them a privileged status over that of the autochthonous Slavs. This so-called 'German law' is not to be understood as an ethnic law, but was rather a technical characterization of the legal framework according to which society was being reorganized. It therefore also extended to cities. Slavic settlers were occasionally awarded the right to use 'German law' for want of Western emigrants. In some places, different legal systems could coexist, until eventually homogeneity was achieved and the Slavs were assimilated. This process was regionally differentiated; it could take generations to complete, and its results were far from uniform. While the Baltic island of Rügen, which had first been conquered and administered by the Danes and had hardly attracted German colonists, would be Germanized in the fourteenth century, the Slavs of the Hanoverian Wendland would continue to speak a Slavonic language until the eighteenth century. As for the Sorbs of the Lausitz area, they still use their Slavonic dialect. Overall, therefore, *Germania Slavica* took shape over many centuries. I hope that I have offered a convincing argument that its significance for German history deserves far more attention than it has received hitherto.

---

[48] English translation in L. and J. Riley-Smith, *The Crusades. Idea and Reality, 1095–1274* (London, 1981), pp. 74–7.

[49] Helmold, *Chronica Slavorum*, ii.110, ed. B. Schmeidler, MGH SRG 32, 3rd edn (Hanover, 1937), p. 218; English translation, *The Chronicle of the Slavs by Helmold, Priest of Bosau*, trans. F. J. Tschan (New York, 1935), p. 281.

[50] W. Kuhn, *Vergleichende Untersuchungen zur mittelalterlichen Ostsiedlung* (Cologne and Vienna, 1973), especially the chapters 'Ostsiedlung und Bevölkerungsdichte' and 'Die Siedlerzahlen der deutschen Ostsiedlung', pp. 173–210 and 211–34; B. Zientara, 'Dzałność lokacyjna jako droga awansu społecznego w Europie środkowej XII-XIV w', *Sobótka* 1 (1981), 43–57.

PART FIVE

REWRITING MEDIEVAL RELIGION

10

DISTANCE AND DIFFERENCE: MEDIEVAL INQUISITION AS AMERICAN HISTORY

Christine Caldwell Ames

In his presidential address to the American Historical Association in 1922, Charles Homer Haskins evaluated the success of the comparatively young American discipline of history – both in comparison to, and when writing about, Europe. Research in the United States, he noted, had especially thrived 'in fields where European and American history touch'.[1] The American student of medieval heresy inquisitions might conclude, with a mix of personal self-satisfaction and professional dismay, that this eliminates her subject, one of the most notorious phenomena of the European Middle Ages. While other colonial Spanish and Portuguese territories in the so-called 'New World' imported inquisitions in order to discipline spiritually new converts to Christianity, inquisition seems to have immediately floundered in Spanish Florida.[2] And while heresy inquisitions were operable in both medieval England and (especially) France, their north-American settlements did not continue the institution. Monarchy, mission, war, trade, and slavery: all were threads, some darker than others, binding European history to its American cousin. But inquisition was a legacy, a history, that happily belonged to Europe alone.

This is only one way in which heresy inquisitions have been a node of distance and difference in medieval historiography, and particularly so in the United States. American medievalists are notoriously troubled by their geographical and genealogical distances from the territory they study. They are accustomed to various forms of difference in their work, centered as it is on a European history that has often been used for nationalist purposes, and located as they are in an America that has sometimes viewed its own national history as assiduously non- or even anti-European. More simply,

---

[1]   C. H. Haskins, 'European History and American Scholarship', *American Historical Review* 28 (1923), p. 220.
[2]   H. C. Lea, *The Inquisition in the Spanish Dependencies* (New York, 1922), pp. 457–9.

some practical challenges (languages, archives, geography and traditions) have long adhered to the American task of writing European history. At the same time, the more specialized history of heresy inquisitions in the Middle Ages – the arrest, investigation, interrogation, torture, and brutal punishment of those who 'do not fear to believe other than the Roman church teaches and preaches', as Pope Lucius III said in 1184 – have frequently symbolized for (and encouraged in) *all* scholars moral distance and difference. That is, the religious repression of inquisition – anti-individual, anti-diversity, anti-freedom – has almost uniquely marked off the medieval from the modern; darkness from enlightenment; bad religion from good. While this moral and ideological distance has existed for American and European historians alike, Americans only could reassure themselves that the inquisitions begun in earnest in the thirteenth century formed no part of their national past and its legacies.

The perspective of 'alterity' in American medieval studies is one manifestation of these venerable distances and differences. Paul Freedman and Gabrielle Spiegel have argued that their generation of American medievalists, trained in the late 1960s and 1970s, fundamentally altered medieval studies in the United States. To summarize: members of the earliest generation in the nineteenth and early-twentieth centuries were 'anti-modernist' romantics who celebrated medieval difference, appealing to the strange in medieval Europe in order to critique an unattractive modernity. Most famously, Henry Adams (1838–1918) dramatically contrasted the ethereal, spiritual otherworldliness of the Middle Ages opposed to, and far distant from, an industrialized, secularized modern age. The 'virgin' and the 'dynamo' were both sources of energy and force, but the former's kind of creative power was alien to the United States.[3] Yet the field's real entrenchment in the twentieth century was effected by historians who rejected this model, and instead depicted the Middle Ages as a site of familiarity, relevance, continuity, and rationality, a recognizable ancestor of twentieth-century America. Two of the best-placed mid-century American medievalists – Charles Homer Haskins (1870–1937) and his student Joseph Strayer (1904–87) – propagated a teleological image of a Middle Ages as both twin to, and the origin of, modernity. To Haskins and Strayer, the medieval was not the illegible, unintelligible other, but simply 'the modern' retrograded into the past. Their heavy influence in the field's growth meant that – to quote Freedman and Spiegel – 'these concerns span virtually the entire length of

---

[3]   Puritan America had forgotten the (sexual) power of women. 'In America neither Venus nor Virgin ever had value as force – at most sentiment. No American had ever been truly afraid of either ... the highest energy ever known to man ... and yet this energy was unknown to the American mind.' H. Adams, *The Education of Henry Adams* (Boston, 1918), pp. 383–4; cf. H. Adams, *Mont Saint Michel and Chartres* (Harmondsworth, 1986 edn, first privately published 1904), pp. 87–102, 137–41, 237–68.

professional medievalism in America, shaping it with notions of scientific methodology, rationality, and progressive ideology'.[4]

According to Freedman and Spiegel, this hegemony was broken by their own generation of medievalists, which abandoned that comforting linearity and familiarity. Estranged from scholarly and personal identifications with the Middle Ages and conscious rather of the fragility and loss of the past, they 'rediscovered' the alterity of the Middle Ages, its difference and strangeness. But instead of Henry Adams's beauty, this new otherness depended upon the grotesque: elements such as contagion, brutality, persecution, and stringent asceticism that could be rebranded as bodily mortification. Scholarly interests in the disgusting, irrational, and bizarre brutally amputated the Middle Ages from historians' modern present. Moreover, Freedman and Spiegel credited this attention to the grotesque – a conscious de-familiarization, de-modernization, and de-rationalization of the Middle Ages – to their generation's receptivity to postmodernism. This was, in turn, engendered partly by demographics: the women, minorities, and students of more economically and socially diverse backgrounds who newly entered the academy in the late 60s and 70s. They could not recognize their familiar in Haskins's familiar, and sought to recover their own images in the past. 'This new generation ... completely *reoriented the study* of medieval history in America, creating a new landscape of concerns that *could hardly have been anticipated* [my emphasis].'[5]

In this turn to 'alterity', both religion and religious persecution were prominent. That generation introduced the grotesque and unfamiliar into what had been a sober vision of medieval Christianity, dominated by the histories of institutional church and theology, often written by clerics. (Interestingly, then, the demographic shifts that drove the incursion of new topics and the interest in alterity – women, minorities, class – merely continued a tradition of identity

[4] P. Freedman and G. M. Spiegel, 'Medievalisms Old and New: the Rediscovery of Alterity in North American Medieval Studies', *American Historical Review* 103 (1998), 677–704 [quotation on p. 689]. This article was a conflation and development of two earlier pieces written separately by the authors: G. M. Spiegel, 'In the Mirror's Eye: the Writing of Medieval History in North America', in *The Past as Text: the Theory and Practice of Medieval Historiography* (Baltimore, 1997), pp. 57–80; P. Freedman, 'The Return of the Grotesque in Medieval Historiography', in *Historia a Debate: Medieval*, ed. C. Barros (Santiago de Compostela, 1995), pp. 9–19. See too the response by E. A. R. Brown, 'Another Perspective on Alterity and the Grotesque', in *Women Medievalists and the Academy*, ed. J. Chance (Madison WI, 2005), pp. 915–32.
[5] Spiegel, *Past as Text*, p. 71; cf. Freedman and Spiegel, 'Medievalisms Old and New', pp. 693, 702. These 'new groups' are defined more specifically elsewhere: 'In addition to the entrance of women and blacks into the American academy for the first time, there was also a new wave of participation among classes and what, for lack of a better word, can be called ethnic groups, among them Jews...constituting a clientele whose interests needed to be addressed'. Spiegel, *Past as Text*, p. 78.

investments in narrative.) Topics now included affective spirituality, mysticism, visionary women, severe asceticism, miracle, and ecstasy.[6] Alterity also entered the study of medieval religion in another, doubled, way, as a view of the Roman church as darkly creating its own 'others' sparked work on dissidence, minorities, repression, and violence. This reflected the influence within medieval studies generally of R. I. Moore's thesis of high-medieval Europe as a 'persecuting society', identifying and then excluding various minorities for purposes of state and clerical power. The church was one instance of institutionalized repression. Heresy was in this model two different things: a sympathetic form of dissent, or a convenient stereotype created by and for power.[7] Regardless, its repression through inquisition was emblematic of anti-individualism, cruelty and fear. To Moore, heretics were perhaps the most important of these new minorities, and Freedman and Spiegel claimed 'the [world] of inquisitorial repression' as one of the 'vividly new postmodern topics in current medieval historiography'. Evocative of earlier anti-modernism, it 'reassert[ed] an older tradition of the grotesque, intolerant character of the epoch, a dark irrationality... [marking] a radical turn in contemporary historical approaches'.[8]

I would like to consider here two genealogies of American scholarly alterity in which heresy and inquisition play featured roles, and which soften our sense of that turn as either 'radical' or unanticipated. Through these genealogies, we see that the scholarly premise of 'otherness' is heir to nuanced and complex imaginings of religious phenomena as markers of past and present, distance and difference. These genealogies remind us that the past's strangeness depends upon how we construct the present, and that American notions of distance and difference from medieval Europe are likewise inseparable from Americans' notions of their own context. A construction of medieval Europe – its religion, its persecutions – as 'other' is only operable within an American religious past and present that is neither bodily nor persecutory. What these genealogies ultimately reinforce, then, is medievalists' enduring difficulty in abandoning self-reflexivity in constructions of the European Middle Ages, and in abandoning our assumptions about what religion is and does.

---

[6] See A. Matter, 'The Future of the Study of Medieval Christianity,' in *The Past and Future of Medieval Studies*, ed. J. Van Engen (Notre Dame IN, 1994), pp. 166–77.

[7] We might also note that some modern scholars of heresy see it as a familiar ancestor of religious dissent in the present, e.g. L. Burnham, *So Great a Light, So Great a Smoke: the Beguin Heretics of Languedoc* (Ithaca NY, 2008).

[8] Freedman and Spiegel, 'Medievalisms Old and New', p. 693. They did briefly consider that their generation's skepticism about state and institutional power could position medieval persecution as 'darkly familiar'. But their final location of inquisition studies within 'alterity' nevertheless assigned it to irrationality, and to that lost past. On persecution, inquisition, and heresy, influenced by Foucault and Moore, 'Medievalisms Old and New', pp. 698–9.

Henry Charles Lea: for a time, he lives in it

Complicating Freedman and Spiegel's insistence upon a 'complete reorientation', 'radical turn', and 'rediscovery' of the medieval grotesque was that their sketch of the early field largely omitted previous scholarly interest in inquisition and heresy. This meant only brief reference was made to Henry Charles Lea (1825–1909), the greatest American historian of heresy inquisitions.[9] The son of a wealthy Philadelphia publisher, Lea combined his studies with a career in the family firm until he suffered a nervous breakdown from overwork. After ceasing to write for a restorative decade, a recovered Lea produced multiple, towering works of medieval grotesquerie, beginning in 1866 with *Superstition and Force: Essays on the Wager of Law, the Wager of Battle, the Ordeal, and Torture*.[10] This was followed (among many other books) in 1887 by the three-volume *A History of the Inquisition of the Middle Ages*; then by *A History of the Inquisition of Spain* (1906-08); and the posthumous *Materials toward a History of Witchcraft* (1939). Although Lea never held an academic post – referring diffidently to his numerous publications as 'what in English we call my hobby' – he was in the full swing of the then burgeoning historical profession in the United States, serving as president of the American Historical Association in 1903.[11]

Lea was a pioneer in tackling the practical problem of the American medievalist's access to European archives. Lea did no research in Europe. Very famously – and unthinkably today – Lea's correspondents in European libraries sent him both copies of, and original, manuscripts. These deliveries were so well

---

[9]   Spiegel's *Past as Text* footnoted Lea as 'the most important writer of medieval history before Haskins', but still exempted him from her genealogy because he 'was not a professor but a publisher'. She did not make explicit that the topics of Lea's 'important work' fit tidily under a rubric of alterity, nor did she cite him in a historiography of heresy. Spiegel, *Past as Text*, pp. 232 n. 17, 237 n. 55. This praise was repeated in 'Medievalisms Old and New', p. 681, which noted that Lea's depiction of the Middle Ages 'asserted its radical difference from the world of the nineteenth century'. As we see, this was partly true. On the professionalization of history as a discipline in the United States, see P. Novick, *That Noble Dream: The 'Objectivity Question' and the American Historical Profession* (Cambridge, 1988), pp. 47–60; for a sketch including Europe, see M. Bentley, 'Introduction: Approaches to Modernity: Western Historiography since the Enlightenment', in *Companion to Historiography*, ed. M. Bentley (London, 1997), pp. 442–9.

[10] E. Sculley Bradley, *Henry Charles Lea: a Biography* (Philadelphia, 1931); E. Peters, *Inquisition* (Berkeley, CA, 1988), pp. 287–92. See also E. Peters, 'Henry Charles Lea (1825–1909)', in *Medieval Scholarship: Biographical Studies on the Formation of a Discipline*, vol. I: *History*, eds. H. Damico and J. B. Zavadil (New York, 1995), 89–99.

[11] It was common, in the nascent discipline, for a non-professional to serve as president of the AHA, which was founded in 1884. It was not until 1928 that the presidency was normally held by PhD-holding university professors. Novick, *That Noble Dream*, p. 49. *Writing the Inquisition in Europe and America: the Correspondence between Henry Charles Lea and Paul Fredericq*, ed. J. Tollebeek (Brussels, 2004), p. 65.

known that Lord Acton's review of *History of the Inquisition* quoted Benjamin Disraeli as complaining that some borrowed manuscripts never came back to England, prompting Lea to deny this rather woundedly in the *English Historical Review*.[12] Yet the archive problem was also an existential one, reminding the American scholar of the kinds of distance that could not be covered by the post. In Europe, the study of medieval inquisition had benefited from the state's role in promoting inquisition history as its own institutional history. For example, what remains one of the most important collections of unpublished inquisition materials, the Doat Collection of the Bibliothèque Nationale de France, owes its origins to Jean de Doat, who spent much of the 1660s touring southern France with a passel of scribes, copying manuscripts. Doat's patron was Jean-Baptiste Colbert, who spent an enormous sum — over fifty thousand *livres tournois* — hoping to gather evidence of the French crown's claim to territory that had been absorbed by the kingdom in the late thirteenth century, as part of the settlement of the Albigensian Crusade in 1229.[13] More immediately comparable to Lea was the travel of his French colleague Charles Molinier, who before Lea's *History of the Inquisition* was published sniffed that the idea of such a comprehensive history was a 'chimera'.[14] While Lea was mail-ordering manuscripts at his own expense, Molinier was sent in 1884 by Armand Fallières, Minister of Public Instruction (and future president) of France's Third Republic, to investigate in Italy 'documents relative to the history of the inquisition'. Molinier spent months seeking sources in Milan, Lucca, Florence, and Rome. (The reason for the commission is unclear, but perhaps it was related to the programme of Fallières's predecessor, Jules Ferry, of laicisation in French public schools?)[15] What was national, institutional origin and ancestry to France could never be so in the United States. In this strict sense, the inquisition was insistently not American history. In Lea's career, identity and origin were a more profound layer of difference superimposed upon the practical challenges of accessing archives.

But other things closed the distance. And Lea offers a kind of past/present 'alterity' to which we should attend in understanding the interpenetrating constructions of inquisition and religion in the making of medieval history. To

---

[12]   Lord Acton, 'Review of Henry Charles Lea, *History of the Inquisition of the Middle Ages*,' *English Historical Review* 3 (1888), 773; H. C. Lea, 'To the Editor of the Historical Review,' *English Historical Review* 4 (1889), 191.

[13]   For comparison, when France sold the Louisiana Territory to the United States in 1803, the agreement's formal conversion rate was one US dollar to five *livres* and eight *sous tournois*. We can roughly (if anachronistically) estimate Doat's costs at about $10,000.

[14]   Acton, 'Review', p. 774.

[15]   When Molinier finally submitted the report in 1886, the minister was René Goblet. C. Molinier, *Études sur quelques manuscrits des bibliothèques d'Italie concernant l'inquisition et les croyances hérétiques du XIIe au XVIIe siècle. Rapport à M. le Ministre de l'Instruction Publique sur une Mission Exécutée en Italie de février à avril 1885* (Paris, 1888).

Lea, the application of a 'scientific method' to history mandated careful research and documentation from the archives, but also a carefully cultivated position of impartiality. He took pains to avoid the 'sensationalism' he believed had impaired previous treatments of the medieval church, ignoring appeals from the – in his term – 'Protestant cranks' who sought more confessionally fervid treatments of inquisition and torture. Lea's presidential address to the American Historical Association in 1903, 'Ethical Values in History', advocated a remarkably complex historical perspective – blending progressivism, contextualisation, distaste, understanding, and relativism – that put past, present, and future in delicate relationship. Lea's talk constituted a response to the 'Lecture on the Study of History' presented by Lord Acton at Cambridge in 1895. As mentioned above, Acton – a prominent English Catholic, friend of Gladstone, and Regius Professor of Modern History at Cambridge – had reviewed Lea's *History of the Middle Ages* in 1888, and was maddened by the fact that 'Mr Lea has a malicious pleasure in baffling inquiry into the principle of his judgments'.[16] Acton's Cambridge lecture, on the other hand, laid bare his own principles, insisting that historians judge their subjects by the (ostensibly self-evident) 'final maxim that governs your own lives'.[17] Acton was an explicit critic of religious persecution, whether medieval or modern, and eight years before his Cambridge lecture had insisted that inquisition 'is the breaking point, the article of their system by which [medieval popes] stand or fall'.[18]

   In his presidential address, Lea disdained Acton's blithe advice. He rejected as methodological practice and principle the historian's assumption of 'a fixed and unalterable standard of morality' now realized in the present and judiciously applied to the past, arguing rather that morality was historically determined and located. There was no 'absolute and invariable moral code by which the men of all ages and... degrees of civilization are to be tried and convicted or acquitted ... [there may be] a universal and inflexible standard of morals ... but

---

[16] Acton, 'Review', p. 786.
[17] Lord Acton, *A Lecture on the Study of History* (London, 1895), p. 63.
[18] 'Indeed it is the most conspicuous fact in the history of the mediaeval papacy, just as the later Inquisition, with what followed, is the most conspicuous and characteristic fact in the history and record of the modern papacy. A man is hanged not because he can or cannot prove his claim to virtues, but because it can be proved that he has committed a particular crime. That one action overshadows the rest of his career. It is useless to argue that he is a good husband or a good poet. The one crime swells out of proportion to the rest. We all agree that Calvin was one of the greatest writers, many think him the best religious teacher, in the world. But that one affair of Servetus outweighs the nine folios, and settles, by itself, the reputation he deserves. So with the mediaeval Inquisition and the Popes that founded it and worked it. That is the breaking point, the article of their system by which they stand or fall.' Lord Acton, *Acton-Creighton Correspondence*, Letter 1 (5 April 1887) <http://oll.libertyfund.org/titles/2254>.

the history of mankind fails to reveal it'.[19] The historian who followed Acton's advice was anachronistic, naive in proclaiming a morality unchanged by time or human situation, unjust towards his subjects, arrogant. Lea did not then reserve judgment but historicized it, encouraging colleagues to acknowledge an intentionality dependent upon context, 'mak[ing] the human conscience the standard of conduct. If a man does wrong, conscientiously believing it to be right, he is justified before God'.[20] (This resembled medieval ecclesiastics' definition of heresy, which depended upon stubbornness and intentionality.) Moralizing distance had to dissolve as the historian entered the ethical world of the past: 'for a time, he is living in it.'[21]

Medieval inquisition then might be evil to the modern eye, but it was not so with any kind of theological or moral absolutism, and it was not irrational. Lea's purple passages impugning inquisition are notorious. It was, for instance, an 'invention of demons', and he concluded *History of the Inquisition* with the hardly apologetic lines that 'the judgment of impartial history must be that the Inquisition was the monstrous offspring of mistaken zeal, utilized by selfish greed and lust of power to smother the higher aspirations of humanity and stimulate its baser appetites'.[22] Yet while this might recall precisely those 'Protestant cranks' he disdained, Lea insisted that a historicized inquisition was a reasonable and pious response to heresy within the framework of medieval orthodox Christianity and its notions of salvation, community, and punishment. Lea's AHA address was chiefly devoted to the religious persecution of Philip II of Spain: If the character and mentality of Philip's contemporary Christianity had produced an environment of repression as piety, the king could not now be condemned for realizing it perfectly. (We might note as an interesting comparison to Henry Adams's romantic contrast of 'the Virgin and the dynamo' – inspired by Adams' visit to the Palais des machines at the Exposition Universelle in Paris in 1900 – that a year after Lea spoke on 'Ethical Values in History' in 1903, the modern was again defined and celebrated at the World's Fair in St Louis. This American city was named after a medieval-European king who, as Lea pointed out in his presidential address, prescribed the sword for unrepentant heresy.)

What legacy, then, did Henry Charles Lea provide for a much later American generation finding 'otherness' in medieval Europe? Obviously, his research treated precisely those 'grotesque' topics that seemed distant to nineteenth-century America's benign 'scientific' rationalism. Yet Lea's wish to avoid polemic, and to contextualize morality, imbued his work with a peculiar perspective of alterity. This was neither Henry-Adams-esque romanticism nor mid twentieth century familiarity and origin – inquisition was indeed a mark of

---

[19]   H. C. Lea, 'Ethical Values in History', *American Historical Review* 9 (1904), 234.
[20]   Lea, 'Ethical Values in History', p. 236.
[21]   Lea, 'Ethical Values in History', p. 237.
[22]   H. C. Lea, *A History of the Inquisition of the Middle Ages*, 3 vols. (New York, 1888), III, 650.

otherness, demonstrating that neither humanity nor Christianity had reached a certain point of evolution. While he carefully owned that Dominic Guzmán and advocates of inquisition were led by a 'sense of duty', Lea explained that in the 'cruel' Middle Ages 'passions were fiercer, convictions stronger ... [people] habitually looked on human suffering with indifference. The industrial spirit, which has so softened modern manners and modes of thought, was as yet hardly known'.[23] Claiming that inquisition was rational in context did not preclude dismissing that context as an unmourned past. But Lea's finely tuned perspective nevertheless recognized that this past had its own rationality and piety, immune to the present's judgment.

Again, this was exactly the complexity – the contrariness? the plain inconsistency? – that had maddened Lord Acton. And we might wonder if Lea was liable to Jonathan Z. Smith's charge that moral relativism in analysing the past obviates the scholar's duty to translate it and to make it intelligible.[24] But we find a resolution, perhaps unexpectedly, in Lea's unfinished present. Crucially, we must reverse here the perspective of past and present, and note how Lea viewed the modern, always an inseparable (if often neglected) component of 'alterity'.[25] If Lea's work was progressive, it nevertheless assumed a modernity that was still too infected by the pre-modern. This meant American and European Catholicism, certainly, which to Lea could disconcertingly appear as the medieval persisting into the present. For instance, one of Lea's many European correspondents was J. J. I. von Döllinger, professor of church history and scholar of the Eucharist, the papacy, and heresy. (Döllinger was also a friend and teacher of Acton.) But Döllinger was also a modern heretic. A Catholic priest, Döllinger was excommunicated in 1871 for denying papal infallibility, proclaimed by the First Vatican Council in 1870 amid the unification of Italy and Pope Pius IX's anti-liberal efforts. In 1886, Lea informed Döllinger that he would donate money to the Old Catholics, the dissenting movement against papal infallibility spurred in part by Döllinger's excommunication.[26]

---

[23] Lea, *A History of the Inquisition of the Middle Ages*, I, 234.

[24] Jonathan Z. Smith, 'The Devil in Mr. Jones', in his *Imagining Religion: From Babylon to Jonestown* (Chicago, 1982), pp. 102–20.

[25] Lee Patterson has, for example, critiqued medievalists' unreflective embrace of alterity: 'To define understanding as the observation of otherness is to assume that the self that does the observing need hardly be taken into account; since the object of study is, by definition, an object, then the subjectivity of the observer is irrelevant. The relationship is entirely technical: medieval culture is an enigma to be solved rather than a living past with claims upon the present.' L. Patterson, 'On the Margin: Postmodernism, Ironic History, and Medieval Studies', *Speculum* 65 (1990), 87–108.

[26] E.-A. Ryan, 'The Religion of Henry Charles Lea', *Mélanges Joseph de Ghellinck, tome II: Moyen Age Époques Moderne et Contemporaine* (Gembloux, 1951), p. 1049. For Döllinger, see *The Oxford Dictionary of the Christian Church*, ed. E. L. Cross, 3rd edn by E. A. Livingstone (Oxford, 2005), p. 499.

But Catholicism alone did not stain, or de-modernize, the present. Other institutions – Protestant ones, American ones – were also enemies of liberty. Lea was active locally and nationally against political corruption, party machines, and local bosses.[27] His AHA address recalled that while Philip II was cruel, corrupt, and deceitful, one should not forget 'the duplicity and the contempt for human rights which have continued to mark the career of statesmen from that time to this'.[28] The chronic, and then-worsening, weaknesses of American democracy were instructive about the Middle Ages, and more narrowly about the experience of medieval heresy and inquisition: about the power of institutions to compel, to control, and to be corrupted; about the limits and looseness of the law; and about how people responded to institutional decadence through dissent and action.

More importantly, Lea well knew that even in progressive nineteenth-century America, religious difference could spur violence against minorities. Lea believed that the Catholicism, and the Europe, of his own day were bound to the history of inquisition as American Protestantism was not. But Lea's AHA address nevertheless reminded his fellow historians that there was nothing uniquely medieval, or Catholic, about religious persecution: 'the Massachusetts law of … 1658 under which Quakers were put to death in Boston Common suffices … to show that this conception of public duty was not confined to one race or to one confession of faith'.[29] An American 'public duty' to eradicate religious minorities had not ended in the seventeenth century. Lea was, perhaps surprisingly for those who have read his work, the son of a Quaker father and a Catholic mother, and was raised as an Episcopalian. In 1844 the young Lea, armed with a gun, had guarded Saint Patrick's Church in Philadelphia during the 'Native American' riots, directed against the city's Irish Catholics, which saw multiple deaths and the burning of two Catholic churches. If 'passions were fierce' in medieval Europe, they could still be so in an America, where only (white) Protestants were 'native' – and in which the chastening, persecutory template of early Puritanism had persisted, and perhaps worsened, amid greater religious and ethnic diversity. From another direction, we can note that Lea was in his prime during the American Civil War, and this had been a stark instance of moral, religious, and biblical relativism, collapsing into an unparalleled American experience of violence and destruction. The war exemplified how the Bible could produce radically opposed and virulently competitive Christian narratives of God's opinions on slavery, killing, the state, and coercion: in the north, abolitionism

---

[27] On this, see J. M. O'Brien, 'Henry Charles Lea: the Historian as Reformer', *American Quarterly* 19 (1967), 104–13; Lea to Fredericq (1905), in *Writing the Inquisition*, pp. 91–2.

[28] Lea, 'Ethical Values in History', p. 241.

[29] Lea, 'Ethical Values in History', p. 240.

and just war; in the south, defences of slavery as biblically compatible and, after 1865, a near-divinized Lost Cause.[30]

Nearly sixty years after the 'Native American' riots, and after his major work on premodern inquisition and torture, Lea's AHA address included some subtle but pointed admissions: 'We of to-day are not lacking in religious convictions, though we are *learning the lesson* [my italics] of toleration...' The West had followed Christ 'in theory' for two millenia, 'yet only within a century or two has there been any serious effort to reduce them to practice ... more significant in its *failures* [my italics] than its successes'. Refusing to judge persecution of the past both highlighted, and helped to end, persecution in the present:

> This is not only the scientific method applied to history, but it ennobles the historian's labors by rendering them contributory to that progress which adds to the sum of human happiness and fits mankind for a higher standard of existence. The study of the past in this spirit may perhaps render us *more impatient of the present* [my italics], and yet more hopeful of the future.

To apply Acton's 'maxim that governs your own lives' to past Christians was, simply, to over-credit the Christianity of the present.[31] Lea's address asked, 'If Elijah is praised for slaying ... 450 prophets of Ba'al [*I Kings* 18:40], how is Philip to be condemned for merely utilizing larger opportunities in the same spirit?' The audience surely did not know – as Lea did – that this biblical allusion was common in medieval inquisitorial texts, used in papal bulls and anti-heretical treatises to justify persecuting and executing heretics.[32] But both Lea and his (probably overwhelmingly Protestant) colleagues were indeed aware that the prophet-slaying Elijah was still there being praised in the Old Testament of 1903, just as he had been in 1593 and 1323. It was not just that Philip's persecution could (and should) be understood in terms of a religious mentality and tradition that embraced violence; it was also that even the most progressive and moderate American Protestant was an equal inheritor of that tradition. Biblical violence was the legacy of any Christian, regardless of any textual criticism or interpretation. The citation confronted Lea's colleagues more subtly with the tradition, traceable to the Puritans, that had posited America as a continuation of the providential history that had begun with the (idolater-slaying) Hebrews.[33]

---

[30] C. R. Wilson, *Baptized in Blood: the Religion of the Lost Cause, 1865–1920*, 2nd edn (Athens GA, 2009).

[31] Lea, 'Ethical Values in History', pp. 235–6, 245.

[32] Lea, 'Ethical Values in History', pp. 238–9. On these biblical allusions, see my *Righteous Persecution: Inquisition, Dominicans, and Christianity in the Middle Ages* (Philadelphia, 2009), pp. 190–8.

[33] Visible, famously, in John Winthrop, *A Modell of Christian Charity*, available at https://history.hanover.edu/texts/winthmod.html.

Lea's perspective was undeniably progressive. But Lea's progressivism, acknowledging failure and looking to the future, realized that the ideal always ran ahead, perhaps unreachable. This was a different kind of 'loss' and 'trauma' than that experienced by Freedman and Spiegel's generation – but loss it was, likewise colouring historical analysis. As Lea reminded his hearers, Acton's confidence of moral rectitude would be replicated by 'every succeeding' age, which consequently from its future post would look back disapprovingly upon the ethical complexion and political actions of Lea and Acton's nineteenth-century world.[34] And it has indeed looked so.

Henry Charles Lea's career demonstrates then that the 'grotesque' slate was not quite blank before the scholarly coming of age of Freedman and Spiegel's generation. More importantly, Lea bedevils any link of intolerance and irrationality, while putting past and present in more complicated relation than 'origin' or 'other' – a relation that crucially included Lea's clarity about modern Christianity, and about his modern United States. Present and past, distance and difference, were entangled in how 'the American' (as Acton called him) wrote the history of heresy and inquisition. To Lea, a resurgent late nineteenth-century Catholicism in the United States had, in a sense, joined forces with what Lea recognized as an American-Protestant history of religious intolerance. Religious persecution was, worrisomely, not unfamiliar. Medieval heresy and inquisitions taught lessons in part because their dangers were not fully past. Much like Lea importing manuscripts from Europe – that is, closing the distance between American historian and European history from an unexpected direction – he closed a more profound analytical and moral distance by drawing his own present nearer to a medieval past of intolerance.

Lea's influence on subsequent American scholarship of inquisition and heresy was heavy: both through *History of the Inquisition*, and through his relationship with Charles Homer Haskins, who wrote a memorial to Lea upon his death. To Haskins, Lea's books 'constitute the most considerable product of any American historian in the European field'. He praised Lea as a 'European' kind of historian, but also noted that 'his career as a man of affairs who trained himself to be an historian was characteristically American'.[35] Haskins followed Lea in spirit and tone in his own (more cursory) attention to heresy and inquisition, arguing: 'That a heretic who persisted in his heresy should be burnt, as a fitting preparation for his fate in the world to come, was to be expected in the thirteenth century.'[36] In 1971, Haskins's student Joseph Strayer wrote his own book on the anti-

---

[34] Lea, 'Ethical Values in History', p. 234.

[35] C. H. Haskins, 'Tribute to Henry Charles Lea', *Proceedings of the Massachusetts Historical Society* 43 (1909), 186; C. H. Haskins, 'European History and American Scholarship' [above, note 1], p. 221.

[36] C. H. Haskins, 'Robert le Bougre and the Beginnings of the Inquisition in Northern France', *American Historical Review* 7 (1902), 437–57 and *ibid.*, 631–52; C. H. Haskins,

heretical Albigensian Crusade (1209–1229). Although Freedman and Spiegel did not discuss these interests in presenting Haskins and Strayer as apostles of the familiar, we should note that Strayer indeed saw medieval religious persecution as a familiar ancestor to modern states, but to repressive totalitarian regimes rather than to constitutional democracies: 'Modern totalitarian governments have made few innovations; they have simply been more efficient.'[37]

Strayer's book on the Albigensian Crusade belonged to a new fashion of heresy and inquisition studies that began in the late 1960s, just as Freedman and Spiegel's generation entered the academy as students. This takes us to our second genealogy of an American scholarly perspective of alterity. It begins in Europe, but delivers us with startling efficiency back to the United States, and to that generational embrace of a lost, strange past.

The Cathars Were Right

On Easter Sunday, 1950, mass at the Cathedral of Notre Dame in Paris was disrupted by four young men. One of these was Michel Mourre, tonsured and dressed in a rented habit of the Dominican order, who leapt upon the altar after the *Credo* and read a 'sermon', shouting that God was dead. The rest of his speech was purposely drowned out by the organist, and the cathedral's guards attacked the protestors with drawn swords, bloodying one in the process. Running out of Notre Dame towards the Seine, Mourre (who blessed the congregation during his escape) and his accomplices eluded lynching by the scandalized congregation only by surrendering to police custody. Mourre was held for repeated psychiatric examinations, which observed among other supposed idiosyncrasies his 'ability ... to travel in an instant through various epochs'.[38]

If the scene reads as near-slapstick, it was not so to its actors. Mourre's career, including this episode, was a performance of themes still lively in medieval scholarship: heresy and Catholic orthodoxy, inquisition, dissent, bonds between state and church, the links between religious mentality, sentiment and psychology, even the Dominican order, that religious order most closely attached to heresy inquisitions as practitioners and theorists. According to Mourre, in a memoir written a few months later, the 'situation' at Notre Dame resulted from a fervent religious passion, alchemized into hate and disillusionment at the moribund Catholicism of the twentieth-century present. The teenaged Mourre had been baptized into a Catholicism that specifically recollected for

'The Heresy of Echard the Baker of Rheims', in his *Studies in Mediaeval Culture* (Oxford, 1929), pp. 245–55, at p. 254.
[37] Haskins, 'Tribute to Henry Charles Lea', pp. 183–8; J. R. Strayer, *The Albigensian Crusade* (New York, 1971).
[38] G. Marcus, *Lipstick Traces: A Secret History of the Twentieth Century* (Cambridge MA, 1990), p. 283.

him two things he conflated: French national identity and the Middle Ages. He
then flirted repeatedly, and impotently, with joining the Order of Preachers –
finally leaving its novitiate in bitter complaint against an order that, he believed,
had abandoned its foundational apostolate (to those tempted by heresy and/
or spiritually abandoned by lax clergy), just as the larger 'church dormant' had
skulked away from a world that, faced with too many meretricious alternatives,
needed it badly. Mourre craved a militant church fearlessly confronting all
claims to truth proffered by modern intellectual and spiritual movements,
confident it alone possessed the truth, proclaimed with vigour and without
embarrassment. Mourre maintained the spiritual value and practical imperative
of zealotry and fanaticism, wishing to 'create fanatics about Eternity and prove
that the craze for Eternity was not yet dead among the people of the West'.[39] The
Middle Ages were a shining site of appeal for that fanaticism, when awareness
of the terrible stakes of God's power prompted a wholly comprehensible and
welcome persecution, by men like Dominic Guzmán, of those shunning divine
and ecclesiastical authority. Debating in cafés, Mourre praised the madness of
Don Quixote, 'being careful, however, to include a parenthetical argument in
favour of the Inquisition, and try[ing] to make our benevolent audience regret
its disappearance'.[40] Yet to Mourre, even medieval heretics were more laudable
than his modern contemporaries; if poisonously wrong, they at least paid more
attention to God than to the movies. Madness was the devotional legacy of the
Middle Ages, a pulsing alternative to the bland, cool emptiness of liberal sanity.
Tolerance, pacifism, and democracy – supposedly superior hallmarks of the
modern West – were to Mourre shameful badges of an atheism that the Catholic
Church brooked with passive indolence.

This is Freedman and Spiegel's secular present versus dark, irrational past:
inverted in its worth and attractions. But the elision of past and present that
marked Mourre's vision – offered by a psychologist as evidence of mental
imbalance – differs importantly from their sense of loss. This temporal collapse,
in which the past drove Mourre's dissatisfaction in a present with which it
co-existed, allowed him to honour a surpassing eternity while also attending to
historically located phenomena. Travelling from the Dominican community in
Montpellier to the order's original house in Toulouse, Mourre mused that, 'this
sunlit road we were on had been trodden countless times by Saint Dominic.
Poor Dominic, barefoot, despised, insulted, wounded by the stones of the little
heretics ... delivering souls from evil ... I felt we might even see him round the
next bend in the road.'[41] The Middle Ages were neither origin (implying the past
and development) nor other (implying difference), but a model that was both

[39] M. Mourre, *In Spite of Blasphemy* (London, 1953).
[40] Mourre, *In Spite of Blasphemy*, pp. 115–16
[41] Mourre, *In Spite of Blasphemy*, p. 133.

absent, and curiously alive, in the present. Like the office of inquisition itself, the medieval period was there to be *reinstalled* in the European present. The distance of time and ostensible 'progress' was erased, just like the distance erased by Mourre's walks across Languedoc. The Inquisition could never be as immediate to Henry Charles Lea, a source probably of both the American's regret and his relief.

Michel Mourre drifted off into calm obscurity. But his confusion of past and present, sameness and strangeness – with inquisition and heresy as emblems – was inherited, if revised, by some cultural revolutionaries who heralded the interrupted mass at Notre Dame as their 'founding crime'.[42] The Situationist International, formed in the late 1950s in Paris, doubted that upheavals in political power and structure alone could ameliorate living in a deadening consumerist, urban culture. They advocated the disclosure and destruction of 'the spectacle', or the mechanizing, enervating totality of human culture erected by capitalism. This happened through the calculated situation: a moment of ridiculousness, of dramatic intervention, like that famous interruption of the mass.

Like Michel Mourre, the Situationists read the medieval past as a site of similarity, and as a model for responding, to modern culture. Yet unlike Mourre, they tended to find that model in heresy, rather than in its ecclesiastical persecution. And heresy was even less banished from the modern world than was inquisition. In their newsletters, the Situationists frequently recalled medieval heresy: the atom bomb validated the supposed anti-materialism of the Cathars (the chief targets of the early Dominican mission, as their lordly supporters were of the Albigensian Crusade). ('The Cathars were Right'.) The mystical, antinomian heretics of the Free Spirit and the strict-poverty movement of the Waldenses were fellow libertine advocates of destruction and of freedom from oppressive society. Conversely, the 'Best News of the Week' in one 1954 newsletter was the death in a car crash of Dominican Master General Emmanuel Suarez, who earlier that year had disciplined the theologians and medievalists M.-D. Chenu and Yves Congar by removing them from their teaching posts. Both Chenu and Congar were suspect to the Holy Office – the modern progeny of the medieval inquisition – for their embrace of the anti-scholastic *nouvelle théologie* and their support of the worker-priest movement.[43] The Situationist leader Guy

---

[42] Mourre and his Notre Dame accomplices were attached to the Lettrist movement. One of these, Serge Berna, was a founder of the Lettrist International, which evolved into the Situationist International.

[43] 'Les Cathares avaient raison': *Potlatch* 5 (20 July 1954), available at http://www.cddc.vt.edu/sionline/presitu/potlatch5.html#Anchor-The-56568. This meant, then, believing entirely as medieval reality what some scholars would now view as clerical constructions. 'All is Revealed: These are the people who are known as 'Lettrists,' as others were known as 'Jacobins' or 'Franciscans,'' *Potlatch* 3 (6 July 1954) – the same issue as the report about Suarez. On the supposed heresy of the 'Free Spirit,' see R.

Debord was explicitly influenced by British historian Norman Cohn's *Pursuit of the Millennium* (1957), a study of dissenting and millenial popular movements in the Middle Ages, which was translated into French in 1962 with the provocative (and Mourre-esque!) title *Les Fanatiques de l'Apocalypse: Courants millénaristes révolutionnaires du XIe au XVIe siècle avec une postface sur le XXe siècle.* Yet Debord departed from Cohn, and echoed Mourre, by conflating past and present: 'modern revolutionary hopes are not an irrational sequel to the religious passion of millenarianism. The exact opposite is true: millenarianism, the expression of a revolutionary class struggle speaking the language of religion for the last time, was already a modern revolutionary tendency, lacking only the consciousness of being historical.' The past was a 'sequel' to the present, not its origin. Medieval popular movements of heresy and millennialism were the compatriots, and not the ancestors, of modern dissent, even if time had finally disposed of 'the language of religion'. [44]

To return to the United States: the Situationists famously enjoyed their greatest success with the student uprising in Paris in 1968. Their influence was most visible in graffiti disseminating their slogans in the city: *Ici spectacle de la contestation. Contestons le spectacle; La culture est l'inversion de la vie; Il est interdit d'interdire.*[45] At the beginning of her career, a young American professor posted on her bulletin board one of these Situationist slogans, *toute vue des choses qui n'est pas étrange est fausse.* This was Caroline Walker Bynum – whom we can fairly describe as the most influential medieval religious historian in the United States – and she has explained that the slogan articulated her desire 'to jolt my ... readers into encounter with a past that is unexpected and strange... whose lineaments are not what we first assume'. Seeking later to synthesize her concerns about the historical profession, she 'returned to this wall slogan. Could a penchant for the strange help us avoid ... a presentist flattening of the past, or ... the danger of being trapped by the multiple readings of texts open to – but, we may fear, reflective only of – us after the linguistic turn?' Bringing us full circle, Freedman and Spiegel saw Bynum's inspiration by this slogan as emblematic of their generation's penchant for alterity in interpreting the Middle Ages.[46] It

---

E. Lerner, *The Heresy of the Free Spirit in the Later Middle Ages* (Berkeley CA, 1972). For Congar (1904–95), who was later re-habilitated, and appointed a cardinal shortly before his death, *Oxford Dictionary of the Christian Church*, p. 401.

[44] Former Situationist leader Raoul Vaneigem later wrote several books on medieval heresy: *Le Mouvement du libre-esprit* (Paris, 1986); *La Résistance au christianisme: les hérésies des origines au XVIIIe siècle* (Paris, 1993), and the *Que sais-je?* volume on heresy, *Les hérésies* (Paris, 1996).

[45] *Les murs ont la parole: journal mural mai 68*, ed. J. Besançon (Paris, 1968).

[46] This piece of graffiti, from the Galerie Lettres at the Sorbonne, was attributed by its writer to the poet Paul Valéry (1871–1945). *Les murs ont la parole*, 100. C. Walker Bynum, 'Wonder,' *American Historical Review* 102 (1997), 1–2; Freedman and Spiegel, 'Medievalisms Old and New,' p. 702 n. 84.

signalled the 'the inaccessibility of that absent other,' the inescapable loss of the past that demanded, in its hopelessness about recovering history as it really was, an optics of the strange.[47]

But as we have seen, that generation's perspective of strangeness, the grotesque, and the loss of the past was not quite that of the Situationists who popularized the slogan, nor of the young Catholic fanatic who had earlier inspired *them*. For these genealogical ancestors, the present was indispensible. Distance was easily crossed. What was 'inaccessible,' and lost, to them? The strange views that had parented and grand-parented this American manifestation were themselves intended to encompass – and to challenge and resist – the present as well as the past, blurring rather than sharpening the lines between them.

The American Religious Present

We have sketched here two fascinating ancestors that lie behind a generation's premise of alterity in viewing the Middle Ages. One was an American scholar attracted precisely by 'grotesque' topics. The other was a batch of young French cultural rebels, casting themselves as medieval inquisitors and heretics, who helped to inspire that American generation's presumption of the strange. (As far as I know, neither Bynum nor Freedman and Spiegel were aware that the movement spawning *toute vue des choses qui n'est pas étrange est fausse* was imbued by images of medieval heresy and inquisition.) These two ancestors of that generational view of 'alterity' show us something other than a shift from familiarity to defamiliarity, origin to other, a connected past to a lost one. To Henry Charles Lea, Michel Mourre, and the Situationists alike, expressing disappointment in the present could be accomplished by crossing the distance to the past.

We also see in these predecessors unusual manifestations of how religion and religious persecution contributed to creating distance and difference. For Lea, religion was, simply, something that (*pace* Durkheim) divided rather than united, one factor among many that, throughout history, determined morality and human behaviour, including its cruelty. Inquisition was evil but rational, unable to be judged as unchristian if properly contextualized (even if the context could be judged!), an element of the past but too close to the present – because, in part, an intolerant *present* was still too close to the past. To Mourre, modernity had evacuated what made 'religion' religious: passion, zeal, that very consciousness of inescapable divine power and eternity. Religion was indeed nothing now but an institution, and nothing now distinguished it from any other tepid bourgeois bureaucracy. (The Situationists he inspired agreed, if evaluating this development more positively.) Mourre and the Situationists consciously

---

[47] Spiegel, *Past as Text*, p. 80.

confused past and present while appealing respectively to inquisitors and to heretics as still-living models to overcome modern torpor. Put simply, inquisition and heresy have a more complicated relationship with the past's alterity, with that 'complete reorientation of medieval studies,' than it may initially seem.

In understanding the role of alterity in an American 'making of medieval history' – and in understanding how religion and religious persecution reinforce alterity – we might also then ask what a strange vision of the medieval past implies about religion in the present, and religious persecution in the past. If American scholars have emphasized the religious grotesque in viewing 'medieval civilization as the West's quintessential 'other', what then does this say about medievalists' conception of the modern religion to which it is compared?[48] To Henry Adams, religion was power, fear, and danger: a force acting upon human action in beautiful, strange, irrational ways foreign to America. (The best way to make Americans understand the importance of medieval cathedrals was to point out how much they cost.)[49] Lea and Mourre both resembled Adams in believing that religion made one do things, even unwise or cruel things, and Lea was keenly aware that religious persecution belonged to American history. We might ask if scholars of alterity — agreeing with Adams about the past's strangeness — depart from his contention of religion's active, even dangerous, power. What is the role in medievalists' 'alterity' of a modern American religious strangeness; of an American history of religious grotesque and repression? Scholarship has pushed back disenchantment, an ostensible hallmark of the modern, chronologically into the Middle Ages.[50] But enchantment persists into the present, and persists in America, as do those aspects of the religious grotesque that putatively de-familiarize medieval Europe: pain, ecstasy, blood, cruelty, irrationality. (We might cite only briefly Christian Pentecostalism and charismatic worship, Santeria, body modification, 'cults', and polygamy.) If American scholars have emphasized a medieval religious grotesque that is

---

[48] Freedman and Spiegel, 'Medievalisms Old and New,' p. 677. See Patterson, 'On the margin' [note 25 above].

[49] Adams, *Mont St Michel and Chartres*, pp. 91–2.

[50] Influential here, of course, is the Weberian premise of 'disenchantment' and modernity. Michael Bailey has argued rather that 'disenchantment' appears in the fifteenth century and earlier, if we mean by that term 'conceptualization of much magical and religious ritual as merely symbolic rather than directly effective'. Disenchantment was not then a process dependent upon the impact of the Reformation: 'Locating some 'disenchantment' prior to the Reformation helps to decouple these processes from modern conceptions of 'magic' and 'religion' that are products of Reformation-era debates.' Bailey's argument still assumes, nevertheless, that 'disenchantment' has indeed taken place in the mentality and practice of the West. M. D. Bailey, 'The Disenchantment of Magic: Spells, Charms, and Superstition in Early European Witchcraft Literature,' *American Historical Review* 111 (2006), 383–404.

unfamiliar and strange, it is only so against a chastened landscape of modern American religion.[51]

This is one way in which – as has always been the case – depictions of medieval religion depend upon how one defines and delimits 'religion'. Moreover, the narrative of a modern secular west to which the Middle Ages is the 'other' can help to govern tacit ideas about what religion is and does. Robert Orsi, a scholar of American Catholicism, has remarked that 'the modernist story only barely masks its prescriptive edge: modernity is the norm, religions must conform'. This means excising from modern religion what medievalists would call the grotesque.[52] Likewise, Talal Asad has contended that modern secularism is not a no-value cipher or default; it is rather assertive, positive, charged and deployed in order to impugn the supposedly 'irrational' in modern religions.[53] Secular modernity does not just depend upon the contention that the West shed religious irrationality. It also polices modern religion, in scholarship and beyond it, by forcibly constructing the religiously legitimate – irenic, tolerant, inclusive, dispassionate, and humanist. A medieval religion 'other' in bodilyness, violence, and persecution helps to preserve our notion of the modern, as distance and difference become a refuge, not a reality.

I have tried above simply to illustrate some of the varieties, subtleties, and complexities of the circumstances against which American scholars draw the Middle Ages, its religion, and its persecution. To Freedman and Spiegel, the perspective of alterity was the latest version of the unavoidable discomfiture of the American medievalist – hampered by languages and geography, keenly feeling the ruptures of the 'New World,' choosing only how to deal most productively with that distance and difference (a more beautiful alternative; origin and ancestor; otherness). With their generation, this misfit was joined, beneficially, to a clear-eyed awareness that the past could never be recuperated, and joined also to the demographic diversity that, they hinted, America could better provide.[54]

Yet in terms of religion and religious persecution, American distance and difference is less than it appears. We can lose sight of the diversity of the American religious present, or the persecutions of the American past, in depicting a strange

---

[51] One may object that these modern religious grotesques are not representative of 'American religion'. But this objection could be turned back to medieval grotesques (pus-drinking, starvation) as emblematic elements of religion in the Middle Ages.

[52] R. Orsi, *Between Heaven and Earth: The Religious Worlds People Make and the Scholars Who Study Them* (Princeton NJ, 2005). See particularly the chapter 'Snakes Alive,' which responds to D. Covington, *Salvation on Sand Mountain: Snake Handling and Redemption in Southern Appalachia* (Reading MA, 1995). Orsi is very much in the model of Adams.

[53] Especially Islam: T. Asad, *Formations of the Secular: Christianity, Islam, Modernity* (Stanford CA, 2003).

[54] Freedman and Spiegel, 'Medievalisms Old and New,' pp. 702–3.

or persecutory European religious history from which it is cleanly disassociated. This was something Lea, say, did not do — with his awareness of a religion that still permitted zeal (as Mourre might approve of). I wonder how closer attention to the strangeness of American religion and of American religious history would affect the sense of distance and difference that has infected medieval studies in America since its inception. The United States had no inquisitions. Yet it has indeed had endogenous and organic religious persecutions, and its fair share of a distinct religious grotesque. Yet Americans, generally so directed towards the future, have tended not to ask what might succeed alterity as an analytic model in medieval studies.[55] What in Americans' 'making of medieval history' might succeed this premise of the Middle Ages, its religion, and its inquisitions as, in Bynum's words, 'radically, terrifyingly, fascinatingly other'?[56] After all, Freedman and Spiegel proclaimed the scholarly dominance of a Middle Ages unfamiliar and strange in its grotesqueness in 1998. This was only a few years before the United States – as Henry Charles Lea might, or might not, be surprised to learn – proclaimed the legality of torture.

---

[55] The boomlet of surveys of the field published in the 1990s tended to see the future only as the current generation of senior scholars.

[56] C. Walker Bynum, 'Why All the Fuss about the Body?: a Medievalist's Perspective,' *Critical Inquiry* 22 (1995), 31.

11

MIND THE GAP:
MODERN AND MEDIEVAL
'RELIGIOUS' VOCABULARIES

Peter Biller

A leitmotif is provided here by the titles of two books. The first was *Five Centuries of Religion* whose first volume was published in 1923.[1] It had its own sub-title, 'St Bernard, His Predecessors and Successors, 1000–1200 AD,' to which the author referred in his preface. 'My title-page will have made it sufficiently clear', he wrote, 'that this volume deals mainly with Religion in the medieval sense, in which the "Religious" was the cloistered soul.'[2] The five centuries of religion are five centuries of religious Orders. We move on to 2005, and the publication of a collection called *Medieval Religion: New Approaches*.[3] Its editor does not define 'medieval religion', and the book contains the secular clergy and laity alongside monasticism. Writing in 1923, George Gordon Coulton assumed the continuing existence of one older meaning of 'religion' and he could expect his reader to put together the word 'religion' and the book's dates and realize that here it meant monasticism.[4] The editor of the 2005 book and its readership, by contrast, are in a semantic-conceptual world where 'medieval

---

[1] 4 vols. (Cambridge, 1923–50).
[2] I, xxxiii.
[3] Ed. C. H. Berman (New York, 2005).
[4] Note the chronology here of generational shifts in one family in the sense of the word religion. First, there is the probable date of the word being taken in by a young Coulton, who was born in 1858. Next there is 1911, the date of Coulton's appointment to a lectureship in Cambridge. He immediately wrote lectures: 'the whole series ran to twelve, upon Monastic History in the later Middle Ages. They aimed at blocking out the whole picture which I have since striven to fill in with my *Five Centuries of Religion*'; G. G. Coulton, *Four Score Years: An Autobiography* (Cambridge, 1943), p. 312. Finally, writing about Coulton's 'religion' shortly after his death in 1947 and under the name Sarah Campion, his daughter Mary Rose Coulton (1906–2002) uses phrases like 'organised religions' and 'religious dogmas', without any sign of awareness of the monastic sense of her father's *magnum opus*; *Father: A Portrait of G. G. Coulton at Home* (London, 1948), pp. 237–8.

religion' has become an omnium-gatherum of things that are 'religious' in a modern but not medieval sense of the word.

How should we think about the relationship between, on the one hand, the words and concepts we have and use in the area of religion, and, on the other, those possessed and used by people in the High Middle Ages? We can help our reflections by looking at one section towards the end of Marc Bloch's *The Historian's Craft* called 'Nomenclature'.[5] Here Bloch looks at the historian and his words - using of course the androcentric language of his time. He begins like this. There is a period in the past, which the modern historian is studying. In that past period people gave names and used words for their actions, their beliefs and various aspects of their social lives. The modern historian thinks about these past people with the categories – and consequently in the words – of his own time. Bloch's first example was modern historians writing of the 'bourgeoisie' when analysing crises of the Roman empire. Neither the word nor the idea could be translated, he suggested, into the language and mental categories of a Roman. Bloch was acutely aware of developments in contemporary thought, especially philosophy and the sciences, and he will have been aware of the philosophical thrust of the thought that was going on in linguistics faculties in Strasbourg and Paris, towards seeing language as in some sense constituting reality.[6] We shall return to Bloch's discussion of nomenclature at the end of this chapter.

The subject of this White Rose series is the way the modern world 'makes' the Middle Ages. This chapter will look at one part of that, the shaping of medieval 'religion' by our language, and it will do this by examining medieval and modern vocabularies in three areas. The first is what we call 'religions', religions as ensembles or entities of faith, cult organization and identity, which we sometimes refer to as 'world religions'. The second is 'popular religion' and the 'religion of the laity', and the third is heretics. One preliminary caveat is that the chapter is written in English and many of its examples are in English. Though some of its propositions about modern English may be applicable to modern French, Italian and German semantic constructions of things medieval, it would be dangerous to assume this.

---

[5] Trans. P. Putnam, with preface by P. Burke (Manchester, 1992), pp. 129–46; in the 1st edn of this translation, with preface by J. R. Strayer (Manchester, 1954), pp. 156–72. *Apologie pour l'histoire ou métier d'historien*, ed. É. Bloch, preface by J. Le Goff (Paris, 1997), pp. 135–46; Le Goff comments on nomenclature in his preface, p. 26. For an account of the transmission of the work and a selection of the bibliography on its reception, see M. Mastrogregori, *Il manoscritto interrotto di Marc Bloch: Apologia della storia o Mestiere di storico* (Pisa and Rome, 1995).

[6] S. W. Friedman, *Sociology and Geography: Encountering Changing Disciplines* (Cambridge, 1996), ch. 6.

Religions

Let us begin with an inaugural lecture delivered at the University of York on 11 February 1981 by a great historian of early modern Christianity, the late John Bossy, subsequently published as an article wittily entitled 'Some Elementary Forms of Durkheim'.[7] Bossy was asking how the words and concepts 'Religion' and 'Society' could have become an equation for Durkheim. And he put forward a short general history of the word and concept *religio*, in three stages. The first was the classical and patristic period, when *religio* principally meant worship. The second was the medieval period, when it mainly denoted monastic and other religious orders, their way of life and their Orders. The earlier sense of worship was being revived in the fifteenth century, and then there came about the major change of the early modern period. Now, in the sixteenth century, *religio* was coming also to mean a particular religion, the Christian religion, the Jewish religion, each of them an ensemble of faith and cult; and religions, a plurality of these. What is important is that in its earliest senses *religio* was an attribute or relation, whereas in its early modern sense *religio* was an entity or thing. What brought about the change in the sixteenth century was the existence of a plurality of embattled and embodied faiths, with the impetus thereby given to see one's way of belief and worship from the outside. The development of meanings of *religio* went hand in hand with a broader development in ways of seeing and thinking.

When hearing this in its own 'Elementary Form' – as a lecture – I took Bossy to be advancing a straight correlation between people having and not having words and their ability or inability to think and express what these words denote. Irritated by the consequence that seemed to follow, the suggestion that people in the High Middle Ages could not think the thoughts of his third period, I set about investigating the case, first of all semantically.[8]

The completion of dictionaries of medieval Latin from individual regions of Latin Christendom will eventually add nuances to Bossy's account of single medieval words for religion and religions, but the broad lines of his early explorer's chart were right. The very rare words *Saracenia* and *Saracenismus* were used in a purely geographical sense, the land of the Saracens,[9] as also was

---

[7] *Past and Present* 95 (1982), 3–18. On Bossy (1933–2015), see P. Jupp, 'John Bossy: A Personal Appreciation', in *Christianity and Community in the West: Essays for John Bossy*, ed. S. Ditchfield (Aldershot, 2001), pp. 294–307.
[8] This led to P. Biller, 'Words and the Medieval Notion of "Religion"', *Journal of Ecclesiastical History* 36 (1985), 351–69.
[9] *Dictionary of Medieval Latin from British Sources*, 17 fascicules (Oxford, 1975–2013), XV, 2935; *Lexicon Latinitatis Nederlandicae Medii Aevi*, ed. J. Fuchs, O. Weijers, M. Gumbert-Hepp, 8 vols. (Leiden, 1977–2005), VII, 4436. Neither word is listed in dictionaries of medieval Latin for Hungary, Poland, Sweden and the former Yugoslavia, though the

Judaismus, Jewry: where Jews lived.[10] The most common way of saying what we call *Judaism* was to put one of the words 'law', 'faith' or 'sect' together with 'Jews', as in 'the law of the Jews', though there are some instances of a use of *Judaismus* in a narrow senses of religion, as 'the cult of the Jews'.[11] Bossy was right about *religio*, as monasticism, a monastic order, or worship. As he suggested, where you found it, the phrase *religio christiana* did not mean the Christian world religion, but Christian cult, worship in a Christian way.[12]

Bossy, however, was overlooking several things, first of all high medieval experience of 'religious' diversity. In the twelfth and thirteenth centuries medieval Christendom was confronted internally with heretics and Jews, and externally with Muslims, and in the middle of the thirteenth century it was trying to learn all it could about about the Mongols, including their 'religion'. In the descriptions which western writers produced, could not the accumulation of categories articulate something like the (allegedly) post-medieval notion of religion as an ensemble? And could not *phrases* do the job that was done later on by the single words Islam and Judaism? Thus there are the categories in the rubric of the 'religion' chapter in the Franciscan John of Pian del Carpine's description of the Mongols, written in the late 1240s: *De cultu Dei, de his que credunt esse peccata, de divinationibus et purgationibus et ritu funeris*, etc. ('On their worship of God, On the things they believe are sins, On their divinations, purgations and funeral rite, etc').[13] And there are the chapter-headings of the Dominican Bernard Gui's description of a sect, in his treatise on the practice of inquisition, finished in 1323 or 1324: *De ejus origine et tempore quo incepit, De triplici … nuncupatione vulgata, De erroribus, De modo seu ritu celebrandi missam, De modo vivendi, De modo dicendi* ('On their origin and the date they began, On the three common ways of naming them, On their errors, On their mode or rite of saying mass, On their way

---

latter's lists *lex Saracenica* in this sense; *Lexicon Mediae Latinitatis Iugoslaviae*, ed. M. Kostrenčić, 2 vols. (Zagreb, 1973–8), II, 1037.

[10] *Dictionary of Medieval Latin from British Sources*, V, 1506–7.

[11] *Lexicon Latinitatis Nederlandicae Medii Aevi*, IV, 2694. There are no entries for *Judaismus* in the Hungarian, Swedish and Yugoslav dictionaries. The Polish dictionary defines it as *religio iudaeorum*, referring to the fifteenth and sixteenth centuries and providing no examples; *Lexicon Mediae et Infimae Latinitatis Polonorum*, ed. M. Plezi (Cracow, 1953-), V, 1089; *Lexicon Mediae Latinitatis Hungariae*, ed J. Harmatta and others (Budapest, 1987-), V, 418: *religio iudaeorum*.

[12] *Dictionary of Medieval Latin from British Sources*, XIV, 2740; *Lexicon Latinitatis Nederlandicae Medii Aevi*, VII, 4247–50; *Lexicon Mediae et Infimae Latinitatis Polonorum*, VIII, 3284–5; *Glossarium Mediae Latinitatis Sueciae*, ed. U. Westerbergh and E. Odelman, 2 vols. (Stockholm, 1968–2002), II, 364–5; *Lexicon Mediae Latinitatis Iugoslaviae*, II, 989, where the monastic meanings include monastic clothing. See n. 61 below.

[13] *Ystoria Mongolarum*, iii, ed. A. van den Wyngaert, *Itinera et relationes Fratrum Minorum saeculi xiii et xiv*, Sinica Franciscana 1 (Quaracchi, 1929), p. 36.

of life, On their way of teaching').[14] Surely the juxtaposition of these categories in systematic and methodical descriptions suggests their authors' and readers' possession of the thought, religion as an ensemble? And as we have already seen with the Jews, medieval writers could use phrases containing 'law of -' 'sect of -' – such as 'the law of Mahomet' and 'the law of the Jews' – to do roughly the job of post-medieval 'Islam' and 'Judaism'.

We can look at a treatise written by William of Auvergne, bishop of Paris (1228–49), *De fide et legibus* (*On Faith and Laws*), which was part of a massive treatise, *Magisterium divinale et sapientiale* (*Teaching on God in the Mode of Wisdom*), begun around 1223 and finished in the 1230s.[15] Here laws are the law of the Jews and the law of Mahomet, and two chapters deal with ideas about the *diversitas legum* (*the diversity of laws*). 'On account of the diversity of these laws and sects', William begins the second of these chapters, ' … not a few have come to this error, believing that anyone is saved in their faith, or law or sect, so long as they believe it is good and from God' (*occasione diversitatis istarum legum atque sectarum … nonnulli in eum errorem devenerunt, ut credant unumquemque in sua fide, vel lege, seu secta salvari, dummodo credit eam esse bonam et a Deo*).[16] Elsewhere, in the section on marriage in his treatise on the sacraments, William grappled with the different relations between Muslim polygamy and Christian monogamy and the populations of Muslim and Christian kingdoms.[17] Here, do we not have individual religions, and something that is approaching what we call 'a comparative approach to religions'?

Let us pause with William of Auvergne. He was very unlike other Paris theologians of the time, writing outside the scholastic form of question, thesis, antithesis and resolution, and using large, swirling and digressive discourses, here perhaps following the style of translated Arabian philosophers.[18] Certainly, in the readiness with which he juxtaposed and thought about the laws of Jews and Muslims and Christians, he was influenced by his reading of an Arabic work of astrology, by Albumasar (Abū Maʿšar), which had been translated into

[14] *Practica inquisitionis heretice pravitatis*, v.2.1-6, ed. C. Douais (Paris, 1886), pp. 244–51. Modern historians have either followed the title chosen by Douais or the French chosen by Guillaume Mollat, *Manuel de l'inquisiteur*, 2 vols., 1st edn (Paris, 1926). Gui's own words when referring to the work were subtly but significantly different *Tractatus de practica inquisitionis* (*Practica*, ed. Douais, p. 1).

[15] William of Auvergne, *Opera omnia*, 2 vols. (Paris, 1674; reprint, Frankfurt-am-Main, 1963), I,1–102; here the treatise is split into two sections, *De fide* (pp. 1–18) and *De legibus* (pp. 18–102), each with autonomous chapter numbers. On William, see *Autour de Guillaume d'Auvergne († 1249): études réunies*, ed. F. Morenzoni and J.-Y. Tilliette (Turnhout, 2005).

[16] William, *De legibus* xx-xxi, *Opera omnia*, I.54–64.

[17] William, *De sacramento matromonii*, *Opera omnia*, I.512–28; analysed, P. Biller, *The Measure of Multitude: Population in Medieval Thought* (Oxford, 2000), ch. 3.

[18] See further discussion of his style in Biller, *Measure of Multitude*, pp. 64–5.

Latin by the 1140s.[19] This work systematically related these laws to stars and their conjunctions, in particular Jupiter and Saturn, making them in a rather abstract sense what one might call 'world religions'.[20]

William of Auvergne was a thinker of great difficulty and daring originality, and a writer who pressed hard on the expressiveness and range of meaning of words. Grappling with law at one point in his treatise *On faith and laws* he approaches a definition of law by listing its seven component parts, beginning with law as witness to truth, and therefore of things to be believed, and ending with ceremonies and divine cult.[21] He is expanding it, and the resulting 'law' approaches post-medieval 'religion'.

This is where we need a reality check, and to get real. We have been foregrounding categories in descriptions of religions and the words and writings of William of Auvergne, in an account of high medieval language. This is misleading. William of Auvergne was an exceptional figure, and a maverick even within his rarefied intellectually elite milieu, high Paris theology. We would do just as well extrapolating from the vocabulary of a few figures at the Institute for Advanced Study at Princeton when investigating the semantic-conceptual mentality of middle-Americans. If we concentrate not on the few pins we have found in the haystack but the haystack itself, we are driven to recognition of the broad accuracy of John Bossy's picture. A writer such as Alan of Lille, addressing individual articles of faith held by Jews, followers of Mahomet, heretics (here mainly meaning Cathars) and Waldensians, is more representative of the haystack.[22] He and the others mainly talked in terms of different faiths: not major or world religions.

Although the discussion so far has concentrated on a few key 'religion' words, much more would need to be taken into account when investigating the semantically frosted glass of modern monographs through which we look, as though through windows, at medieval phenomena. Take as an example two modern works on Islam and Judaism in the Middle Ages. In R. W. Southern's

[19] Abū Maʿšar, On Historical Astrology. *The Book of Religions and Dynasties (On the Great Conjunctions)*, ed. K. Yamamoto and C. Burnett, 2 vols. (Leiden, Boston and Cologne, 2000).

[20] See J.D. North, 'Astrology and the fortunes of Churches', *Centaurus* 24 (1980), 181–211. Within the article 'Churches' becomes 'Churches and Religions'.

[21] *De legibus* i, *Opera omnia*, I,19.

[22] *De fide catholica*, PL 210, cols. 305–430. Written in the late twelfth century; the best account is M.-T. d'Alverny, *Alain de Lille. Textes inédits* (Paris, 1965), pp. 156–62. There are fine studies of two books in the treatise: M.-T. d'Alverny, 'Alain de Lille et l'Islam le "Contra Paganos"', *Cahiers de Fanjeaux* 18 (1983), 325–50; J. H. Pearson, 'The anti-Jewish polemic of Alan of Lille', *Alain de Lille, docteur universel*, ed. J.-L. Solère, A. Vasiliu and A. Galonnier, Société Internationale pour l'Étude de la Philosophie Médiévale Rencontres de Philosophie Médiévale 12 (Turnhout, 2005), pp. 83–106.

Western Views of Islam what is at issue is the attempt 'to get to grips with Islam'.[23] Two chapters are entitled 'The Century of Reason and Hope' and 'The Moment of Vision'. The religious cliché in the 1960s was 'dialogue between religions'. Its largest and most famous expression in the Catholic Church was at the Second Vatican Council (1962–5), and, on this point, the Council's 'Declaration of the Relation of the Church with Non-Christian Religions'. Issued in 1965 under the name *Nostra Aetate* (*In our time*), the decree's sonorous Vatican Latin parades over and over again the –ism religion names – *Buddismus, Hinduismus, Judaismus* and so on – as it extends to these world religions positive understanding and recognition, the ground for which had been prepared by a large vast production of historical theology on Christianity's relations with other world religions, written especially by French and German scholars. When we turn to Southern's *Views of Islam* we see the scholarship and brilliant lecturer's skills of Oxford's Chichele Professor of Medieval History. But the Southern of these years - who was a convert to Christianity in the 1930s and a lay preacher at the University Church of St Mary's - is also there in the melancholy and almost plangent language which he used to describe the medieval moments of opportunity for Christianity to obtain a real vision of Islam.[24] This chance had been lost: but what about now?

In 1998 Dominique Iogna-Prat provided an account of a twelfth-century Cluniac abbot who wrote *Against the Jews, Against the sect of the Saracens* and *Against the Petrobrusians* (*Adversus Iudeos, Contra sectam Sarracenorum* and *Contra Petrobrusianos*). In the modern French title the individuals become the –isms of religions, in the title *Ordonner et exclure: la société chrétienne face à l'hérésie, au judaïsme et à l'islam*, which became in English, *Order and Exclusion: Cluny and Christendom face Heresy, Judaism and Islam*.[25] The language of analysis is that of sophisticated Paris medievalism and R. I. Moore's *Persecuting Society*, while references to 'terroristes islamiques' and 'les mécanismes infernaux qui, tel l'antisémitisme, rendent l'homme étranger à l'homme' supply the vocabulary of the reflections with which Iogna-Prat frames his book.[26] The words of Southern and Iogna-Prat – for whose modern preoccupations I have great respect – are deeply coloured by their worlds.

---

[23] R. W. Southern, *Western Views of Islam in the Middle Ages* (Cambridge MA, 1962), p. 104. See p. 2, where Southern allusively evoked a parallel in the global political problem of his time, communism and western democracy.

[24] See A. Murray, 'Richard William Southern, 1912–2001', *Proceedings of the British Academy* 120 (2003), 413–42. Southern discussed Christianity and his own conversion in a TV debate, an edited version of which appeared in 'Looking at History: Professor R. W. Southern and M. Foot, MP, talk with Jenny Isard', *Dialogue with Doubt*, ed. G. Moir (London, 1967), pp. 9–28.

[25] (Paris, 1998; Ithaca NY, 2002).

[26] *Ordonner et exclure*, pp. 15, 367.

'Religion of the people *or* of the laity'

Let us look at the vocabulary used about the laity at three times, in (i) the High Middle Ages, (ii) the 1960s–1970s, and (iii) the 1980s-now, taking them out of order: (ii), (iii), (i).

We look first at the mid-twentieth century. As is well known, the laity were the hot item in the Christianity of the 1950s and 1960s.[27] The World Council of Churches erected a Department for the Laity, while in 1965 the Second Vatican Council issued its most important decree, *Apostolicam Actuositatem* (*Apostolic Activity*), on the apostolate of the laity. While theologians argued for expansion in the role and ministry of the laity, historians were providing the laity with its own history. The World Council of Churches commissioned historians, and in 1963 published their results in a book called *The Layman in Christian History*.[28] Expressive of the Christian ecumenism of the period is that each historian's affiliation was spelled out, Orthodox, Methodist, Catholic etc.[29] – and they include Southern, defined as an Anglican, valiantly trying to find evidence about the laity in the dark ages.[30] Catholic historians and historical theologians, including the conciliar father, and subsequently Cardinal, Yves Congar, had been at work historically resurrecting the laity.

All this went hand in hand with developments in vocabulary, especially in French. *Peuple* and *populaire* were getting increasing employment for lay as opposed to clerical, and they now came to be paired with another noun and adjective. The fundamental manifestation of this was a title chosen in 1964 by Canon Etienne Delaruelle: *La vie religieuse du peuple chrétien*.[31] Eleven years later the annual Colloque de Fanjeaux that had been held every year since 1965, devoted to the Histoire religieuse du Languedoc au XIIe et au début du XIVe siècle,[32] turned away from its usual topics of monasticism, secular clergy and heretics. Instead it looked

---

[27] See 'The Rise of the Laity', in P. Biller, 'Popular Religion in the Central and Later Middle Ages', in *Companion to Historiography*, ed. M. Bentley (London, 1997), pp. 221–46 (225–7); see n. 37 below.

[28] Subtitled *A Project of the Department on the Laity of the World Council of Churches*, and ed. S. Neill and H.-R. Weber (London, 1963). *Laymen* in the title may be rooted not only in androcentricity and the gender of Gratian's definition, but also the canon-legal tautology of 'lay women'.

[29] In the 'Contents', pp. 5–6.

[30] 'The Church of the Dark Ages, 600–1000', pp. 88–134.

[31] E. Delaruelle, E.-R. Labande and P. Ourliac, *L'Église au temps du Grand Schisme et de la crise conciliaire (1378–1449)*, *Histoire de l'Église depuis les origines jusqu'à nos jours*, ed. A. Fliche and V. Martin, 21 vols. (Paris, 1934–64; vol. 11 not published). A very nuanced discussion of what Delaruelle meant by *populaire* and *peuple* was provided by A. Vauchez in his 'Étienne Delaruelle historien: II', É. Delaruelle, *La piété populaire au moyen âge* (Turin, 1980), pp. xiii-xix.

[32] Its proceedings, which usually appear a year after each conference, began with *Saint Dominique en Languedoc*, Cahiers de Fanjeaux I (Toulouse, 1966).

at the laity. The title was *La religion populaire en Languedoc*. The figure of Canon Delaruelle and what he had done in 1964 was evoked in the opening address by the Dominican historian Marie-Humbert Vicaire,[33] and the conference was presided over by André Vauchez. Vauchez was becoming one of the most important of all historians of his generation in this area; although his masterpiece was his *thèse d'État* on later medieval sanctity, the laity would also eventually elicit a book from him.[34] In his conclusion to the conference he struggled brilliantly and perceptively with the meanings of *religion populaire*. Its currency was deeply connected, said Vauchez, with the deep sea-change introduced by the Second Vatican Council and debates and controversies within the Church.[35] He evoked and discussed three images of what people thought when they heard the phrase, one of them rites and practices that belonged more properly to folklore, another spontaneous outbreaks of such movements as the shepherds' crusade and the processions of flagellants. On these, Vauchez was acting as a descriptive lexicographer. When he turned to the third, there was a note of advocacy. This third image was the piety and practices of the Christian faithful, within the structures and in particular the parishes of the Church: lay people. This was what Delaruelle had meant.

The language came to England. *Past and Present* held a conference on 'Popular Religion' in 1966. One very influential paper was delivered there by John Bossy and published by *Past and Present* in 1970. Bossy faced up to Delaruelle's presentation of massive evidence about the piety of the laity and his phrase for this. And he provided a panoramic view of 'the popular religion of Catholic Europe' – meaning lay people in parishes – from the Middle Ages to the Counter Reformation and later.[36]

From the 1980s until now we see a massive diffusion of the vocabulary of medieval religion and medieval popular religion.[37] Some of the authors and editors side-step definition, while others raise it as a topic. Here a theological construction of the middle of the twentieth century produces the question – 'What was popular medieval religion?'[38] There is epistemological creep here.

---

[33] 'Liminaire: l'apport d'Etienne Delaruelle aux études de spiritualité populaire médiévale', *La religion populaire en Languedoc du XIIIᵉ siècle à la moitié du XIVᵉ siècle*, Cahiers de Fanjeaux 11 (Toulouse, 1976), pp. 23–36.

[34] *Les laïcs au moyen âge* (Paris, 1987).

[35] 'Conclusion', *La religion populaire en Languedoc*, pp. 429–44 (429–33).

[36] John Bossy, 'The Counter-Reformation and the People of Catholic Europe', *Past and Present* 47 (1970), 51–70.

[37] See for example R. and C. N. L. Brooke, *Popular Religion in the Middle Ages: Western Europe 1000–1300* (London, 1984); *Medieval Popular Religion, 1000–1500: A Reader*, ed. J. Shinners (Peterborough, Ontario, 1997). The title of P. Biller's chapter, 'Popular Religion in the Central and Later Middle Ages', in *Companion to Historiography*, ed. M. Bentley, pp. 221–46, was decided by the editor.

[38] Chapter 4 in the Brookes' *Popular Religion* poses the question 'What is Popular Religion' and provides no definition. In the introduction to his anthology *Medieval*

Once formulated, the question inches along, until popular religion seems itself to be an entity in the past, needing definition and explanation.

We have already seen, at the beginning of this chapter, that medieval popular religion has become a hold-all. It also often has an inherent tendency towards positiveness. It is interesting in this light to look at one narrower stream of scholarship that has concentrated more narrowly on medieval definitions and vocabulary. Fundamental within this is a semantic-conceptual account by Karl Schreiner,[39] and, in the wake of this, articles by Sethina Watson[40] and Peter Biller.[41] Watson's illuminating and important article was devoted to the medieval Church's low requirements of the laity. Interesting here is the darker view taken by those scholars who have concentrated more on medieval vocabulary and ideas. It is time to remind ourselves of these. Let us now go back in time, beginning with medieval canon law, and the fundamental definitions provided in Gratian's *Decretum*.

> There are two sorts of Christians. There is one sort that is given over to the divine office, dedicated to contemplation and prayer... There is another kind of Christians – these are the lay. For the λαὸς is the people. These [the lay] are allowed to possess temporal things ... They are permitted to marry, till the earth, judge between man and man, litigate, place offerings on altars, pay tithes, and they can be saved thus [doing these things and leading this form of life] if they have done good and avoided sins. (*Duo sunt genera Christianorum. Est autem genus unum, quod mancipatum divino officio, et deditum contemplationi et orationi ... Aliud vero est genus Christianorum, ut sunt laici. Λαὸς enim est populus. His licet temporalia possidere ... His concessum est uxorem ducere, terram colere, inter uirum et uirum iudicare, causas agere, oblationes super altaria ponere, decimas reddere, et ita saluari poterunt, si uicia tamen benefaciendo euitauerint*).[42]

Popular Religion, pp. xv-xix, discusses definitions, suggesting readers look at the book's documents to answer the question. A sophisticated historiographical discussion has been provided recently by L. A. Smoller as an answer to a section entitled 'What is "popular" religion?', within her chapter '"Popular" religious culture(s)', *The Oxford Handbook of Medieval Christianity*, ed. J. H. Arnold (Oxford, 2014), pp. 340–56 (341–3).

[39] 'Begriffsgeschichtliche Prolegomena', *Laienfrömmigkeit im späten Mittelalter: Formen, Funktionen, politisch-soziale Zusammenhänge*, ed. K. Schreiner, Schriften des Historischen Kollegs, Kolloquien 20 (Oldenburg, 1992), pp. 1–78.

[40] Together with N. Tanner, 'Least of the Laity: The Minimum Requirements for a Medieval Christian', *Journal of Medieval History* 32 (2006), 395–423.

[41] 'Intellectuals and the Masses: Oxen and She-Asses in the Medieval Church', *Oxford Handbook of Medieval Christianity*, ed. J. H. Arnold (Oxford, 2014), pp. 323–39; see also his 'Popular Religion', cited in n. 37 above.

[42] C.12 q. 1 c.7, ed. E. Friedberg, *Corpus iuris canonici*, 2 vols. (Leipzig, 1879), I, col. 678; the quotation is attributed, with some uncertainty, to St Jerome.

In his treatise *On the Instruction of Preachers*, written probably between 1270 and 1274, Humbert of Romans provided 100 model sermons to be addressed to the two kinds of Christians. They are in descending order, the first group (up to no. 70) being addressed to the clergy and religious, the second group (72–100 to lay people. Among the latter women come last. In sermon 71, Humbert switches away from the clergy and religious and towards the lay. He makes this the occasion for a general statement about the two sorts of Christians. Just as Heaven is superior and earth inferior, just as souls are superior and bodies inferior, similarly:

> there are two kinds of men among the faithful of Christ, that is to say the clergy, who are superior in dignity and have to be more intelligent through their knowledge and holier than lay people, who abound less in these things. Further, in order to denote this distinction there are two parts in the churches of Christians, the choir which pertains to the clergy and the nave which pertains to lay people. Further, as regards lay people, it should be noted that they ought not to reach up towards the scrutiny of the secrets of the faith which the clergy hold. Rather they should adhere implicitly, in accordance with this passage from Job – 'The oxen were ploughing and the she-asses feeding beside them', which Gregory expounds thus, saying that the she-asses, that is to say the simple, ought to be content with the doctrine of their elders. (*inter fideles Christi sunt duo genera hominum, scilicet clerici, qui sunt superiores dignitate et magis intelligentes per cientiam, et sanctiores habent esse quam laici, qui in his minus abundant. Ad notandum autem istam distinctionem sunt in ecclesiis Christianorum duo partes, scilicet chorus, qui ad clerum pertinet, et navis quae ad laicos. Notandum autem circa laicos, quod ipsi non debent ascendere ad scrutandum secreta fidei, quae tenent clerici, sed adhaerere implicite, iuxta illud Iob, 'Et boves arabant et asine pascebantur iuxta eos'* [Job 1.14], *quod exponit Gregorius,*[43] *dicens quod 'asinae', id est simplices, debent esse contenti doctrina suorum maiorum*).[44]

Here Humbert was distilling a passage in Peter Lombard's *Four Books of the Sentences*, about the simple in the Church and their faith, and theologians' reflection on this, which had led by the early thirteenth century to the phrase and notion of *fides implicita*, implicit faith. Alongside a minimal grasp of five or six articles of faith, what sufficed for a lay person was implicit faith, essentially believing what priests told one to believe. In university theology lectures, Peter

---

[43] Gregory the Great, *Moralia in Job* ii.30, ed. M. Adriaen (Turnhout, 1979), pp. 88–9.
[44] *De eruditione praedicatorum* ii.71, 'Ad omnes laicos', *Maxima Bibliotheca Veterum Patrum*, ed. M. de la Bigne, 28 vols. (Lyons, 1677–1707, XXV, 491. On the text and its date see Humbert of Romans, *Legendae sancti Dominici*, ed. S. Tugwell, Monumenta Ordinis Fratrum Praedicatorum Historica 30 (Rome, 2008), pp. 325–8.

Lombard was the set text alongside the Bible from the 1220s until Martin Luther.[45] Over these centuries the definition, a crisp vocabulary and the clear ascription of an inferior role were hard-wired into the minds of theology students: two kinds of Christians: the lay, the simple, and their implicit faith; and the biblical imagery of oxen and she-asses. The asses were she-asses. Their gender combined with misogyny to suggest the stock-figure in the brain-teaser put forward by commentators on this passage in the *Sentences*. This was the *vetula*, the little old woman. What should one make of the belief of a *vetula* who in her stupidity and lack of education believes in what her parish priest teaches, not knowing some of what he says is error?[46]

The pages of modern monographs are crowded – rightly – with many pious lay individuals and movements of lay piety. But modern vocabulary threatens to veil one large element in medieval clerical views of the laity: massive condescension.

Medieval Heretics

We conclude with the heretics and heresies of the High Middle Ages. The background is best evoked through Arno Borst, the founder of modern semantic awareness in this area. His masterpiece *Die Katharer*, published in 1953, provided studies of the two medieval vocabularies, words used by 'heretics' about themselves and their rituals, and words used by the Church about them.[47] Its account of approaches to medieval heretics adopted between c. 1520 and 1950 sketched the thought and scholarship that were articulated in a long line of post-medieval phrases for them.[48] They have been the following: 'witnesses to truth' to Protestants; forerunners of proletarian revolutionaries, in their opposition to feudalism, to Friedrich Engels; Occitan separatists, to proponents of a culture crushed by northern France and the Church; and, after Borst's time, and in the writings of historians at the Karl-Marx Universität in Leipzig in the 1960s, articulators of the ideology of the plebs and helpers in the fight for women's rights.[49]

---

[45] The wide diffusion of these notions was extensively established by G. Hoffmann, *Die Lehre von der* fides implicita *innerhalb der katholischen Kirche* (Leipzig, 1903).

[46] Biller, 'Intellectuals and the Masses', 328–31.

[47] *Die Katharer*, Schriften der Monumenta Germaniae Historica 12 (Stuttgart, 1953).

[48] *Ibid.*, pp. 27–58. P. Biller provided a version of Borst's schema, geared to the theme of heresy and women, in 'Cathars and Material Women', *Medieval Theology and the Natural Body*, ed. P. Biller and A. J. Minnis, York Studies in Medieval Theology 1 (York, 1997), pp. 61–107 (71–81).

[49] M. Erbstösser and E. Werner, *Ideologische Probleme des mittelalterlichen Plebejertums: Die freigeistige Häresie und ihre sozialen Wurzeln*, and G. Koch, *Frauenfrage und Ketzertum im Mittelalter: Die Frauenbewegung im Rahmen des Katharismus und des Waldensertums und ihre sozialen Wurzeln (12.–14. Jahrhundert)*, Forschungen zur mittelalterlichen Geschichte

For Engels, since the Church's theology sanctioned feudal domination, 'all the general and overt attacks on feudalism, in the first place attacks on the church, all revolutionary, social and political doctrines, necessarily became theological heresies'.[50] It is easy to pass by these formulations quickly, because of their age, the crudeness of their language, and memory of the years when the wretched medievalists of the German Democratic Republic were forced to quote them like scripture. But it is not wise to do so. the translation of heresy into socio-political protest has remained one of the most persistent of all habits among medieval historians, though they have learnt to do it in subtler language. It sometimes accompanies extension in the meaning of a word whose use in this context seems at first sight so appropriate: 'dissent'. In his *The Origins of European Dissent*, published in 1977, R. I. Moore's careful survey of heretics of the High Middle Ages builds up to the socio-political analyses of the concluding pages and then a sophisticated example of this translation. 'Since religion was often the most potent expression of group solidarity and the most acceptable instrument for resolving tensions and dislocations within the group, the struggle thus precipitated between local enterprise and the prerogative of distant lordship was often conducted in religious terms.'[51]

Given the growing awareness in recent decades that heresy and its repression should be studied together, the modern vocabulary of both needs scrutiny. Two later works by R. I. Moore have been fertile in producing the vocabulary that is current now. The first of these appeared in 1985, *The Formation of a Persecuting Society*. This has been an extraordinarily influential work.[52] Before

---

7, 9 (Berlin, 1960, 1962). This lay behind a phrase in a book addressed to a more popular market in East Germany, S. Harksen, *Die Frau im Mittelalter* (Leipzig, 1974), in whose English translation it became the proposition that 'heretical movements and the fight for women's rights went hand in hand'; S. Harksen, *Women in the Middle Ages*, trans. M. Herzfeld (New York, 1975), p. 38.

[50] <www.marxists.org/archive/marx/works/1850/peasant-war-germany/ch02.htm> (accessed 13 September 2016); es ist klar, dass hiermit alle allgemein ausgesprochenen Angriffe auf den Feudalismus, vor allem Angriffe auf die Kirche, alle revolutionären, gesellschaftlichen und politischen Doktrinen zugleich und vorwiegend theologische Ketzereien sein mußten; K. Marx and F. Engels, *Werke*, Institut für Marxismus-Leninismus beim ZK der SED, 46 vols. (Berlin, 1960–89), VII, 343–4. Cf. the different translation in F. Engels, *The Peasant War in Germany*, trans. V. Schneierson (Moscow, 1956), p. 42.

[51] *The Origins of European Dissent* (London, 1977), pp. 282–3. Editors of compendia lean towards allocating to contributors chapters on heresy with 'dissent' in the title; see e.g. P. Biller, 'Women and Dissent', in *Medieval Holy Women in the Christian Tradition, c. 1100–c.1500*, ed. A. Minnis and R. Voaden (Turnhout, 2010), pp. 133–62.

[52] *The Formation of a Persecuting Society: Power and Deviance in Western Europe , 950–1250* (Oxford, 1987); 2nd edn with altered sub-title, *Authority and Deviance in Western Europe, 950–1250* (Oxford, 2007). It attracted a volume of studies, *Heresy and the Persecuting Society in the Middle Ages: Essays on the Work of R. I. Moore*, ed. M. Frassetto (Leiden and Boston, 2006). The phrase has acquired general academic usage; see for example

its appearance, historians studying actions taken against heretics looked first of all at individual people, events and texts from the past: popes and their bulls, church Councils legislating against heretics, writers of polemical treatises and inquisitors. A sociological abstraction replaces these. Once 'The Persecuting Society' is located as an entity in the High Middle Ages, attention shifts towards it, the laws according to which it worked, and in particular its inherent need to find groups to persecute, regardless of their identity. Some blurring of vision is a consequence. As The Persecuting Society looked out on the world there was conflation, for example of heresy and leprosy. Moore's most recent work on medieval heresy took this further. There was a clever echo of the phrase used by President George W. Bush, 'The War on Terror', in his title, *The War on Heresy*.[53] Could 'heresy' have been as intangible as 'Terror', and as malleable by medieval Churchmen's nightmares as 'Terror' by the fear and imagination?[54]

The vocabulary of some French historians had been moving in sympathy with this, emphasizing the Church's construction of what was there, in *L'hérétique imaginé* (*The Imagined Heretic*)[55] and *Inventer l'hérésie?* (*Inventing Heresy?*).[56] The erosion of heretics' identity in Moore's *The War on Heresy* was also being helped by Mark Pegg's *Corruption of Angels*,[57] a study of the people of the Lauragais in Languedoc interrogated by inquisitors in 1245–6. With Mary Douglas as his beacon, Pegg provided an anthropological account, which ultimately reduces heresy to an expression of what is local. The semantics of this were not provided by a punchy headline, but the 'thick description' of the prose of the whole book, which is a *tour de force* of highly coloured evocation of the culture, customs, touch, feel and sounds of a small region.[58]

In the foreground of Moore's *War on Heresy*, where it turns to analysis and explanation, is the modern vocabulary of his social analysis of communities.

Beyond the Persecuting Society: Religious Toleration before the Enlightenment, ed. J. C. Laursen and C. J. Nederman (Philadelphia, 1998).

[53] *The War on Heresy: Faith and Power in Medieval Europe* (London, 2012).

[54] This chapter does not tackle the controversy about the reality and identity of medieval dualist heretics. See on this *Cathars in Question*, ed. A. Sennis, Heresy and Inquisition in the Middle Ages 4 (York, 2016).

[55] A. Trivellone, *L'hérétique imaginé: Hétérodoxie et iconographie dans l'occident médiéval, de l'époque carolingienne à l'inquisition*, Collection d'Études Médiévales de Nice 10 (Turnhout, 2009); see pp. 21–2, where Trivellone sets her work within the context of the shifts brought about by Moore's *Persecuting Society*.

[56] *Inventer l'hérésie? Discours polémique et pouvoirs avant l'inquisition*, ed. M. Zerner, Collection du Centre d'études médiévales de Nice 2 (Nice, 1998); see pp. 7–13 for Zerner's account of the book's intellectual origins and its various interpretations of *inventer*.

[57] M. G. Pegg, *The Corruption of Angels: The Great Inquisition of 1245–1246* (Princeton NJ and Oxford, 2001).

[58] See further analysis of Pegg's language in P. Biller, 'Goodbye to Catharism?', *Cathars in Question*, ed. Sennis, pp. 274–304.

At the same time the only medieval words that survive directly from the 'Cathar' heretics of Languedoc – those contained in the extensive fragments of a theological treatise written in Latin by one of them around 1220[59] and in a manuscript containing in Occitan the forms of some of their rituals – are kept out of the book.[60] The most terrible of all themes in heresy and its repression in the thirteenth century is the execution of heretics by burning. Why did men and women voluntarily embrace this death? And how is this expressed in medieval and modern vocabularies? It pre-occupied the theologians William of Auxerre (writing between 1215 and 1229) and Roland of Cremona (writing probably around 1229–33). They raised it in formal questions about why and how a heretic could bear such 'appalling torments' (*immania tormenta*) 'on behalf of his false faith' (*pro fide falsa; pro sua infidelitate*).[61] Moore raises it too. 'What was it that brought these people to embrace their terrible fate?'[62] At the end of his book he gives an answer. 'A striking proportion of those who went willingly to the holocausts described in these pages did so as the defenders of values, a community or a way of life under threat.'[63] The thirteenth century saw them dying for their faith. The early twenty-first century sees them dying as defenders of community values.

The *Historian's Craft* is sacred because of its author's heroic death. At the same time it is sometimes undervalued. Readers can be misled by its unfinished state into thinking, 'Oh, it was just a product of the last year or two of Bloch's life, thought up while he was on the run.' They can be misled by its apparently informal and conversational style. Anglophone readers may be further misled by the translator's unfortunate decision to turn the sub-title, *métier de l'historien*, into the title, while omitting *Apologie de l'historien*. Through this omission they

---

[59] *Un traité cathare inédit du début du xiiie siècle d'après le* Liber contra Manicheos *de Durand de Huesca*, ed. C. Thouzellier, Bibliothèque de la Revue d'Histoire Ecclésiastique 37 (Louvain, 1961), translated in *Heresies of the High Middle Ages*, ed. W. Wakefield and A. P. Evans (New York, 1969), pp. 494–510. The treatise is better understood when read together with the polemical treatise in which it was copied and by which it was criticized. See *Une somme anti-cathare: Le* Liber contra Manicheos *de Durand de Huesca*, ed. C. Thouzellier, Spicilegium Sacrum Lovaniense, Études et Documents 32 (Louvain, 1964), and the translation of extracts from both in *Heresy and Inquisition in France, 1200–1300*, ed. J. H. Arnold and P. Biller (Manchester, 2016), pp. 20–8.

[60] An edition of the Occitan ritual is going to appear in the Concordance of Medieval Occitan. Meanwhile the text is available on-line – 'Cathar ritual', ed. M. R. Harris, at <www.rialto.unina.it/prorel/CatharRitual/CathRit.htm> – and it is translated in *Heresies of the High Middle Ages*, ed. Wakefield and Evans, pp. 483–93.

[61] William of Auxerre, *Summa aurea*, iii.LXIII.2, ed. J. Ribailler, 4 vols. in 7, Spicilegium Bonaventurianum 16–20 (Paris and Grottaferrata, 1980–87), XVIIIb, 825; *Summae Magistri Rolandi Liber Tercius*, q. 377, ed. A. Cortesi (Bergamo, 1962), pp. 1132–3. Note that Rolando talks about a heretic's trust in his *religio*; *ibid.*, p. 1133.

[62] *War on Heresy*, p. 254.

[63] *Ibid.*, p. 330.

are so much less likely to have precedents of *Apology* floating through their minds – Thomas More's *Apology*, or Plato's *Apology for Socrates* – and therefore less likely to meditate on the artfulness of Bloch's prose. The result is seeing the book as simply artless jottings: practical tips and useful information from the workshop.[64] In fact Bloch had been 'cooking' these ideas for a very long time, as the notebooks he filled with reflections on history in 1906 and 1907 show.[65] The workshop examples are paraded in order to bear upon the nature of history; and in its purpose the prose is Socratic, to stimulate thought and reflection.

Bloch's discussion of words in 'Nomenclature' did not have at its core a strenuous argument, and it did not recommend the simple reproduction or copying of the terminology of the past. Rather, as it moved from one point to another, it was doing what its author intended: encouraging meditation on historians and language. The scrutiny of the relationship between medieval and modern religious vocabularies provided in this chapter is in part a tribute – however inadequate – to the greatest practitioner of our craft. It is in part an attempt, written in the spirit of his discussion of nomenclature, to remind all of us to 'mind the gap'.

---

[64] It is 'A couple of hours conversation with a great historian talking about his craft', wrote Maurice Powicke in his review, and 'a model piece of humane sagacious practical advice, and, as it proceeds, of information, as in the most interesting study of nomenclature'; *History* n.s. 35 (1950), 197–201 (pp. 198, 200).
[65] C. Fink, *Marc Bloch: A Life in History* (Cambridge, 1989), p. 35.

INDEX